HERBERT EDGAR DOUGLASS

TRUTH
Matters

An analysis of the *Purpose Driven Life* movement

Pacific Press® Publishing Association
Nampa, Idaho
Oshawa, Ontario, Canada
www.pacificpress.com

Design by Ken McFarland
Cover photo by dreamstime.com

Additional copies of this book are available by calling toll free
1-800-765-6955
or online at <www.adventistbookcenter.com>.

Unless otherwise noted, all Scripture quotations are from the
New King James Version of the Bible, © copyright 1979, 1980,
1982, Thomas Nelson, Inc., Publishers.

Author assumes responsibility for the accuracy of quoted material.

ISBN 13: 978-0-8163-2156-8
ISBN 10: 0-8163-2156-6

06 07 08 09 10 • 5 4 3 2 1

WHAT OTHERS ARE SAYING ABOUT
TRUTH MATTERS

"Events around the world are moving rapidly towards the climatic ending foretold in Revelation and *The Great Controversy*. These events include false revivals and well-meaning, but misguided religious activities. Douglass's new book shows the results of programs not fully based on Scripture and how they subtly lead away from truth. Read *Truth Matters* and learn to lean more completely on Jesus and His Word as we anticipate His soon return."

—Ted N. C. Wilson., Ph.D.
General Vice President,
General Conference of Seventh-day Adventists

"Many Christians are confused over 'truth.' Is it absolute, or relative? For some, 'truth' is linked to either legalism or absolute perfection. Still others wince at the thought that only one church has 'the truth.' Should we not applaud the worldwide thrust of the Purpose-Driven movement?

"If any of these issues have crossed your mind, or that of your friends, you owe it to yourself to read this book. In clear, easy to understand language. Herb Douglass has done a masterful job of comparing popular religious thinking with Scripture. *Truth Matters* includes the clearest explanation of the complete gospel I have ever read."

—Tom Mostert, M.A.
President, Pacific Union Conference

"*Truth Matters* should not be seen as an attack on a man, an organization, or an institution. Douglass, however, brilliantly addresses the serious implications of many of these popular church phenomena for those living in the end of the end time. From the 'Jesus only' emphasis to the new ecumenism, this book delineates the pitfalls for Adventists, while demonstrating the juxtaposition beautifully of our own reason for existence."

—Jere Patzer, M.B.A., D.Min.
President
North Pacific Union Conference

"*Truth Matters* challenges much of conventional religious thinking that has become acceptable in the Adventist denomination today. With fine scholastic skills honed and refined by his years of study, writing, speaking and editing, Herb Douglass has exposed a contemporary challenge facing pulpits everywhere, thus helping us to re-establish in our minds the core of the mission and message of Seventh-day Adventists. This book helps us to recognize anew that, indeed, *Truth Matters*."

—Ricardo Graham, D.Min.
  Executive Secretary
  Pacific Union Conference

"Dr. Douglass has done careful research and is well acquainted with the books, philosophy, and beliefs of the Purpose Driven Movement. He has been generous in his recognition and affirmation of Rick Warren's love for Christ and passion to reach the world with the gospel. At the same time he presents a careful analysis of concerns of which Adventists should be aware. His presentation of the complete biblical gospel and its application for today is the best I have read. Growing Christians should find this book both interesting and helpful in distinguishing truth from compromised truth. *Truth Matters* is a 'must read' for these last days."

—Larry L. Caviness, M.Div.
  President
  Southern California Conference

"Herb Douglass has written a friendly and insightful critique of the theological underpinnings of Rick Warren's work. His gracious tone does not muffle his clarion concern that Adventists embrace at their peril key presuppositions of *The Purpose Driven Life*."

—Dale Martin, M.A.
  Pastor
  Ocala, Florida

CONTENTS

"But what matter," said Charmides, "from whom I heard this?"
"No matter at all," I [Socrates] replied: "for the point is not who said
the words, but whether they are true or not." —*The Dialogues of
Plato*, Jewett, vol. 1, 11 (161).

"If anyone wants to do His will, he shall know concerning the
doctrine, whether it is from God or whether I speak on My own
authority." —John 7:17, NKJV.

INTRODUCTION

Nothing I write or say has any intention of questioning Rick Warren's motives or his sincerity. I have no reason to believe Warren is a wolf in sheep's clothing, as some in the Protestant world have suggested. Many have condemned him for a host of reasons—most of which are groundless in my opinion. Many books have been written, and the Internet is rampant with their condemnations. Most of these condemnations are simply the result of either contrary presuppositions or careless research.

The purpose of this book is threefold: first, to urge many Seventh-day Adventists who have felt blessed with Rick Warren's signature book, *The Purpose Driven Life,* to take a second and longer look at the Purpose Driven life movement. The movement is more than one book. Warren's seminars, workshops, weekly sermons, etc. spell out even more clearly his theological direction as he continually offers much that is practical.

Second, to urge others who have seen some of the dangers in the Purpose Driven life movement to do more than take a negative stance, recognizing that many around the world have found spiritual nourishment in its program. Attacks that are only negative breed negative reactions; nothing is gained except deeper gulfs between those who should be friends.

Third, to urge all to recognize that basic error is defeated, not by heated arguments, but by quiet truth—not partial truth, not compromised truth, but truth wrapped up in the big picture that Adventists call the great controversy theme. In some instances, Rick Warren stands on tiptoes, as he sees further than most other evangelicals. Perhaps one of these days he may lead the charge in making the core truths of the great controversy a worldwide choice for the truth-seekers.

However, the Bible encourages us to examine all things as did the Bereans (see Acts 17:10, 11) and to be discerning. No one is above this biblical examination.

My favorite author once wrote, "True Christian love cherished in the heart and exemplified in the life, would teach us to put the best possible construction upon the course of our brethren. We should be as jealous of their reputation as of our own. . . . That which one may be ready to construe into grave wrongs, may be no more than we ourselves are chargeable with every day."[1]

The same author wrote, "It is important that in defending the doctrines which we consider fundamental articles of faith, we should never allow ourselves to employ arguments that are not wholly sound. These may avail to silence an opposer, but they do not honor the truth. We should present sound arguments, that will not only silence our opponents, but will bear the closest and most searching scrutiny."[2]

Adventists, especially, have the responsibility of discerning in last-day revivals and other church phenomena those concepts that may speed along a movement that will unite Protestants, Catholics, and others in establishing a worldwide equivalent of a United States national Sunday law and its consequences. The main issue in the end time is the proclamation of the "everlasting gospel" (Revelation 14:6). Cosmic forces aligned with global groups on planet Earth will force the question of who best represents the God of the universe. How people respond to these unprecedented issues in the end of the end times will depend on how they respect freedom and God's plan to redeem people who can be entrusted with eternal life. Such issues will be discussed in chapters 13 through 17 especially.

Herbert Edgar Douglass
Lincoln Hills, California
April 2006

---

1.   Ellen White, *Review and Herald*, April 15, 1880.

2.   Ellen White, *Counsels to Writers and Editors*, 40.

ONE

The Purpose Driven Life Phenomenon

Who is Rick Warren?

By all accounts, Rick Warren is a modern phenomenon. No appearances on Oprah's world stage,[1] no financial or sexual scandals that have catapulted other well-known religious leaders to the front page or evening news programs, no news conferences on the Supreme Court steps, not even his own TV or radio programs. For many he is a lovable, unpretentious teddy bear with a "global target."[2]

Warren and his wife, Kay, with their three children, live in a home similar to his church members' and drive their own four-year-old Ford SUV.[3] Just a fun-loving man without a boat, private plane, or beach house. But he was featured on the cover of *Time* magazine (February 7, 2005) and listed in its cover story as one of the twenty-five most influential evangelicals for 2005! Weeks later (April 18, 2005), *Time* included Warren as one of the hundred most influential persons in the world! Some meteoric trajectory for a person only fifty-one years old and with only twenty-five years of professional life behind him!

Warren was among a select panel of advisers that President George W.

---

1. However, during the week of October 3–7, 2005, Rick Warren appeared on Oprah Winfrey's TV program promoting both *The Purpose Driven Life* and Ashley Smith's new book on how *The Purpose Driven Life* helped her to cope with the murderer in her home. Since his much-chronicled trips to Africa and after announcing his P.E.A.C.E. Plan, Warren seems to be everywhere—on radio, on TV, and in various news magazines.

2. "I've got a target. It's called the globe. The whole Gospel for the whole world."—*USA Today* 7/21/2003.

3. As of December 2005.

Bush consulted for "discussion and prayer" as he prepared his speech commemorating the first anniversary of September 11 in New York and Washington.

Born in 1954, Warren has been pastor of Saddleback Church in Lake Forest, southern Orange County, California, since 1980. He earned his master of divinity degree from Southwestern Theological Seminary and his doctor of ministry degree from Fuller Theological Seminary. Since 1980, he has been the chief architect of the Purpose Driven ministry movement.

During his last year in seminary, he and Kay drove west to visit Robert Schuller's Institute for Church Growth. "We had a very stony ride out to the conference," Warren says, because such nontraditional ministry scared her to death. Schuller, though, won them over, "We were captivated by his positive appeal to nonbelievers. I never looked back."[4]

On graduation from seminary, Warren was offered the pulpit of a five thousand–member Texas church, but he had larger plans in mind! He and Kay took off for Southern California with no money, just a dream.

On April 6, 1980, twenty-six-year-old Warren spoke to 205 strangers who had responded to his advertisement for an Easter Service at Laguna Hills High School and announced his dream of building a church with twenty thousand members on fifty acres of land, sending out hundreds of career missionaries, and starting at least one daughter church a year. Boldly, he declared, "I stand before you today and state in confident assurance that these dreams will become reality. Why? Because they are inspired by God!"[5]

On April 17, 2005, at Angel Stadium, home of the Angels baseball team, Warren and his Saddleback Church celebrated their twenty-fifth anniversary. Thirty thousand people listened to Warren announce a new worldwide spiritual awakening for the twenty-first century. And his dream continues to grow. His P.E.A.C.E. Plan, he believes, will mobilize one billion foot soldiers for the Christian church in missions by 2020.

Warren is on a roll. Since 1980, more than four hundred thousand pastors and leaders in 162 countries have been trained in Purpose-Driven seminars; more than forty thousand churches in 117 countries on all seven continents are in his global network.[6] His email newsletter,

---

4. Tim Stafford, "A Regular Purpose-Driven Guy," *Christianity Today*, November 18, 2002. See chapter 11 for Warren's disclaimers that Robert Schuller was his mentor or that Warren modeled his ministry after Schuller.

5. Ibid. See also "Forty Days of Purpose"/Rick Warren Biography (<www.ynew.org/pur­pose/boo.html>).

6 . <www.pastors.com/aboutus/> 10/22/04.

Ministry Toolbox, reaches more than eighty-five thousand church leaders![7] More than thirty thousand churches around the world have completed his Forty-Day study plan. When six hundred senior pastors were asked to name the people they thought had the greatest influence on church affairs in the United States, Warren came in second only to Billy Graham.[8]

More than eighty thousand names are on Saddleback's church roll. Church staff members number more than 300 full- and part-time workers while the Purpose Driven Ministries has 250 staff members. Saddleback Church launches a daughter church annually. It expects to reach a weekly attendance of thirty thousand while not building a worship center larger than its current three-thousand-seat auditorium. How is that done? The church is like a cineplex with multiple smaller venues using a videotaped sermon and live music in different styles to please as many people as possible. One is never late because another service is about to begin somewhere in the complex.

Warren speaks of his training of these four hundred thousand pastors as his "stealth strategy." He intends to change the world—not through himself on TV or radio—but through pastors. "We train more pastors than all the seminaries combined,"[9] he says.

More than twelve thousand churches from all fifty states and nineteen countries have reported that these Purpose-Driven seminars were the most transforming event in their congregation's history.

Forbes magazine declared that "were it a business, Saddleback church would be compared with Dell, Google or Starbucks."[10]

Warren pictures the pastor as a team player who uses as many colleagues as possible. His leadership at Saddleback reflects this philosophy. For example, during the seven months he was writing *The Purpose Driven Life (PDL),* he preached only Christmas and Easter services.

Warren packs *PDL* with lists and exhortations, rarely with anecdotes. His superb sense of organization and pithy admonitions grows out of his self-awareness: "I was just wired by God to see how things relate to each other. I'm a synthesizer and systematizer."[11] Anyone who listens to his

7. Richard Abanes, *Rick Warren and the Purpose That Drives Him* (Eugene, Ore.: Harvest House Publishers, 2005), 8.

8. *Time,* February 7, 2005.

9. Stafford, op. cit.

10. February, 2, 2004.

11. *USA Today,* 7/21/2003.

sermons or to his lectures at the Purpose-Driven seminars knows exactly what I mean.

Warren compares his "Purpose-Driven paradigm" as the Intel chip and the Windows system for the Christian church in the twenty-first century.[12]

How do people recognize him? In his pulpit he often wears a Hawaiian-style shirt, with deck shoes and without socks. Interestingly, though, when he was photographed with President Bush, he wore his business suit with tie. And on Neil Cavuto's TV news show (June 23, 2005), when Rick Warren was interviewed a day before Billy Graham's meetings in New York City, he was wearing a regular suit and tie!

Warren is more concerned with people than with numbers. In 2004, more than 3,000 people accepted Christ as their Savior at Saddleback; of that number, 2,029 were baptized.[13]

Let's now focus on how dramatically his ministry and his writings have taken the world by storm.

What has been the impact of Warren's Purpose Driven Life?

In his recent survey (May 2005) on books that have most influenced pastors, George Barna discovered that Rick Warren's two books topped the list, with one out of every five senior pastors (21 percent) naming *The Purpose Driven Life (PDL)* and *The Purpose Driven Church (PDC)* as the most helpful in the last three years. *PDL* is the most popular of the religious titles among evangelicals (60 percent of whom have read the book), and it also did well among nonevangelical, born-again Christians (25 percent). Within those markets, *PDL* is a hit particularly among upscale baby boomers. Conservatives were twice as likely to have read Warren's tome as other groups surveyed.[14]

In a later Barna survey (June 2005), the three best-selling, fiction and nonfiction religious books in the past few years have been the books in the *Left Behind*™ series by Jerry Jenkins and Timothy LaHaye, *The Da Vinci Code* by Daniel Brown, and *The Purpose Driven Life* by Rick Warren. *The Da Vinci Code* was the best-known, being familiar to four out of five adults surveyed; *PDL* was known to almost two-thirds of religious readers.[15]

---

12. Timothy C. Morgan, "Purpose Driven in Rwanda," *Christianity Today,* October 2005, 36.

13. Abanes, 8.

14. Barna Group Update email, May 30, 2005.

15. Barna Group Update email, June 28, 2005.

THE PURPOSE DRIVEN LIFE PHENOMENON • 13

As of June 2005, *PDL* was the best-selling nonfiction hardback book in history, with sales of more than twenty-six million copies—clearly a book that has taken the world by storm. This is an astounding achievement. This means Warren has had more exposure to the general public, as well as to Christians, than any other Christian author. Clearly, when he speaks, others listen. Imagine—*PDL* is listed as "one of the one hundred Christian books that changed the twentieth century!"[16]

PDL has been topping the *New York Times* bestseller list for nonfiction for more than 115 weeks (as of June 2005). It has been translated into many languages and sells well in developing countries, notably China.

On a full-page advertisement in *Christianity Today,* Christianbook. com's "Top Ten Bestsellers" lists *PDL* as number 1; number 2, *Your Best Life Now,* is authored by Joel Osteen, the pastor of another megachurch, in Houston, Texas.[17]

Bruce Ryskamp, president of Zondervan Publishing, declares that *PDL* and *PDC* are more than bestsellers, they are a movement.[18]

Rich Karlgaard, publisher of *Forbes* magazine, called *PDL* "the best book in entrepreneurship, business, and investment in a long time." He then compared Warren's success by comparing it to the growth of Dell or Starbucks, saying that Warren had the ability to "identify a consumer need—a religious consumer need—and fill it." What was that need? The need of the unchurched.[19]

The cover story of *Christianity Today,* October 2005, featured Rick and Kay surrounded by hundreds of Africans under the legend, "Rick Warren has a sweeping plan to defeat poverty." The cover story, "Purpose Driven in Rwanda," features the Warrens' July 2005 trip to Kigali, Rwanda, accompanied by forty-two other American evangelicals, where the group joined nine thousand Rwandan Christians "in launching the first Purpose Driven Nation initiative to harness business people, politicians, and pastors against the nation's biggest social problems."[20]

These amazing statistics and undebatable popularity may numb the doctrinal discernment of many.

---

16. <www.pastors.com/aboutus/>

17. As of June 2005.

18. <www.assistnews.net/STORIES/2004/s04120087.htm> 12/23/04. That is precisely what they call themselves, "Purpose Driven movement"—see Pastors.com.

19. Abanes, op. cit., 82.

20. Morgan, op. cit., 32.

What have been the marketing techniques that have succeeded so well?

Warren's consultant in his management process is CMS, a full-service marketing agency. CMS says, "We view it as our mission to help our clients grow their businesses. We do this by working with each client identifying opportunities and developing innovative, creative and profitable services which assist them in the execution of effective marketing, sales and communications program. . . .

> "We are best able to serve clients when they allow us to act as partners. . . . CMS is made up of a team of talented individuals whose dedication and expertise have earned them a solid reputation for creating results."[21]

CMS clients include Quaker, Isuzu Motors America, City of West Covina, Purpose Driven Ministries, Saddleback Valley Community Church, Smalley Relationship Center, and Walk Thru the Bible, a project headed by Bruce Wilkinson, author of *The Prayer of Jabez*.[22]

Peter Drucker, dean of American management, calls Rick Warren "the inventor of perpetual revival" and Saddleback's organizational model "the most significant sociological phenomena of the second half of this century."[23]

Why bring in Peter Drucker? Drucker, legendary management guru, was the first to help business leaders understand that they had to define their businesses from a customer's perspective. Drucker did much to help Japan rethink its business strategy in the last twenty years; since these principles worked so well with corporations, they were also echoed in church management. And the race was on.

Obviously, focusing on a "customer's perspective" brings "success" wherever tried. People feel satisfied, and they come and buy. That's how advertisers lure customers—by focusing on "felt needs." Drucker's management skills worked well for Robert Schuller, the possibility thinker who called Mikhail Gorbachev a Christian disciple despite the protests of this unrepentant Communist. And if these management principles worked so well for Robert Schuller, they surely should work well for Saddleback and Rick Warren.

---

21. <www.christian-ministry.com/default.htm>; <www.christian-ministry.com/aboutus_who.htm>.

22. <www.christian-ministry.com/clients.htm>.

23. <www.Saddlebackfamily.com>.

Who have been most critical of PDL?

Many evangelicals who oppose Rick Warren work from a Calvinist framework. John F. MacArthur wrote, "The philosophy that marries marketing techniques with church growth theory is the result of bad theology. It assumes that if you package the gospel right, people will get saved. It is rooted in Arminianism, which makes the human will, not a sovereign God, the decisive factor in salvation. It speaks of conversion as a 'decision for Christ.' "[24]

What makes this criticism more than interesting is that Warren, while working with certain Arminian-Wesleyan concepts, has also adopted several aspects of Calvinism, including man's depravity, the eternal security of the saints, and, at times, the unconditional election of certain persons for salvation. However, all of this is a mixed bag for Warren—the Arminian—because he seems to promote the teaching that Christians cannot lose their salvation after they "accept" Jesus. "You didn't do anything to earn your salvation," he says, "and you can't do anything to lose it."[25]

Another Grand Canyon divide comes from the verbal inerrantists, those who believe that every word of the Bible is God dictated. This group is the largest group to have written extensively against Rick Warren's program, it seems to me.

Others, both Calvinist and Arminian, wonder why Warren does not preach against specific sins such as homosexuality or abortion. But he does, although not in his books. Warren does believe abortion and sexual infidelity are wrong, categorically wrong.[26]

---

24. *Ashamed of the Gospel: When the Church Becomes Like the World* (Wheaton, Ill.: Crossway Books, 1993), 84, 85. Probably to confuse MacArthur further, Warren wrote (in his contribution to *From the Ashes—A Spiritual Response to the Attack on America* [Emmaus, Pa.: Rodale Press, 2002]), "God has given us a free will. Made in God's image, we have been given the freedom to decide how we will act and the ability to make moral choices. . . . We must choose to do God's will every day. It isn't automatic. . . . We were made for relationship with God, but he waits for us to choose him." 130, 131.

25. "What We Believe: If I Accept Jesus Christ Is My Salvation Forever?" <www.saddleback.org>.

26. In Warren's pulpit sermon titled "Maintaining Moral Purity," he said, "God's standards have never changed. Premarital sex is unacceptable to God. It always has been. It always will be. Living together without getting married is unacceptable to God. It always has been. It always will be. Adultery, having an affair, being unfaithful to somebody you're married to is unacceptable to God. It always has been and it always will be. Homosexuality is unacceptable to God. It always has been. It always will be. Pornography is unacceptable to God. It always has been. It always will be. Every one of those things brings a judgment. If you have been guilty of one or all of these things I've just mentioned you've come to the right place. This is what Saddleback's all about. A place for

Which brings up an observation that I think is being overlooked. *PDL* is not Warren's systematic theology any more than any of my books, in themselves, contain everything I believe on theological subjects. *PDL* is a devotional guide meant primarily for (1) unbelievers, (2) those who have lost an earlier relationship with God, and (3) the average Christian seeking a simple daily reading plan.[27] Of course, with such a wide array of readers, it is hard to distinguish between what is aimed at the unbeliever and that which is aimed at the postconversion believer.

If one wants to know what Warren's doctrinal beliefs are, his Saddleback Web sites are easy to read. Any reader will quickly discover that Warren takes a high view of biblical doctrines, as he understands them. Adventists will note those key areas where Calvinism circulates through his theological system.

Others have spoken freely about Warren's spiritual fast-food and junk food—that it feeds people what they are clamoring for and that it compensates for their lack of true repentance. These critics believe that when we use energizing music, emotional stimuli, and short, light messages to satisfy the flesh with its "felt" needs, we tend to obscure our deeper spiritual needs.

Let's now try to see why Rick Warren's Purpose Driven ministry has satisfied such a broad spectrum of many hundreds of thousands of laypeople, as well as tens of thousands of Christian pastors.

---

healing, forgiveness, restoration. God says, 'I want to give you a chance to come clean and start over and make the rest of your life the best of your life.' . . . What is the pathway back to purity? Repent. Repent means 'to change your mind.' . . . It means I change my mind and say, 'You are right, God, it was wrong. It's sin.' I don't rationalize it. I don't excuse it. I don't say everybody's doing it. I say, 'It was wrong.' "

27. Abanes, op. cit., 77.

TWO

What Many Find Appealing in the Purpose Driven Ministry

Rick Warren desires to make Christianity friendly to those turned off by conventional, traditional church programs.

Early in his young ministry, one of Warren's first decisions was to figure out how best to attract people to his Sunday services. His primary desire was to attract those who had either been burned out in conventional churches or those who had never felt that Christianity had anything to offer. That is, he saw a world of people "stuck with the past."[1] Further, life for both groups already seemed self-fulfilling—they didn't need church connections. How could he get their attention?

So Warren declared to the world, "We are unapologetically contemporary!" His next step was obvious:

> "I passed out a three-by-five card to everybody in the church, and I said, 'You write down the call letters of the radio station you listen to.' I wasn't even asking unbelievers. I was asking people in the church, 'What kind of music do you listen to?' When I got it back, I didn't have one person who said, 'I listen to organ music.' Not one. . . . So, we made a strategic decision that we are unapologetically a contemporary music church. And right after we made that decision and stopped trying to please

---

1. At Super Conference 2003, held at Falwell's Liberty University, Warren spoke to more than thirteen thousand ministers and students on "Attracting a Crowd to Worship." At one point, "Falwell and Warren switched their characteristic dress, with Falwell donning a Hawaiian shirt and Warren wearing a business suit. Falwell acknowledged the two were cultures apart, but it takes different people to reach all people for Christ. Warren added that regardless of any differences, we all serve one Spirit, one Lord, and one God."—*Evangelical News*, October 10, 2003.

everybody, Saddleback exploded with growth. . . . I'll be honest with you, we are loud. We are really, really loud on a weekend service. . . . I say, 'We're not gonna turn it down.' Now the reason why is baby boomers want to feel the music, not just hear it. . . . God loves variety."[2]

Of course, it took more than removing the organ and turning up the speakers with Christian rock. Warren is a master at preparing sermons that speak directly to what his audience think they need. And he organized his user-friendly church services to meet various age groups and particular interests.

Warren recognized that many boomers have no concept of being filled with the Holy Spirit or how to make sense out of the Bible. For decades, diversity of style, opinion, and prejudices have pervaded our postmodern generation. He believes that this diversity demands simplified Bibles that have been paraphrased, reinterpreted, and made appealing to the modern mind.

When asked about his muting of sin and judgment, Warren replies that rather than threaten sinners, "we believe in attraction evangelism. We believe in loving people into the kingdom." Warren sees worldly, weary people in need of self-esteem, interpersonal relationships, mood enhancement, and motivation for success—not more judgment and guilt. In other words, Saddleback Sam (a researched composite of people in Southern California) is offended by "outmoded" forms of evangelism.

As part of his "attraction evangelism" to make newcomers feel at home, Warren does away with standard religious symbolism, even basics like crosses and pews.

One of the first ways he makes visitors feel comfortable is to reserve the best parking places for them! And then they are personally greeted as they walk into church.

Dress must be casual. "Worshipers" and staff alike shun ties, suits, and dresses. Warren comes in his casual shirt, khakis, and loafers and tells ministers in his seminars, "Get comfortable. This is as dressed up as I get in this church. My idea of winter is to put on socks."

Later in this book we will compare Warren's approach to the secular marketing strategy principles of a typical management training seminar— one must provide a product that will meet the perceived needs of the consumer, requiring a survey of the community and then developing programs to meet those needs. Saddleback Sam must feel comfortable, helped, and encouraged, which explains Warren's use of Christian rock and backup

2. Dennis Costello, *Foundation*, March–April 1998.

bands that accentuate the driving beat the unchurched are used to.

Another "appealing" aspect of his ministry is Warren's emphasis on ecumenicity—the joining of all Christians in a worldwide movement. In one of his Saddleback Seminars, he said: "You're a group today of over 45,000 pastors and church leaders that have gone through this conference, from Europe, from Asia, from South America." To emphasize the ecumenical mood, he suggested, "It really doesn't matter your denomination, folks. We're all on the same team if you love Jesus."[3]

Another marketing principle that fits with Warren's emphasis on ecumenicity is to eliminate mental barriers such as denominational labels. Thus his Southern Baptist church is known as Saddleback Community Church. All across North America one sees a similar approach—the People's Church, Willow Creek Community Church, etc. In other words, minimize doctrinal differences.

When changing over a "traditional" church program to this emphasis on reaching Saddleback Sam, resistance often arises. In such collisions, Warren is ready with answers that are being duplicated in many churches following his program.

First, Warren's program works best when starting up a new congregation; it is not designed for churches already in place. In fact, Warren has made it clear that the "unchurched" are his unique market. This has removed the fear of "sheep-stealing" from surrounding churches.

Second, for those who are troubled with the fallout from this contemporary program, Warren is emphatic:

> "Be willing to let people leave the church. And I told you earlier, the fact is that people are gonna leave the church no matter what you do. But when you define the vision, you're choosing who leaves. You say, 'But Rick, they're the pillars of the church.' Now, you know what pillars are. Pillars are people who hold things up. . . . And in your church, you have to have some blessed subtractions before you have any real additions."[4]

Which leads to the question, should evangelistic attention to the unchurched (unsaved) become the pattern for the church life of the committed? Might these two biblical concerns that together fulfill our Lord's commission (evangelizing the unsaved and edifying the believers) be worked out in two different venues until there is a natural merging of interests? Shouldn't Christian truths be made attractive and appealing to both the unchurched *and* the converted believers?

---

3. Costello, op. cit.

4. Ibid.

Rick Warren speaks to people who long for a sense of purpose and meaning to life

Warren knows well that satisfactory incomes, two cars, a boat, and vacation trips are not ultimately satisfying to most people. Along with other thoughtful Christians, ministers and laity alike, Warren recognizes that most people, deep within, do long for a sense of purpose and meaning to life.[5]

According to Barbara Becker Holstein, psychologist in Long Branch, New Jersey and author of *Recipes for Enchantment: The Secret Ingredient Is You*, "It would be like asking, 'Why do we need to eat?' or, 'Why are there males and females on earth?' It is so intertwined with what we have been given as human beings." She explains that having purpose stabilizes us and is important for physical, mental, and spiritual well-being. "We need the infusion. This is biology tied into the human species—maybe God put it in us. We need the stimulation of a group to feel we're on track. So a group is an ideal mechanism when it's used properly. It gives us the resiliency."[6]

Although many seem to disagree, Warren's message in *PDL* sets him apart from typical religious motivational authors. From the get-go, he re-routes readers' minds from themselves to God: "It's not about you," he tells them. In other words, you won't discover life's purpose or meaning by looking within. The first chapter sets the tone for the rest of this bestseller: "The purpose of your life is far greater than your own personal fulfillment, your peace of mind, or even your happiness. It's far greater than your family, your career, or even your wildest dreams and ambitions. If you want to know why you were placed on this planet, you must begin with God. You were born *by* his purpose and *for* his purpose."[7]

And the last chapter ends with these words: "Imagine what it is going to be like one day, with all of us standing before the throne of God presenting our lives in deep gratitude and praise to Christ. Together we will say, *'Worthy, O Master! Yes, our God! Take the glory! The honor! The power! You created it all; It was created because you wanted it!'* (Revelation 4:11, *Message*). We will praise him for his plan and live for his purpose forever!"[8]

---

5. "Half of all unchurched and non-Christian adults admit that they are seeking meaning and purpose in their life proving a meaningful entry point for evangelizers." Barna research, <www.crossroad.to/charts/church-statistics.html>, 5/30/2005.

6. Frederica Saylor, "American churches embrace purpose-driven movement."—*Science and Theology News;* <www.stnews.org/rlr-316.htm>.

7. Rick Warren, *The Purpose Driven Life (PDL)* (Grand Rapids, Mich.: Zondervan, 2002), 17.

8. Ibid., 319.

Who could possibly argue with these insights? Warren's third chapter outlines five benefits of "purpose-driven living": (1) Knowing your purpose gives meaning to your life; (2) Knowing your purpose simplifies your life; (3) Knowing your purpose focuses your life; (4) Knowing your purpose motivates your life; and (5) Knowing your purpose prepares you for eternity.

In one sense, *PDL* is full of practical truths that even believers tend to ignore or forget. True, indeed—our time on earth is short, and our fruitfulness now will count for eternity. Warren emphasizes the importance of humility and servanthood, the reality of temptation, and that spiritual victory over temptation is possible.

With this kind of freshness and direction, no one should wonder why more than twenty-five million people have bought *The Purpose Driven Life*!

Rick Warren sees his ministry as continuing the honorable line of aggressive spiritual salesmanship as modeled by the great evangelists since the apostle Paul

Rick Warren's ministry is an outgrowth of the Church Growth movement (CGM) that is often credited to the innovative techniques of Donald McGavran of Fuller Theological Seminary, who, in turn, borrowed the techniques from Charles Finney, a noted Methodist evangelist in the first half of the nineteenth century. "Church Growth is that science that investigates the planting, multiplication, growth, function, health, and death of churches. It strives to apply the biblical and social principles in its gathering, analysis, displaying, and defending of the facts involved in implementing the great commission. The heart of the Church Growth movement involves research into growth to establish principles to guide others in the harvest."[9]

The CGM began as an international phenomenon—a product of American missions. It found its way back to the United States using new names and terms such as "seeker-sensitive" and "seeker-friendly." Like its foreign counterparts, the American CGM focused on pragmatic means by which to influence the lost with the gospel.[10]

Obviously, Warren finds nothing inherently dishonorable about aggressive proselytizing and spiritual salesmanship. He intentionally models

---

9. See John Muether, "Contemporary Evangelicalism and the Triumph of the New School," *Westminster Theological Journal* 50/2 (Fall 1998), 343.

10. See Appendix B: Relationship Between the Rick Warren Ministry and the Church Growth Movement (CGM).

himself after such Christian spokesmen as the apostle Paul; John Wesley, George Whitefield, and Dwight L. Moody. For example, he feels indebted to Wesley's emphasis on small-group ministries that helped set the dramatic spread of Methodism.

At the same time, Warren disdains unscrupulous evangelists such as Elmer Gantry, Jim and Tammy Faye Bakker, and others. This is one reason that Warren avoids a television ministry. "The spotlight blinds you," he says.[11]

Rick Warren builds five elements into his church program based on his understanding of the "Great Commission" and the "Two Great Commandments"

The five elements, or five fundamental purposes—fellowship, spiritual maturity, service, evangelism, worship—are not different from those motivating any other alert Christian church, large or small. Warren's emphasis is that none of these five should get out of balance or be neglected.

Actually, it seems so obvious why thousands of pastors get excited about Warren's emphasis. A young pastor of a Christian Reformed church in Alameda, California, said, "My biggest challenge is to convince people that this really is Reformed. It's pretty hard to argue with the Great Commission and the Great Commandment," from which Warren's five purposes are drawn.[12]

Baseball diamond. Warren likes to simplify things, especially with diagrams. One of his diagrams features a baseball diamond that depicts the flow of his church into the lives of its adherents. Here's how it works: Vast crowds attend his services, but they reach the *first base of fellowship (membership)* only if they sign a covenant card of commitment to Christ and the church. They reach the *second base of spiritual maturity (maturity)* when they sign the next card, committing themselves to daily quiet time, tithing, and attendance at a small group. The *third base of service (ministry)* is reached when members commit to serving actively in one of dozens of church ministries—after being individually interviewed. *Home base is evangelism (mission)* when the members commit to active evangelism. At the center of the diamond is *worship (magnification).* Warren's concept begins with the unchurched experiencing church services for the first time and then deciding to commit themselves. When the un-

---

11. Tim Stafford, "A Regular Purpose-Driven Guy," *Christianity Today,* November 18, 2002.

12. Ibid.

saved become believers, they begin to "run the bases." As they run, they begin to realize that everything in the diagram centers on glorifying God in genuine worship.

Concentric circles. Warren's second diagram is one of concentric circles. These circles outline the target audiences for each of the bases in his first diagram. The largest circle is evangelism's main target—the general *community*. The next circle (and smaller) is the *crowd*—those who come to the seeker-sensitive church and experience *worship.* The next smaller circle represents the *congregation*—those who commit their lives to Jesus and become church members and are making certain commitments with their time and money. The next smaller circle is for the *committed*—those who are giving evidence of spiritual growth. The inner core represents those actively committed to at least one of the church's active ministries.

Truly organizational! But organization was one of the secrets of John Wesley's methods (hence the name, *Methodism*). Warren calls these five purposes the "Intel chip" of the church. That is, these five principles function as an invisible architecture that any church can build on in a variety of ways, as long as it keeps the principles in balance.[13]

Warren's sermons, often lasting for forty-five minutes to an hour, are more than motivational exercises; they are training seminars. His congregations feel part of a serious learning experience. They are provided printed outlines and asked to fill in blanks, read Bible texts out loud, and circle important words. Warren aims at simplicity (as evident in his two diagrams). He aims to be thoroughly understood, not just with knowledge but with knowledge to change lives, change the world. That's part of the stealth that he believes will change the world. Foreign countries may not know English, but they understand the diamond, and thus the five purposes, in their own languages.

Of course, Warren does not do all this by himself. Saddleback's 175 full-time, paid staff members are very busy every day of the week; each of them is required to take on an overseas mission project plus a twenty-six-week systematic theology course. All thirteen Saddleback pastors have seminary degrees.[14]

Saddleback's staff practices what they preach. They are fulfilling Warren's dream and promise: Warren launched his first daughter church after Saddleback's first year of existence and has continued to launch at least one new daughter church every year since—some record!

---

13. Ibid. Verified in a personal phone call with a Saddleback pastor.

14. Ibid.

Warren helps churches of all denominations to "balance" the five components of a healthy church

Pastors often describe how their healthy churches have grown when balanced attention is given to worship, fellowship, discipleship, service, and missions. Many churches have focused on worship and fellowship with one another. These are strengths, but when they focus with equal attention on the next three purposes, a fresh breeze of new energy develops. In other words, one-dimensional, or even two-dimensional, churches are comfortable for the older members, but they are not yet an open door to the unchurched.

Warren and other pastors advise that churches must give themselves permission to change—especially with the question, What are we willing to give up to make this change? And often that means that the pastor has to be willing to "give up" long-time members who leave for other churches that better fit their expectations. In other words, to make a Purpose Driven church succeed, one must create a safe place for people to begin their journey—and not focus primarily on what long-time members expect. Such is the success of many growing churches on more than one continent.

Much of Rick Warren's material feeds thousands of pastors with helpful principles and models of sermon building and delivery— actual sermons that are preached throughout the world— small-group networks, and formation of seeker-friendly Bible classes

Warren's influence is astonishing. He considers Saddleback to be a "teaching church" with the responsibility to pass on the principles that have made it a religious phenomenon. He says that he has "trained more pastors than all the seminaries combined." More than four hundred thousand pastors worldwide have come under his influence and have multiplied that influence in their home churches.

Warren calls himself a "toolmaker," and he believes that the tools he provides will change the world. One of his tools that he shares with more than sixty thousand to one hundred thousand pastors *daily* is his *Ministry Toolbox*—an online newsletter on pastors.com.[15] This newsletter provides tips on recruiting new members as well as help in balancing individual worship and discipleship, sample sermons, and general suggestions on improving sermon technique.

---

15. <www.pastors.com>

One of the features of this toolbox is "The Sermon Vault Talk," where the busy pastor can find his next week's sermon! In fact, if he or she is wondering about what to preach for Christmas, there is a special "vault" under holiday sermons—"Looking for ideas for a holiday sermon this year? Check out these thirty-four holiday sermon transcripts from Rick Warren. Not only will you find Christmas sermons, but you'll be ahead of the game when Easter comes around!"[16] Talk about continuing education! What could be more helpful for busy pastors?

Rick Warren divides his ministry into two foci: (1) seeker-friendly services that focus on the unchurched, and (2) the five elements in his church program that focus on the postconversion life.

Warren's detractors rarely understand this double focus. His seeker-friendly methods focus on unbelievers, or the unchurched. His "five purposes" (illustrated by the baseball diamond analogy) are for those in the postconversion experience. Detractors should let Warren speak for himself: "The style of preaching that I use in our seeker service is very different than the style I use to teach believers. The style of communication that most church members are used to is counterproductive in reaching most of the unchurched."[17]

When preaching to believers, Warren teaches from the books of the Bible, verse by verse. He said that he took two and a half years to go through Romans—after believers have accepted the authority of the Bible and are motivated to learn the Scriptures.

But not so with unbelievers. "With the unchurched, you will not establish common ground by saying, 'Let's open our Bibles to Isaiah, chapter 14, as we continue in our study of this wonderful book,' "[18] Warren warns.

His clear distinction between these two groups, and the preaching methods each group needs, strongly suggests that pastors *should not try to marry these two groups in a typical weekly worship service.*

Rick Warren holds his church members accountable with annual commitments

Saddleback is far more serious about its membership roles than most other Protestant churches regardless of denomination. Those who commit

---

16. November 30, 2005.

17. Rick Warren, *The Purpose Driven Church (PDC)* (Grand Rapids, Mich.: Zondervan Publishing House, 1995), 294.

18. Ibid., 294, 295.

their lives to Jesus and want to learn more are asked to sign a commitment before they are permitted to go to the next "base." And each move to the next "base" is preceded by another written commitment.

In a move that is definitely unusual, each Saddleback church member is asked to sign an annual commitment regarding the purposes of the church and his or her participation. In other words, membership at Saddleback is not a vast fishing net that embraces everyone who shows up on Sunday morning. Every year, each member must renew his or her commitment to definite beliefs and participation in church activities.

Rick Warren's vision of a global network of interlocking churches stimulates loyalty and the sense of belonging to a movement that is enriching the world.

As already noted, Warren has fulfilled many of the dreams that he announced on April 6, 1980, to 205 strangers attending an Easter Service at Laguna Hills High School. Part of his vision was to build a church with twenty thousand members on fifty acres of land, send out hundreds of career missionaries, and start up at least one "daughter" church a year.[19]

But Africa is on his mind along with 117 other countries. In 2003, he and Bruce Wilkinson went to Africa with Kay (who was the first to catch the vision regarding the millions who are orphaned due to AIDS) to train ninety thousand pastors using digital satellite downlinks.

After the Purpose-Driven Conference, he wanted to see a little village for himself. There he met a pastor in his tent church of about seventy-five people (twenty-five children orphaned by AIDS and fifty adults). The pastor said, "I know who you are."

Warren asked, "How do you know who I am?"

The pastor said, "I get your sermons every week [on the Internet in the post office]." Then he added, "You're the *only* training I've ever had."

That's when Warren made up his mind to give "the rest of my life to these guys." Then Warren realized that his African pastors needed more than church training. They needed help in such areas as how to handle poverty, spiritual emptiness, egocentric leadership, illiteracy, business training, education, and health issues. Here was the beginning of his P.E.A.C.E. Plan.[20]

19. Stafford, op. cit. Warren's Saddleback Vision, presented in his first sermon to sixty attendees on March 30, 1980, is printed on page 43 of *The Purpose Driven Church.*

20. I am extending this overview of Warren's dramatic plan to go global because I believe that this step-up in his world vision will have enormous implications in last-day events. See chapter 16.

In an October 27, 2003, email that Warren titled, "God's Dream for You—and the World," Warren said that his Saddleback empire had arrived at its "moment of destiny"—that in this P.E.A.C.E. plan, God would "change history" and that it "is going to happen."

He announced that on the next weekend he would begin a "series of five messages on God's dream to use you globally." Continuing, he said, "Only one other time in my life have I felt this deep conviction—and that was the day God called me at age twenty-five to begin Saddleback Church with no money and no members."

On November 2, 2003, Warren unveiled his five-step P.E.A.C.E. Plan to Saddleback Church and to everyone watching on the Internet. He reviewed his "forty-year commitment" to Saddleback Church and to the community. He would devote the first ten years to "local blessings." The next ten years, to "national" interests, training more than 250,000 churches around the United States through seminars and other training resources.

But now we are in the twenty-first century, and it is time to go "global." His wife, Kay, identified the "giants" that needed to be subdued—spiritual lostness, the lack of servant leadership, poverty, disease, and ignorance. Warren said that Saddleback was uniquely prepared to take on these "global giants."

Where did Warren get biblical affirmation for his P.E.A.C.E. Plan? Unfortunately, he used a fairly new Bible translation that renders poorly 2 Corinthians 5:18, 19: "God sent Christ to make peace between himself and us. And he's given us the work of making peace between himself and others. God was in Christ offering peace and forgiveness to the people of this world. And now he has given us the work of sharing his message about peace" (CEV). Tens of thousands heard these words as Warren's heavenly endorsement on his P.E.A.C.E. Plan.

But that was not what Paul wrote! Warren stopped before verse 20, which, if included, would have dramatically changed his message that day.[21]

Warren said that he had been thinking about this plan since his first visit to Africa and that he had talked to world leaders, getting their opinions.

Further, he said that his P.E.A.C.E. Plan would provide the foundation for world peace that everyone craves and that it would hasten the return of Jesus by fulfilling the Great Commission (see Matthew 28:19, 20).

On Larry King's TV program, March 22, 2005, Warren outlined more of how his plan would be implemented. He first would organize pilot pro-

---

21. See chapter 7 for a review of Warren's often misuse of Scripture.

grams in sixty-seven countries over a two-year test program (that would extend into 2006). He wants to assist the poor, care for the sick, and educate the next generation on a massive scale involving many millions of dollars and thousands of trained supervisors.

One of Warren's observations is that the world is baffled by the lack of qualified leaders on all levels. Most of those now leading are focused on themselves and their cronies. In other words, there are many top leaders, but few servant leaders. Furthermore, in many underdeveloped countries, such as in Africa, the dilemma is how to make Christian leaders out of those who have never been to the equivalent of high school. There can be no real Christian leaders, Warren believes, until they have been trained. That is why he is zeroing in on the plague of poverty, widespread illness, and illiteracy that produces ignorance. The bottom-line question: Otherwise, how will these people ever learn about Jesus?

Advantage over government agencies. Warren clearly sees that the church has the advantage over government agencies. Churches have the widest distribution system, and they have the moral authority to face up to these widespread sources of misery—something no government is able to do.

So what does the P.E.A.C.E. Plan mean?

"P" is for "plant churches"—the first step in combating evil. When Warren outlined this plan to his church, he introduced nine people in the audience who started the Saddleback Church twenty-five years before. Why? He wanted to demonstrate that a church could be started by a small group who said, "We're just people. Let's start a church." They weren't pastors or missionaries, just people. But they had a vision. Since then, the Saddleback Church has "planted" thirty-six other churches in Southern California and has helped thousands of others get started.

"E" is for "equip leaders"—good leaders who can train others to be good leaders. Like whom? Like Jesus—not necessarily like the world's great business leaders.

"A" is for "assist the poor." The test of faith is in how we treat the poor. Warren cites a World Vision study that found there are six hundred million poor in the world that could get out of poverty if someone would just loan them a little money.

"C" is for "cure the sick." Each day twenty-seven thousand children die from *curable* diseases! Every year, fourteen million children become orphans due to AIDS. The answer will be found not in more money from governments but from people who care.

"E" is for "education"—training the next generation to live better.

There is nothing new in any aspect of his plan, yet Warren says his plan is *revolutionary*.[22] He has seen his plan work on a smaller scale, sending out forty-five hundred people on a mission project such as Clinic-in-a-Box. Next to ramp up will be Church-in-a-Box and School-in-a-Box. The bottom line is that Saddleback members "all go, all pray, all pay."

Warren's appeal is simple: "All we need is the will to do it. When I was a twenty-five-year-old, and God said, 'Go to California and start a church,' everybody said, 'You're nuts. You have no members, no money, no building, nothing.' I feel as confident about this as I did the day we started Saddleback Church, and look what has happened. I believe God brought you here to this church—you're not here by accident—you're not here to sit, sulk, and sour. God wants to use you, and I'm coming after you. What if each of you adopt a village and do what average people can do—un-average things with extraordinary results!"[23]

We have been describing a worldwide ecumenical umbrella that will sweep the nations of the world under the gospel according to Rick Warren. Nobody really doubts that Warren's dream will succeed.

Warren chooses not to make a super megachurch complex[24] that will outrival all others

As mentioned previously, another of Warren's goals is to increase Saddleback's attendance while not building an auditorium larger than its current three-thousand–seat capacity in his main church. He is doing this with multiple smaller venues, using a videotaped sermon and live music in different styles to fit the expectations of different groups. In other words, the main church will function like a cineplex where one may feel free to choose the kind of worship environment where one is most comfortable, at whatever time one is able to get to "church." Like a cineplex, there would be a service about to begin somewhere in the complex throughout the day.

How does Warren personally do it? This is amazing. Saddleback has six services on the weekends—Saturday at 4:30 and 6:30 P.M.; Sunday at 9:00 and 11:00 A.M. and 4:30 and 6:30 P.M. Warren preaches at all six services

---

22. Warren acknowledges all five elements of his P.E.A.C.E. Plan are being done by great organizations but "nobody has been able to do them through the local church together, combined. That's what makes the PEACE Plan unique."—Morgan, op.cit., 36.

23. George Mair, *A Life With Purpose* (New York: Berkley Books, 2005) 195.

24. Megachurches are those whose attendance is two thousand or more weekly. In 1980, the United States had 80 megachurches; in early 2005, there were 880!

on twenty-one to twenty-four weekends annually! His team of preachers takes turns on the other weekends. There are no slouches at Saddleback!

Warren's unique church-building philosophy is characterized by frugality

"Being intelligently frugal" is a remarkable Rick Warren mode of operation. Rather than spending "borrowed money," he carefully invests "earned money." His record shows that he doesn't build a big church and then work hard to fill it up—he finds the people first. His twenty-five-year history at Saddleback reveals how many times he has cycled through this "people first" principle. When he reaches a certain number of followers, he then builds a bigger accommodation. That is truly unusual in the history of church growth! And he builds the church for "durability and functionality rather than something competing for a Frank Lloyd Wright Architectural Award."[25]

Warren's personal life is his best witness

Few internationally known preachers live as modestly as Rick and Kay Warren. He drives his own four-year-old Ford (in 2005). He, Kay, and their three children live in a house similar to those of his church members. He does not own an ocean-view dream house or a vacation home in Montana. From the very beginning of his ministry he has paid back all that his church has paid him from the very beginning—he serves his megachurch for free! He refuses to walk the road of a television star or conduct a radio ministry. He says that such public exposure "blinds" one. Warren and Kay are reverse tithers—that is, they now give away 90 percent of their income from their books to Warren's various foundations and other charities and live on 10 percent of their income.[26]

I find it easy to believe that Warren's public testimonies are sincere and contagious. An example is his personal witness before a "Leadership Conference," September 29, 2000: "When I humble myself and say, 'God, break me. I want to die to my ambitions. I want to surrender my whole being for Your purpose'—that's a purpose-driven life. 'I want to surrender to Your purpose. For the rest of my life from this day forward I want to go Your way. I want to be purpose driven, not profit driven, not pleasing-other-people driven, but personally dedicated to You. I want to be purpose driven.' "[27]

---

25. Abanes, op. cit., 85.

26. Abanes, op. cit., 20.

27. Ibid., 7.

THREE

What I Especially Like About Warren's Messages

In a quick overview of *PDL*, **I found myself applauding certain teachings** *that are not as clearly presented in many other Christian denominations.*[1] One of the reasons so many people are impressed with *PDL* is that the book is full of practical truths that even genuine believers tend to ignore or forget. Here are some that are worthy of anyone's study. The page number(s) are given in parentheses at the end of each quotation.

Chapter 1

"God is not just the starting point of your life; he is the *source* of it. To discover your purpose in life you must turn to God's Word, not the world's wisdom. You must build your life on eternal truths, not pop psychology, success motivation, or inspirational stories" (20).

Chapter 2

"If there were no God, we would all be 'accidents,' the result of astronomical random chance in the universe" (25).

Chapter 3

"God specializes in giving people a fresh start" (28).

"Real security can only be found in that which can never be taken from you—your relationship with God" (29).

---

1. However, Warren mingles these positive and treasured insights with a faulty use of Bible texts and unwise references to those who do not accept the New Testament gospel, as we will see in succeeding chapters.

Chapter 4

"This life is not all there is.

"Life on earth is just the dress rehearsal before the real production. You will spend far more time on the other side of death—*in eternity*—than you will here" (36).

Chapter 5

"*Every* day is an important day, and every second is a growth opportunity to deepen your character, to demonstrate love, or to depend on God" (43).

Chapter 6

"To make the best use of your life, you must never forget two truths: First, compared with eternity, life is extremely brief. Second, earth is only a temporary residence. You won't be here long, so don't get too attached" (47).

Chapter 7

"It's all for him.

"The ultimate goal of the universe is to show the glory of God. It is the reason for everything that exists, including you. God made it *all* for his glory. Without God's glory, there would be nothing" (53).

Chapter 8

"When we worship, our goal is to bring pleasure to God, not ourselves" (66).

Chapter 9

"There are no *unspiritual* abilities, just misused ones. Start using yours for God's pleasure" (75).

Chapter 10

"We aren't God and *never* will be. We are humans. It is when we try to be God that we end up most like Satan, who desired the same thing" (79).

Chapter 11

"God wants to be your best friend" (85).

Chapter 12

"Like any friendship, you must work at developing your friendship with God. It won't happen by accident. It takes desire, time, and energy. If you want a deeper, more intimate connection with God you must learn to honestly share your feelings with him, trust him when he asks you to do something, learn to care about what he cares about, and desire his friendship more than anything else" (92).

Chapter 13

"God doesn't want a part of your life. He asks for *all* your heart, *all* your soul, *all* your mind, and *all* your strength. God is not interested in halfhearted commitment, partial obedience, and the leftovers of your time and money. He desires your full devotion, not little bits of your life" (100).

Chapter 14

"The deepest level of worship is praising God in spite of pain, thanking God during a trial, trusting him when tempted, surrendering while suffering, and loving him when he seems distant" (107).

Chapter 15

"Because God is love, he treasures relationships. His very nature is relational, and he identifies himself in family terms: Father, Son, and Spirit. The Trinity is God's relationship to himself. It's the perfect pattern for relational harmony, and we should study its implications" (117).

Chapter 16

"Love should be your top priority, primary objective, and greatest ambition. Love is not a *good* part of your life; it's the *most important* part" (124).

Chapter 17

"While your relationship to Christ is personal, God never intends it to be private. In God's family you are connected to every other believer, and we will belong to each other *for eternity*" (130).

Chapter 18

"Authentic fellowship is not superficial, surface-level chit-chat. It is genuine, heart-to-heart, sometimes gut-level, sharing. It happens when people get honest about who they are and what is happening in their lives.

They share their hurts, reveal their feelings, confess their failures, disclose their doubts, admit their fears, acknowledge their weaknesses, and ask for help and prayer" (139).

Chapter 19

"Cultivating community takes honesty. You will have to care enough to lovingly speak the truth, even when you would rather gloss over a problem or ignore an issue. While it is much easier to remain silent when others around us are harming themselves or others with a sinful pattern, it is not the loving thing to do" (146).

Chapter 20

"Peacemaking is not *avoiding conflict*. Running from a problem, pretending it doesn't exist, or being afraid to talk about it is actually cowardice. Jesus, the Prince of Peace, was never afraid of conflict. On occasion he *provoked* it for the good of everyone. Sometimes we need to avoid conflict, sometimes we need to create it, and sometimes we need to resolve it. That's why we must pray for the Holy Spirit's continual guidance" (153).

Chapter 21

"Divorcing your church at the first sign of disappointment or disillusionment is a mark of immaturity. God has things he wants to teach you, and others, too. Besides, there is no perfect church to escape to. Every church has its own set of weaknesses and problems. You'll soon be disappointed again" (163).

Chapter 22

"You were created to become like Christ" (171).

"Let me be absolutely clear: You will never become God, or even *a* god. That prideful lie is Satan's oldest temptation. Satan promised Adam and Eve that if they followed his advice, *'ye shall be as gods.'* Many religions and New Age philosophies still promote this old lie that we are divine or can become gods" (172).

Chapter 23

"God wants you to grow up.

"Your heavenly Father's goal is for you to mature and develop the characteristics of Jesus Christ. Sadly, millions of Christians *grow older* and never *grow up*. They are stuck in perpetual spiritual infancy, remaining in diapers and booties. The reason is that they never *intended* to grow" (179).

Chapter 24

"The truth transforms us.

"Spiritual growth is the process of replacing lies with truths. Jesus prayed, *'Sanctify them by the truth; your word is truth.'* Sanctification requires revelation. The Spirit of God uses the Word of God to make us like the Son of God. To become like Jesus, we must fill our lives with his Word" (185).

Chapter 25

"What happens outwardly in your life is not as important as what happens *inside* you. Your circumstances are temporary, but your character will last forever" (197).

Chapter 26

"On the path to spiritual maturity, even temptation becomes a stepping-stone rather than a stumbling block when you realize that it is just as much an occasion to do the right thing as it is to do the wrong thing. Temptation simply provides the choice. While temptation is Satan's primary weapon to destroy you, God wants to use it to develop you. Every time you choose to do good instead of sin, you are growing in the character of Christ" (201).

Chapter 27

"You may sometimes feel that a temptation is too overpowering for you to bear, but that's a lie from Satan. God has promised never to allow more *on* you than he puts *within* you to handle it. He will not permit any temptation that you could not overcome" (209).

Chapter 28

"There are no shortcuts to maturity.

"It takes years for us to grow to adulthood, and it takes a full season for fruit to mature and ripen. The same is true for the fruit of the Spirit. The development of Christlike character cannot be rushed. Spiritual growth, like physical growth, takes time" (217).

Chapter 29

"You weren't created just to consume resources—to eat, breathe, and take up space. God designed you to make a difference with your life. While many best-selling books offer advice on how to 'get' the most out of life, that's not the reason God made you. You were created to *add* to life on earth, not just take from it. God wants you to give something back" (227).

Chapter 30

"Whenever we forget these basic truths about [spiritual] gifts, it always causes trouble in the church. Two common problems are 'gift-envy' and 'gift-projection.' The first occurs when we compare our gifts with others', feel dissatisfied with what God gave us, and become resentful or jealous of how God uses others. The second problem happens when we expect everyone else to have our gifts, do what we are called to do, and feel as passionate about it as we do. The Bible says, *'There are different kinds of service in the church, but it is the same Lord we are serving'* " (237).

Chapter 31

"There is no 'right' or 'wrong' temperament for ministry. We need all kinds of personalities to balance the church and give it flavor. The world would be a very boring place if we were all plain vanilla" (245).

"You will be most effective when you use your *spiritual gifts* and *abilities* in the area of your *heart's desire,* and in a way that best expresses your *personality* and *experiences.* The better the fit, the more successful you will be" (248).

Chapter 32

"The best way to discover your gifts and abilities is to *experiment* with different areas of service. . . .

"Many books get the discovery process backwards. They say, 'Discover your spiritual gift and then you'll know what ministry you're supposed to have.' It actually works the exact opposite way. Just start serving, experimenting with different ministries, and then you'll discover your gifts. Until you're actually involved in serving, you're not going to know what you're good at" (250, 251).

Chapter 33

"Faithfulness has always been a rare quality. Most people don't know the meaning of commitment. They make commitments casually, then break them for the slightest reason without any hesitation, remorse, or regret. Every week, churches and other organizations must improvise because volunteers didn't prepare, didn't show up, or didn't even call to say they weren't coming" (261).

Chapter 34

"Unfortunately, a lot of our service is often self-serving. We serve to get others to like us, to be admired, or to achieve our own goals. That is manipulation, not ministry. The whole time we're really thinking about ourselves and how noble and wonderful we are. Some people try to use service as a bargaining tool with God: 'I'll do this for you God, if you'll do something for me.' Real servants don't try to use God for their purposes. They let God use them for *his* purposes" (266).

Chapter 35

"Humility is not putting yourself down or denying your strengths; rather, it is being honest about your weaknesses. The more honest you are, the more of God's grace you get. You will also receive grace from others. Vulnerability is an endearing quality; we are naturally drawn to humble people. Pretentiousness repels but authenticity attracts, and vulnerability is the pathway to intimacy" (276, 277).

Chapter 36

"God is at work in the world, and he wants you to join him. This assignment is called your *mission*. God wants you have a ministry in the Body of Christ and a mission in the world. Your ministry is your service to *believers*, and your *mission* is your service to *unbelievers*" (281).

Chapter 37

"Your testimony is the story of how Christ has made a difference in your life. . . . This is the essence of witnessing—simply sharing your personal experiences regarding the Lord. In a courtroom, a witness isn't expected to argue the case, prove the truth, or press for a verdict; that is the job of attorneys. Witnesses simply report what happened to them or what they saw" (290).

Chapter 38

"You have a choice to make. You will be either a *world-class* Christian or a *worldly* Christian.

"Worldly Christians look to God primarily for personal fulfillment. They are saved, but self-centered. They love to attend concerts and enrichment seminars, but you would never find them at a missions conference because they aren't interested. Their prayers focus on their own needs, blessings, and happiness. It's a "me-first" faith: How can God make *my* life more comfortable? They want to use God for their purposes instead of *being* used for *his* purposes.

"In contrast, world-class Christians know they were saved to serve and made for a mission. . . . World-class Christians are the only *fully alive* people on the planet" (297, 298).

Chapter 39

"A small reading group provides many benefits that a book by itself cannot. You can give and receive feedback about what you're learning. You can discuss real-life examples. You can pray for, encourage, and support each other as you begin to live out these purposes" (307).

Chapter 40

"How do you know when God is at the center of your life? When God's at the center, you worship. When he's not, you worry. Worry is the warning light that God has been shoved to the sideline. The moment you put him back at the center, you will have peace again" (314).

Conclusion

In this sampling of *PDL,* we can understand why so many readers have felt nourished and why so many keep attending Rick Warren's church services. Warren is very clear about emphasizing that our time on earth is short and that fruitfulness now will count for eternity. Every believer should appreciate his emphasis on the importance of humility and servanthood, the reality of temptation, and the assurance that spiritual victory over temptation is possible.

In our next chapter, we will take another look at what Rick Warren seems to mute or overlook in *PDL.* In fact, much of the criticism of *PDL* focuses on what he *doesn't* say or emphasize. Much of this criticism comes from those who claim Warren doesn't emphasize the sovereignty of God enough, while others say he is too committed to a view that God has predestined every facet of our lives. And they are both right—but for the wrong reasons. Others, from both sides, scold him for not being as forthright about various sins that are as prominent in our day as they were in Christ's time or that of the apostle Paul.

But let's be fair. Who can fault Warren for his insightful description of the way that a genuine believer's life should reflect our Lord's character? My main concern is that his readers will laud Rick Warren for those statements that appear so positive and obvious, but that in their appreciation, they will not be led into seeing a bigger biblical picture regarding what God really has in mind for planet Earth and its inhabitants.

After saying this, we must recognize that Warren had a specific goal in mind in writing *PDL* and that he might have much more to say on other subjects should he write *PDL 2*. That bigger picture would involve the great controversy between God and Satan, the state of human beings after death, why Jesus came and died, the urgency resting on the Christian church to be more explicit about its responsibility in the end times, and how God brings closure to human history.

FOUR

What Is So Special About "Forty Days"?

One of the most appealing, most compelling, first few pages of any book I have ever read is Rick Warren's introductory chapter in *PDL*, "A Journey With Purpose."[1]

Those looking for a freshness in their spiritual journey are swept into the book with its first paragraph:

> "This is more than a book; it is a guide to a *40-day spiritual journey* that will enable you to discover the answer to life's most important question: What on earth am I here for? . . . Having this perspective will reduce your stress, simplify your decisions, increase your satisfaction, and, most important, prepare you for eternity."

Then Warren makes this astounding statement: "The Bible is clear that God considers 40 days a spiritually significant time period. Whenever God wanted to prepare someone for his purposes, he took 40 days."

What is happening here? For the average reader, *forty* becomes built in to whatever Warren wants to prove. The average reader is set up to be blown away with Warren's (sometimes amazing) logic and assertions! Nowhere in the Bible do we find that God will take forty days to prepare someone for His purposes. This is another example of Warren misusing the Bible to back up his presuppositions—in this case, persuading the reader that forty days with his book will lead to a remarkable "spiritual journey."

Let's examine how Warren "proves" that the Bible is clear that whenever God wanted "to prepare someone for his purposes, he took 40 days:

---

1. *PDL*, 9–12.

▶ Noah's life was transformed by 40 days of rain.

▶ Moses was transformed by 40 days on Mount Sinai.

▶ The spies were transformed by 40 days in the Promised Land.

▶ David was transformed by Goliath's 40-day challenge,

▶ Elijah was transformed when God gave him 40 days of strength from a single meal.

▶ The entire city of Nineveh was transformed when God gave the people 40 days to change.

▶ Jesus was empowered by 40 days in the wilderness.

▶ The disciples were transformed by 40 days with Jesus after the resurrection."[2]

Then Warren makes his promise: "The next 40 days will transform *your* life."

For the lonely, weary, frazzled reader, young or old, this line of reasoning is captivating! *Nothing else seems to be working. Why not give the next forty chapters my best shot?*

How many readers will pause to ask such questions as, Is all this true? Did God use the forty-day plan in Noah's experience (and in all the other instances Warren cites) to "transform" him? Is this a valid premise?

Let's take a look! Nothing in the Genesis story suggests that Noah was transformed by forty days of rain. God chose Noah because he was *already prepared* for God's assignment. Noah was being transformed before the Flood came. "Noah found grace in the eyes of the LORD. . . . Noah was a just man, perfect in his generations. Noah walked with God" (Genesis 6:8, 9). Rain was on the earth for "forty days and forty nights" (Genesis 7:12) as a judgment on the world of "wickedness" wherein "every intent of the thoughts of [mankind's] heart was only evil continually" (Genesis 6:5).

No, Noah was not "transformed by forty days of rain"; the planet was.

What about Moses on Sinai? "Moses went into the midst of the cloud and went up into the mountain. And Moses was on the mountain forty days and forty nights" (Exodus 24:18). "He was there with the LORD forty days and forty nights; he neither ate bread nor drank water. And He [God] wrote on the tablets the words of the covenant, the Ten Commandments" (Exodus 34:28). Moses had this identical experience twice!

---

2. Ibid., 10.

Again, we find nothing in these two references to Moses being on Sinai for forty days to suggest that he was especially transformed. Of course, he was greatly blessed as no man ever before or since. God gave Moses this terrific experience because, like Noah, Moses *had already been transformed.*

Were the spies transformed by forty days in the Promised Land (see Numbers 13:25)? The sad story of those twelve spies is told in Numbers 14 and 15. Only two remained faithful; ten were not! All twelve surely had their trust in God tested. The reader of *PDL* would hardly want to use these "forty days" to prove that his or her next forty days would be a glorious adventure!

Was David transformed by Goliath's forty-day challenge? "And the Philistine drew near and presented himself forty days, morning and evening" (1 Samuel 17:16). If anything transforming happened to anyone in the Valley of Elah during those forty days, it would have happened to Goliath—not David. During these forty days of taunting, David made his way to the camp to bring food from home, knowing nothing about Goliath's forty days. He told his brothers—and then King Saul—that he was ready to meet Goliath and remove the "reproach from Israel" (verse 26). In other words, David heard Goliath's challenge that had been going on for forty days. This forty-day period had nothing to do with David's decision to meet Goliath face to face. David "transformed" Goliath, but it didn't take forty days!

Elijah was running for his life after Queen Jezebel had sent out her secret agents to find and kill him (see 1 Kings 19). He ran from Mount Carmel to Horeb—a long way. Terrified, he believed he was forsaken by man and God—a failure! After the forty days of flight, God called to him in a Horeb cave: "What are you doing here, Elijah?" (1 Kings 19:9). A forty-day flight does not constitute God's way of transforming Elijah!

Jonah had a searing message for Nineveh: " 'Yet forty days, and Nineveh shall be overthrown!' " (Jonah 3:4). Remarkably, Nineveh did listen, and God was pleased with Jonah's preaching and Nineveh's repentance (see verse 10). So it could be said that Nineveh responded to the message of doom during the forty-day period. But Jonah's message to Ninevah may not be the kind of message that Rick Warren would give in his book.

When Warren suggests that Jesus was "empowered by 40 days in the wilderness," one has to wonder what his words mean. I suppose that anyone who goes nose to nose with Satan and is not overcome must surely be an empowered person. But Jesus was already transformed in His thirty years of preparation for His earthly ministry.

It's true that Jesus was with the disciples for forty days after His resurrection, before His ascension (see Acts 1:3). It had to be a remarkable, unrepeatable experience! Pentecost was approaching, the fiftieth day after the Passover. Jesus spent this time preparing the disciples for the witnessing possibilities they would have when Jews from countries afar would gather in Jerusalem to celebrate. Perhaps this is one parallel that Warren is justified in using as a template for what he hopes his book will do for his readers.

But is there some deep spiritual message in the biblical use of a forty-day period? The answer, as we have seen, is no. With one possible exception, Warren has used faulty exegesis to back up his preconceived plan to persuade people that he has a divine injunction to pass on to his readers— that "by the end of this journey [of forty days] you will know God's purpose for your life and will understand the big picture—how all the pieces of your life fit together."[3]

The Bible refers to other forty-day periods that Warren doesn't mention. What is the significance of these? For example, what is the spiritual significance of the forty days a mother must wait to be purified from bleeding after giving birth to a boy (see Leviticus 12:1–4)? Or the forty days spent embalming Jacob's body (see Genesis 50:3)? Think of the quiet time of forty years during Gideon's judgeship (see Judges 8:28). Is there any spiritual meaning here? Or is there any spiritual transformation attached to the reign of King David over Israel for forty years (see 1 Kings 2:11)?

In chapter 7, we will examine the various ways Rick Warren uses biblical texts. However, in the next chapter, let's move on to analyze whether New Testament preachers used pragmatic techniques.

---

3. Ibid., 9.

FIVE

Did Biblical Preachers Use Pragmatic Techniques?

Rick Warren believes that Christian preaching can find a style to fit the occasion, whatever it may be, but that the substance must remain the same.[1] That surely is a common-sense rule. But when we read *PDL* and *PDC*, we sense that he picks and chooses what he means by "substance."

When Warren's picture of a seeker-friendly church coupled with a pastor that preaches to "felt" needs[2] is matched up with the example of biblical preachers such as Jonah or Paul, we surely have a disconnect or, as some say, a cognitive dissonance. I am not saying that Warren's sermons are all fluff. Hardly! They are highly motivational. They have their place in "growing" Christians. I, personally, have been rewarded with fresh insights in Warren's sermons. I can easily see why so many "feel" good and encouraged with his messages.[3]

But now the disconnect! Think about one of the greatest revivals in

---

1. *PDC*, 61.

2. "Felt" needs in the twenty-first century usually include loneliness, sense of failure, low self-esteem, anger, and resentment. These character problems are behind virtually all addictions, whether drug, alcohol, sex, or tobacco. But lying further behind these problems is the pervasive sin problem that all men and women must face up to. Treating these commonly described "felt" needs without dealing with the sin problem only postpones genuine, long-lasting relief and recovery.

3. Some of the recent newspaper clippings advertising user-friendly churches include "There is no fire and brimstone here. No Bible-thumping. Just practical, witty messages." "The sermons are relevant, upbeat, and best of all, short. You won't hear a lot preaching about sin and damnation and hell fire. Preaching here doesn't sound like *preaching*. It is sophisticated, urbane, and friendly talk. It breaks all stereotypes." "Our pastor is preaching a very upbeat message. . . . It's a salvationist message, but the idea is not so much being saved from the fires of hell. Rather, it's being saved from meaninglessness and aimlessness in this life. It's more of a soft-sell."—John E. MacArthur, op. cit., 47.

recorded history—that of Jonah in Nineveh (see Jonah 3:4, 5). What kind of a seeker-friendly approach did Jonah make as he sought to satisfy the Ninevites' "felt" needs? Did he walk around the city to see what music the Ninevites listened to before he opened his meetings, so that they would feel comfortable with him? Did Jonah gather poll data to find out how best to reach the young people?

Think of two other great biblical preachers with a terrific message. What did Ezra and Nehemiah do that brought about a great revival? Did they ask the churched or unchurched how they, as their leaders, should serve their "felt" needs? Nehemiah and Ezra preached the Word—without entertainment, gimmicks, dramas, worldly music, etc.—and it caused the people to weep (see Nehemiah 8:8, 9).

Turn again to the many sermons of Jeremiah (see Jeremiah 2:1–37; 3:1–25; 4:1–31; 5:1–6:16, etc.). Think of his ringing appeals:

> "And from the prophet even to the priest,
> Everyone deals falsely.
> They have also healed the hurt of My people slightly,
> Saying, 'Peace, peace!'
> When there is no peace.
> Were they ashamed when they had committed abomination?
> No! They were not at all ashamed;
> Nor did they know how to blush. . . .
>
> "Stand in the ways and see,
> And ask for the old paths, where the good way is,
> And walk in it;
> Then you will find rest for your souls" (Jeremiah 6:13–16).

What was Jeremiah's success record? Should we measure his success by counting those who came to thank him and call him blessed? What if Jeremiah had attended a church growth seminar or one of Saddleback's many seminars and learned about preaching that really worked! Do you think he would have changed his sermons in order to get more appreciation for his efforts?

We can't overlook John the Baptist, whom Jesus called "more than a prophet" (Matthew 11:9); in fact, Jesus said that no one born of a woman is "greater than John the Baptist" (Matthew 11:11). Honored with the greatest assignment ever given to a preacher, he bore "witness of the Light [Jesus]" (John 1:7).

How did John get the attention of the educated, the military, and the common laborer? "And he went into all the region around the Jordan, preaching a baptism of repentance for the remission of sins." He told his hearers, "Therefore bear fruits worthy of repentance." "And with many other exhortations he preached to the people" (Luke 3:3, 8, 18).

How did Jesus appeal to the masses?

Then there's Jesus! Warren notes that Jesus "began with people's needs, hurts, and interests."[4] He refers to our Lord's first sermon in Nazareth, where Jesus announced His preaching agenda by quoting from Isaiah 61, closing with His application to His listening audience.

But Warren does not read on! What kind of reception did Jesus get? Luke wrote, "Then all those in the synagogue, when they heard these things, were filled with wrath, and rose up and thrust Him out of the city; and they led Him to the brow of the hill on which their city was built, that they might throw him down over the cliff" (Luke 4:28, 29).

Did Jesus give His hometown a smooth message? He gave them what they needed to hear, but not what *they* "felt" to be important. If He had stressed only the love and mercy of God and avoided sin and judgment, He would not have turned off the home crowd. But Jesus was forthright and straightforward about what it took to follow Him. Unlike the seeker-friendly approach, Jesus was not afraid of turning off people.

Among other instances of Jesus speaking to His audience's real needs, not merely its "felt" needs, look at Luke 11. Of course we do not have all the circumstances surrounding this occasion; we have only Luke's condensed message. But Christ's words are not ambiguous: "And while the crowds were thickly gathered together, He began to say, 'This is an evil generation. It seeks a sign, and no sign will be given to it except the sign of Jonah the prophet. . . . The lamp of the body is the eye. Therefore, when your eye is good, your whole body also is full of light. But when your eye is bad, your body also is full of darkness. Therefore take heed that the light which is in you is not darkness' " (verses 29, 34, 35).

And the chapter continues to unfold in even stronger condemnations, using harsh language to describe many in His audience.

John 6 speaks of a great multitude that followed Jesus wherever He went. As the day wore on, He fed five thousand men plus their wives and children. They wanted to make Him king. The next day, after Jesus secretly sailed across the Sea of Galilee, the crowds caught up with Him. He preached another sermon in which the conditions for salvation became even clearer. The result? "From that time many of His disciples went back and walked with Him no more" (John 6:66).

Mark 10 gives us a few instances in which Jesus answered certain questions put to Him by the Pharisees and by the rich, young ruler. Jesus surely

---

4. *PDC*, 224, 225.

had His chance to ingratiate Himself with both men. But each time He said what had to be said, not what they wanted to hear. And they turned away, either mad or sad.

Of course Jesus knew how to speak to "felt" needs. He knew how to appeal to rough fishermen and sophisticated academicians. He pierced their conventional thinking, made them think "out of the box"—*way* out of the box. When He gently said, "Come to Me, all you who labor and are heavy laden, and I will give you rest" (Matthew 11:28), the high and the low felt a fresh voice from heaven.

The point is, however, that Jesus mixed His new revelations of what God was really like with a piercing picture of what human beings are like. He never blurred the line between His invitational appeals and the conditions of salvation. He never confused genuine repentance with mere confession.

The world today is awash with an ocean of various gospels. Did Jesus really understand the gospel? Mark thought He did: "Now after John was put in prison, Jesus came to Galilee, preaching the gospel of the kingdom of God, and saying, 'The time is fulfilled, and the kingdom of God is at hand. Repent, and believe [have faith] in the gospel' " (Mark 1:14, 15).

Are we today more sophisticated than Jesus? Are we smarter in recognizing how to build a church? Are we wiser and more urbane in making the good news appealing? *In Jesus' day and ours there is something about the clear gospel that divides an audience.*

Paul's ministry and his counsel to young Timothy

User-friendly gurus will have difficulty relating to Paul's ministry or his advice to young preachers. Even a casual review of Paul's two letters to Timothy makes one wonder today how young Tim would have fared in a twentieth-century, market-driven ministry.

Paul knew that his young intern (now with the church Paul had established in Ephesus) was up against severe trials. Many Ephesians wanted a watered-down gospel regarding church standards and discipline and what the good news should change in a believer's life. Note some of Paul's counsel to Timothy:

▶ Correct those teaching false doctrine and call them to a pure heart, a good conscience, and a sincere faith (1 Timothy 1:3–5).

▶ Fight for divine truth and for God's purposes, keeping your own faith and a good conscience (1:18, 19).

▸ Recognize the source of error and those who teach it, and point these things out to the rest of the church (4:1–6).

▸ Faithfully read, explain, and apply the Scriptures publicly (4:13, 14).

▸ Teach and preach principles of true godliness, helping the people to discern between true godliness and mere hypocrisy (5:24–6:6).

▸ Pursue righteousness, godliness, faith, love, patience, and gentleness (6:11).

▸ Fight for the faith against all enemies and all attacks (6:12).

▸ Keep all the Lord's commandments (6:13–16).

▸ Hold tightly to the truth and guard it (2 Timothy 1:12–14).

▸ Be a teacher of apostolic truth so that you may reproduce yourself in faithful men (2:2).

▸ Suffer difficulty and persecution willingly while making the maximum effort for Christ (2:3–7)

▸ Lead with authority (2:14).

▸ Interpret and apply Scripture accurately (2:15).

▸ Refuse to be drawn into philosophical and theological wrangling (2:23).

▸ Face dangerous times with a deep knowledge of the Word of God (3:1–15).

▸ Understand that Scripture is the basis and content of all legitimate ministry (3:16, 17).

▸ Preach the Word—reproving, rebuking, and exhorting with great patience and instruction (4:1, 2).[5]

Does any of this counsel sound like pragmatic marketing techniques? Read the dozens of books available today on church growth and the modern ministry. Many of them do their best to find "something" in Scripture that will support their modern business techniques, their psychological concepts and management theories. Rarely do any even refer to Paul's counsel to Timothy!

In fact, with prophetic vision, Paul could see our day: "For the time will come when they will not endure sound doctrine; but according to their own desires, because they have itching ears, they will heap up for themselves

---

5. Taken from a larger analysis in MacArthur, op. cit., 25–27.

teachers; and they will turn their ears away from the truth, and be turned aside to fables" (2 Timothy 4:3, 4). Why do listeners "have itching ears"? Because they don't want to be confronted with the full gospel! They don't want to be convicted! They want to feel good with motivational lectures, heavy-beat music, and positive-thinking sermons.

Further, Paul never told Timothy how to measure his success. "Just stay committed, Tim. Stay faithful to the gospel that I have shared with you, the gospel that I received from our Lord Jesus and from the apostles. Don't worry about how the world measures success; just keep pursuing excellence in following my example."

In summary, Paul is telling all New Testament gospel preachers to "preach the Word." Meet each generation, each new culture, with the simple gospel that turns sinners into willing believers. Don't let each new culture, each new world situation, determine the substance of preaching or even the method—if it means not preaching the whole everlasting gospel.

First-century Christian church as a model

Remember when Luke recorded how envious Jews described early Christians? They "turned the world upside down" (Acts 17:6). Some say that in our day, the world is turning the church upside down!

Consider an event in the Jerusalem church, which had been growing rapidly; thousands had already joined, nourished by the sound preaching of the apostles. Many were selling assets to care for those who were less fortunate, especially those who lost their jobs because of their commitment to the crucified Jesus. Some, like Barnabas, shared liberally.

But then, there were Ananias and Sapphira (see Acts 5), who conspired to look good in front of their fellow church members. They sold some property but "kept back part of the proceeds" (verse 2). Greed and deceit appeared in the early church because their hearts were filled with Satan's spirit (see verse 3). Ananias and Sapphira didn't have to sell their property— the sin was their lie. Peter said to Ananias, "You have not lied to men but to God" (verse 4). The husband and wife died in one day, perhaps out of sheer shock.

Many today give offerings under false pretenses. Jesus called it "the leaven of the Pharisees" (Luke 12:1). Greed and deceit are dangerous infections anywhere, but especially in the Christian church. God dealt harshly with deception. How did the young church react? "Great fear came upon all those who heard these things" (Acts 5:5).

What was God's message? "I don't play church. There are more important issues in proclaiming the gospel than trying to be only user-friendly. To sincerely profess Christianity is to reject sin; greed and deceit are not trivial matters."

What was the general impact of the death of Ananias and Sapphira? "So great fear came upon all the church and upon all who heard these things" (verse 11). And what happened to the church? The result turned the typical user-friendly philosophy upside down: "Believers were increasingly added to the Lord, multitudes of both men and women" (verse 14).

What kind of a God did Christians represent? A God who helped them do "many signs and wonders . . . among the people" (verse 12). A God who was revealed through Jesus Christ, their " 'Prince and Savior, to give repentance to Israel and forgiveness of sins. And we are His witnesses to these things, and so also is the Holy Spirit whom God has given to those who obey Him' " (verse 31). A God of judgment who hates sin and a God of great compassion who loves and re-creates sinners! A great message for those who really need help for all their addictions, loneliness, and resentments. But for all those who do not want to confront their self-absorption and inner desires for power and self-gratification, this kind of a message will not seem user-friendly.

Was Paul a marketing expert in being "all things to all men"?

George Barna, whom many compare with George Gallup in taking reliable polls, wrote in 1988 that "Paul provided what I feel is perhaps the single most insightful perspective on marketing communications, the principle we call *contextualization* (1 Corinthians 9:19–23). Paul . . . was willing to shape his communications according to their needs in order to receive the response he wanted."[6]

Does that sound like Paul was a pragmatic preacher? After all, he did write:

"For though I am free from all men, I have made myself a servant to all, that I might win the more; and to the Jews I became as a Jew, that I might win Jews; to those who are under the law, as under the law, that I might win those who are under the law; to those who are without law, as without law (not being without law toward God, but under law toward Christ), that I might win those who are without law; to the weak I

---

6. George Barna, *Marketing the Church* (Colorado Springs, Colo.: NavPress, 1988), 33. Barna has changed his emphasis and would modify these thoughts today. His new direction appeared in his remarkable volume *Think Like Jesus* (Brentwood, Tenn.: Integrity Publishers, 2003). Barna is searching for a new strategy that would recall the vitality of the early church in Jerusalem. "His constant surveying of the American public reveals no turning back from moral and spiritual relativism [in the American public]."—Stafford, *Christianity Today*, August 5, 2002.

became as weak, that I might win the weak. I have become all things to all men, that I might by all means save some. Now this I do the for the gospel's sake, that I may be partaker of it with you" (1 Corinthians 9:19–23).

What should we think about all this? When I read Paul's letters and follow his journeys through the book of Acts, I surely do not find a modern user-friendly, people-pleasing preacher. How should we understand Paul's "marketing techniques"?

I like John MacArthur's description: "He was Christ's ambassador, not His press secretary. Truth was something to be declared, not negotiated. Paul was not ashamed of the gospel (Romans 1:16). He willingly suffered for the truth's sake (2 Corinthians 11:23–28). He did not back down in the face of opposition and rejection. He did not compromise with unbelievers or make friends with the enemies of God."[7]

But still, what did Paul mean by becoming "all things to all men that I might by all means save some" (1 Corinthians 9:22)? Let's look at his whole statement in context.

Whatever it took, Paul would sacrifice—not his message, but himself. He would be a "servant" (Greek: "slave") to all men if that is what preaching the gospel took. He gave up his enviable status as a highly respected member of the Sanhedrin with all its material benefits. He turned from being greatly honored by his countrymen. He would be without the income he had been accustomed to. All this so that he could devote his mental, emotional, and physical energies to proclaiming the good news to the weak as well as the strong, the Gentile as well as the Jew.

Although Paul enjoyed Christian liberty, free from Jewish legalism, he would do his best not to offend the Jew. His Christian liberty kept him from unending wrestling with Gentile philosophers, although he could also speak to their minds with logic meeting logic (see Acts 17). But he did not tailor his message to his audience in order to make it more pleasing. When he got the people's attention, using obvious illustrations of good will, he led them to the gospel before he ended his sermons. He didn't needlessly offend the Gentiles.

He was willing to mingle with Jews in observing Old Testament rituals in order to get their attention regarding what those rituals meant. He made it clear that he was not neglecting God's holy laws, which he proclaimed on many occasions. And he was not modifying his message to make it more pleasing. He simply did not want to unnecessarily offend the Jews—he wanted their attention.

---

7. MacArthur, op. cit., 91.

Paul explains his own paradox: He is a free and willing servant unto Christ and His righteousness, and he is also free to restrict his own liberties that he might win others to Christ.

When Paul speaks of winning, he is not looking at external rewards; he wins souls for the kingdom of God. He emphasized this to Timothy: "I endure all things for the sake of the elect, that they also may obtain the salvation which is in Christ Jesus with eternal glory" (2 Timothy 2:10).

So what's Paul's point? He is not explaining a marketing plan or advocating *contextualization.* He is simply revealing the principles that motivated his life as a Christian preacher.

Still, specifically, what did Paul mean when he said, "To the weak I became as weak, that I might win the weak" (2 Corinthians 9:22)? Earlier, in his letter to the Romans, he defined whom he regards as "weak" (see Romans 14:1–23): "Receive [have fellowship with] those weak in faith but not for the purpose of passing judgment upon their scruples" (Romans 14:1, literal translation).

In Romans 14, the "weak," for Paul, are those who have personal opinions regarding food and drink that are more strict and austere than the opinions of others. Yet, their real offense was not their stricter dietary principles but their censorious attitude toward other church members who were not as strict. In turn, the less strict were contemptuous of their "weaker" church members. Not a good, loving situation!

Paul's appeal to both groups is "Stop it! Who are you to judge another, especially those who are Christ's servant?"

Whatever the reason for bickering and judgment from either side, "Let each be fully convinced in his own mind. . . . Why do you judge your brother? Or why do you show contempt for your brother? For we shall all stand before the judgment seat of Christ. . . . So then each of us shall give account of himself to God. Therefore let us not judge one another anymore, but rather resolve this, not to put a stumbling block or a cause to fall in our brother's way. . . . Therefore let us pursue the things which make for peace and the things by which one may edify another" (Romans 14:5, 10, 12, 13, 19).

So how does this fit Paul's preaching methodology? His first principle is not to offend anyone needlessly, either the super scrupulous or the contemptuous. Jews and Gentiles were in both groups; it was a new situation for everyone in the young Christian community. But Paul was free from the pangs of conscience felt by the young Jewish Christian and from the superstitions of the Gentiles who once had offered food to idols.

When Paul says, "That I might by all means save some . . . for the gospel's sake" (1 Corinthians 9:22, 23), he is certainly not compromising to follow some kind of pragmatic technique. He is using his Christian liberty in order to avoid offending anyone with his personal lifestyle choices. But Paul didn't preach a cheap gospel in order not to offend: "We are not, as so many, peddling the word of God; but as of sincerity, but as from God, we speak in the sight of God in Christ." "We have renounced the hidden things of shame, not walking in craftiness nor handling the word of God deceitfully, but by manifestation of the truth commending ourselves to every man's conscience in the sight of God" (2 Corinthians 2:17; 4:2).

Paul would not water down the gospel to please the Jew who considered his good news about Jesus "a stumbling block" or to please the Gentile who considered the good news "foolishness" (see 1 Corinthians 1:23). But he would practice Christian love in deference to their ways of thinking in order to get their attention and to hold that attention as long as he could. In other words, Paul was not trying to win a popularity contest.

Paul on Mars' Hill is the template for preachers everywhere

Those who extol "contextualization" and seek cultural identification and relevance in their preaching often point to Paul at the Areopagus in Athens (see Acts 17). But those who would make Paul into a savvy marketer of the gospel do not read very far into his monumental sermon. He was simply being Paul, becoming "all things to all men, that I might by all means save some" (1 Corinthians 9:22).

He began his sermon in Athens with the time-honored salutation that sophisticated Athenians would appreciate: "Men of Athens!" Then he jolted them, actually surprised them: "I perceive that in all things you are very religious; for as I was passing through and considering the objects of your worship, I even found an altar with this inscription: TO THE UNKNOWN GOD" (Acts 17:22, 23). Here was perfect identification with his audience; he showed them respect and got their favorable attention.

Then Paul set forth his first premise that they would never forget: "Therefore the One whom you worship without knowing, Him I proclaim to you" (verse 23). He is following a marvelous preaching technique—leading his audience from the known to the unknown.

I wish we knew everything Paul said that day; we have only the digest of what must have been a magnificent sermon. But the outline we have is almost sufficient. Paul doesn't wander into philosophical oratory; he answers the question he has placed in their minds regarding the identity of this "Unknown God." He tells them that the God they worship unknowingly is the Creator of the world and everything in it (see verses 23, 24), and with a sweep of his hands in a magnificent gesture, he points to the Acropolis and the Parthenon on an adjoining hill—the temple of the goddess Athena— the goddess of Wisdom. What an illustration!

Paul knew that he was talking to men and women who were drenched in Greek mythology and philosophy, persons who were accustomed to debating the principles and observations of Plato, Aristotle, and dozens of others who had opined on how this world came to be. Paul's incisive contribution could not be ignored!

And his logic was masterful. All men and women grope to get a clear understanding of God. In fact—and here Paul was marvelously tactful—he quoted two of their own Greek poets, Epimenides and Aratus (or Aradus), who wrote that we are "offspring" of this unknown God whom Paul will shortly introduce.

Then standing on the grounds of the highest court in Greece, he told them that the God he represents "will judge the world in righteousness." That really got their attention!

The suspense must have been electric! How will this all happen? Paul continued by pointing out that God had already ordained "the Man" who will do the judging! Paul's God was not just another in the pantheon of gods—the Greeks might even accept that!

Now this is where Paul really was no longer "user-friendly." He declared that this Man that the Creator had ordained had already lived on planet Earth. In fact, He had been killed, but the Creator resurrected Him!

That did it! In all their literature, in all their philosophy, no one had ever been resurrected from the dead! Their only response was to "mock" Paul— they had no logic with which to argue further. What Paul said did not fit their worldview! They waved him off.

Imagine, calling for the Epicureans and the Stoics to repent! "Repent from your self-centered, pleasure-loving lives, Epicureans! Repent from your self-satisfied, self-disciplined philosophies, Stoic friends! God is winking at your many years of ignorance—but judgment is coming for all of us!"

Was Paul a big flop in Athens? Was his attempt at blending respect and courtesy and graciousness with a clear picture of God a big failure that should never be tried again? Hardly! Would not every preacher be grateful if in even one sermon he or she could win "some," including Dionysius, one of the members of the Athenian Supreme Court, and Damaris, probably an influential woman (see verse 34)? It was a great start for the church in Athens!

Going back to Paul's preaching principle—becoming all things to all men that he might win some—how did he do in Athens? Just as he did in the Jewish synagogues, where he became "Jewish" in tone and illustration, so in Athens, Paul became Grecian in tone and illustration. He showed respect and deference for whatever audience he could find. He adjusted his message to gain the attention of his audience, but he never adapted his message to please his audience.[8]

The Athenian sermon is a masterful template of what Christian preaching should—and must—be today. Successful preaching technique, such as Paul modeled, always has eternal results.

Paul was forever sorry that He didn't have the opportunity in Athens to speak more about Jesus of Nazareth and the meaning of His death and resurrection (1 Corinthians 1:1, 2). Yet, he knew that with the audience he had, he had no other choice.[9]

---

8. One of the basic assumptions of Saddleback and Willow Creek is that "adaptation" is a governing principle. Obviously, Christian history has many examples of "constructive adaptation." Os Guinness points out that "in the nineteenth century Hudson Taylor founded the China Inland Mission and scandalized Europeans [missionaries] when he took the gospel right into the interior of China, not just to the treaty ports where other Westerners stopped. Taking the incarnation as their pattern, and without ever compromising the gospel, he and his fellow missionaries set out to become as Chinese as they could. In the process, they learned not just Mandarin but also local Chinese dialects, wore Chinese dress rather than Western, and adopted Chinese customs whenever appropriate."—*Prophetic Untimeliness* (Grand Rapids, Mich.: Baker Books, 2003), 61.

9. "See Paul at Athens before the council of the Areopagus, as he meets science with science, logic with logic, and philosophy with philosophy. Mark how, with the tact born of divine love, he points to Jehovah as 'the Unknown God,' whom his hearers have ignorantly worshiped; and in words quoted from a poet of their own he pictures Him as a Father whose children they are. Hear him, in that age of caste, when the rights of man as man were wholly unrecognized, as he sets forth the great truth of human brotherhood, declaring that God 'hath made of one blood all nations of men for to dwell on all the face of the earth.' Then he shows how, through all the dealings of God with man, runs like a thread of gold His purpose of grace and mercy. He 'hath determined the times before appointed, and the bounds of their habitation; that they should seek the Lord, if haply they might feel after Him, and find Him, though He be not far from every one of us' (Acts 17:23, 26, 27.)"—E. G. White, *Education,* 67.

SIX

Some Troubling Features

The user-friendly approach to the gospel will surely meet modern man's "felt" needs as individuals see them, but will it truly meet their modern "deepest" needs?

Putting it in the most positive sense, the user-friendly, positive gospel will surely meet the "felt" needs of men and women for affirmation, identity, and a sense of belonging. It especially fits our postmodern culture! Most men and women feel either guilty or lacking in self-esteem (as psychologists are quick to tell us) and thus are predisposed to believe in a tolerant, nonjudgmental God.

But God doesn't promise to make us comfortable or pamper our feelings in our search for meaning and purpose. He does promise, however, that He will speak to the causes of our sense of guilt and low self-esteem. Further, God promises personal help to meet each day's challenges. Even further, as we persevere in faith, we will hear Him whispering, "My grace is sufficient for you, for my power is made perfect in your weakness" (2 Corinthians 12:9). This power of grace may have little to do with today's "felt" needs—but everything to do with our "deepest" needs.

We must realize that unregenerate "believers" who hold to the ways of the world will naturally seek a church that fits that world. But the church in worship should not reinvent itself simply to make unregenerate "believers" feel at home and to satisfy curious seekers. Of course, as they lovingly share the uplifting truths of the everlasting gospel, churches should make searchers for truth feel welcome; that should always be the mark of a Spirit-led church.

But leading the curious into a knowledge of the holy Lord of the universe and what He has in mind for each person, young and old, *is* primarily the

57

function of an appealing *evangelistic service*. Here, without any embarrassment, the unregenerate should be led step by step into a personal acceptance of Jesus, their crucified Savior.

We could also ask, Does God really love today's cultural variety? Is He pleased when we feed our cravings for emotional stimulation? Paul reminds us that those things that happened in the Israelites' experience are recorded "as examples, and they were written for our admonition" (1 Corinthians 10:11). When the Israelites became bored, they embraced a wide variety of cultural and spiritual thrills. God disciplined them severely, even comparing them to a "wild donkey . . . that sniffs at the wind in her desire" (Jeremiah 2:24).

Could it be that the spiritual fast-food and "gospel lite" for which people clamor is merely a substitute that compensates for their lack of true repentance? When we use energizing music, emotional stimuli, and light messages to satisfy the flesh with its "felt" needs, we tend to obscure our deeper spiritual needs. When holiness, absolute truth, and God's direct commands (as reflected in both the Old and New Testaments) are toned down, "believers" are deprived of the spiritual armor they need to stand against the wiles of Satan (see Ephesians 6:10–18). If negative themes are not welcome, how would church members ever know about the spiritual deception that Paul warns about, including the role of false prophets, the rise of antichrist, and last-day events?

Warren tends to minimize the sobering reality behind God's warnings and to inflate God's promises

Warren's preference for *The Message* paraphrase of John 3:36 is more than interesting: *"Whoever accepts and trusts the Son gets in on everything, life complete and forever!"* (*PDL*, 58). What does "gets in on everything" mean? A more literal translation of John 3:36 would be, "He who accepts and trusts the Son has everlasting life; and he who does not obey the Son shall not see life, but the wrath of God abides on him."

Unfortunately, one of the most politically incorrect words in the English language today is "judgment." And to say that God will judge sinners on the basis of a "right-wing" conservative's use of biblical texts is considered a passé scare tactic.

My point is, God's love is unconditional; His promises and acceptance are not. But for the most part, Warren leaves out the conditions and warnings. The reader of *PDL* gets the idea that everyone seems OK in the eyes of Him who "passionately" loves and accepts all of us as we are.

By trivializing the authority of God's Word, Warren bends our view of

God's high standards for our lives—standards that are possible to us only through cooperation with His Holy Spirit. Although Warren quotes God's promises, while ignoring His warnings, he unintentionally builds presumptive assurance—not a genuine "obedience to the faith" (see Romans 16:26). Most *PDL* readers would come away hardly knowing what to obey!

Warren's definition of sin is so general that individuals will not sense genuine guilt

Warren defines sin as follows: "All sin, at its root, is failing to give God glory. It is loving anything else more than God. Refusing to bring glory to God is prideful rebellion, and it is the sin that caused Satan's fall—and ours, too. In different ways we have all lived for our own glory, not God's. The Bible says, *'All have sinned and fall short of the glory of God'* " (Romans 3:23).[1]

True, but this general view of sin, which applies to all humanity, will hardly cause modern believers to sense any genuine, personal guilt or a personal need for what Jesus did for human beings on the cross and what He wants to do in us through His Holy Spirit.

The issue for Warren is to "bring glory to God," and he points to "Jesus who told the Father, 'I brought glory to you here on earth by doing everything you told me to do.' " Warren chose the right text, but he leaves unanswered the question How do we sinners know, specifically, what God requires of us? If Warren does emphasize obedience to God's will as expressed in His commandments, I have not discovered it. Nor have I seen any reference by him to 1 John 3:4—"Sin is the transgression of the law."

When sin becomes generalized, it is easy to lapse into a comfortable half-truth: "Sin is a normal part of life, and I'm just as good as everyone else—maybe a little better. Besides, God understands and loves me as I am." This leads to dismissing "sin" as old-fashioned legalism; eyes become shut to sin's corrupting power.

Warren does outline well how to bring glory to God: (1) by worshiping Him; (2) by loving other believers; (3) by becoming like Christ; (4) by serving others with our gifts; (5) by telling others about Him.[2] This is a general picture of a genuine Christian, but the details that have much to do with genuine worship are lacking. Where, for example, are repentance, acknowledgement of need, or confession of personal sin? Where is the emphasis on why Jesus died? It seems that we are saved merely from a purposeless life, not from the bondage of sin.

---

1. *PDL*, 54, 55.

2. Ibid., 55–57.

Most people who call themselves Christians have little understanding of the gospel. Postmodern "believers" may be full of the excitement of a fresh purpose in their lives but woefully short on spiritual awareness.

George Barna is a remarkably efficient, trustworthy pollster and commentator on contemporary life. He (Barna Research Group, Oxnard, California) has written a number of books in the past fifteen years reflecting what he discovers in his research.

Moving from his analysis and former encouragement to the church growth movement and pragmatic marketing to a painful examination of what all this has accomplished generally, his last two books—*The Second Coming of the Church*[3] and *Think Like Jesus*[4]—are remarkable in their analysis of spiritual life in the United States of the twenty-first century. They cry out for serious readers.

In a *Christianity Today* interview (August 5, 2002) Barna said, "In the last quarter-century it seems that we have learned how to sell Bibles, but not how to sell what's in the Bible. Increasingly, people pick and choose the Bible content they like or feel comfortable with, but ignore the rest of God's counsel."

Further, "Christianity has no cost in America. We've made it way too easy to be 'born again'—perhaps much easier than Jesus intended. When do we get to the point at which we accept smaller numbers of intensely devoted people rather than feverishly investing in filling auditoriums and stadiums with massive numbers of the lukewarm 'Christians' that Jesus will need to reject (Rev. 3:16)?"

Tim Stafford, providing the interview, said of Barna, "His constant surveying of the American public reveals no turning back from moral and spiritual relativism."

In his book *The Second Coming of the Church*, Barna compared the remarkable similarities between "born-again" Christians and non-Christians in such areas as prevalence of divorce, using drugs for depression, watching R-rated movies, giving money to a homeless person, etc. He then concluded, "Americans have taken to piecing together a customized version of faith. Consider how we have repositioned spirituality. Faith used to revolve around God and His ordinances and principles; the faith that arrests our attention these days is that which revolves around us. We have demystified God, befriended Jesus, abandoned the Holy Spirit. . . . Few Americans possess a sense of awe, fear,

---

3. *The Second Coming of the Church* (Nashville: Word Publishing, 1998).

4. *Think Like Jesus* (Nashville: Integrity Publishers, 2003).

or trembling related to God. To increasing millions of Americans, God . . . exists for the pleasure of humankind."[5]

Barna is right! There seems to be a pervasive reluctance among many contemporary Christian leaders, including Rick Warren, to use the word *fear* when referring to God. The Bible is unambiguous regarding an un-compromising God with little tolerance for our lukewarm "obedience" and self-pleasing "worship." *Fear* clashes with today's attempt to market God to postmodern masses, but *fear* of God is not "cowering trepidation." *Fearing God* includes awe, a sense of unworthiness, recognition of the consequences of sin. I fear the look on God's face if and when I embarrass Him, even as I fear my wife's face if I should embarrass her.

Postmodern Christians prefer a more likable God who resembles a permissive parent—for many, *fear* and *righteous* are judgmental terms!

I could wish that Warren had used one of the clearest biblical texts regarding the relationship of *fear* to one's total commitment to God:

> "Trust in the Lord with all your heart,
> And lean not on your own understanding;
> In all your ways acknowledge Him,
> And He shall direct your paths.
> Do not be wise in your eyes;
> Fear the LORD and depart from evil.
> It will be health to your flesh,
> And strength to your bones" (Proverbs 3:5–8).

In *The Barna Update* for December 1, 2003 ("A Biblical Worldview Has a Radical Effect on a Person's Life"), Barna wrote, "Most Americans have little idea how to integrate core biblical principles to form a unified and meaningful response to the challenges and opportunities of life. We're often more concerned with survival amidst chaos than with experiencing truth and significance."

In other words, the religion of many is an inoffensive gospel that is defined so vaguely that it can be accepted by virtually everybody; sin and its dreadful consequences are rarely mentioned. This happens when the full implications of Jesus' death on the cross and His heavenly ministry are not explicitly proclaimed. Others have called this the fallout of "cheap grace."[6]

Today, most Christians emphasize the receiving part of the gospel and

---

5. Ibid., 6.

6. Dietrich Bonhoeffer, *The Cost of Discipleship* (New York: The Macmillan Company, 1959) 45–59.

overlook the repenting parts. Further, confession is not repentance. Only a clear definition of sin produces genuine repentance (a "turning around") that leads to peace and genuine assurance.

A proper understanding of Warren's message is even more important than focusing on his methodology

Many of Warren's detractors focus primarily on his methodology. They worry about his marketing techniques. They fret over his methods, such as his music, his sermon-lite, etc. Rarely seen in the many books analyzing the Warren phenomenon (other than those coming from the Calvinist side of Protestantism or from extreme fundamentalism) is a careful examination of his message.[7] For example, if the content of Warren's gospel (or anyone else's gospel) is incomplete, then the movement will never meet biblical criteria, no matter how orthodox or "successful" the methods. What good is it to speak the language of secular people and gain their attention if we lose or distort God's message in the process?

From another standpoint, it is one thing to sound orthodox on paper. But often, in the attempt to be biblical, it is easy to de-emphasize certain parts of New Testament theology—choosing to focus only on those parts of the message that sound enticing to potential seekers.

This kind of "gospel" preaching fits the pragmatic approach of the Christian growth movement, which avoids "sticky" or unpopular theological issues.[8] One way to do this is to replace verse-by-verse exposition with topical messages that focus on the "felt" needs of the audience. Such preaching may sound like a biblical message, but if one downplays God's judgment, holiness, and righteousness—and focuses almost exclusively on His paternal love—a very important part of the everlasting gospel is lost. If one focuses on the promise of peace, prosperity, and life-fulfillment in this world, it is very likely that these goals will overshadow the eternal consequences of one's personal response to Christ.

---

7. Both the Calvinist and the Fundamentalist have their own incomplete understanding of the gospel.

8. See Appendix B—"Relation Between the Rick Warren Phenomenon and the Christian Growth Movement."

SEVEN

Faulty Use of Biblical Passages

Many of Warren's detractors, even in his own denominational circle, are troubled by his seeming disregard for generally accepted hermeneutical principles. As I read both of his books, *The Purpose Driven Life* (*PDL*) and *The Purpose Driven Church* (*PDC*), it didn't take me more than a few pages to come to the same conclusion. Warren used many texts that are either flawed, incomplete, or contrary to the meaning of their contexts.[1]

Hermeneutics is the word used to describe how we should interpret literary documents. We use the term when we attempt to understand secular writers such as Plato and Shakespeare, as well as inspired writers such as Moses, Paul, and John. Hermeneutical rules help us to understand what writers meant by what they said.

For example, readers should do their best to "see" and "hear" what the writer saw and heard. That, of course, depends on how much we can learn about the character, personality, and historical milieu of the writer. Amos, the sheepherder, would express himself differently than Isaiah, a statesman and counselor of kings.

Further, we should try to discover, as far as possible, what the contemporaries of these writers understood their writings to mean (if the messages were directed to them). This will protect the Bible student today from "seeing" in the Bible only what he or she is looking for. When one reads his own meaning into a biblical text, we call that misuse of Scripture eisegesis (putting *our* thoughts *into* what we want the Bible to say). Those who are faithful to the rules of hermeneutics practice exegesis—that is, they try to *bring forth* to their listeners what Bible writers actually meant.

---

1. For many examples of Warren's faulty use of biblical texts, see Appendix D: Examples of Faulty Use of Biblical Texts.

In other words, don't look "to get" a message from the Bible; rather, "seek" the message of the Bible.

One of the astonishing features of Warren's two books is his copious use of fifteen different Bible translations to ensure that his points are supported. In *PDL,* one must travel through forty chapters to find Appendix 3 where he can read what Warren should have explained in his introduction regarding why he used so many translations, paraphrases, and versions! In Appendix 3, Warren writes, "I have deliberately used paraphrases in order to help you see God's truth in new, *fresh* ways." [2]

Obviously, the use of modern paraphrases provides a "new, *fresh* way" to read the Bible! But what really happens in this free use of paraphrases and translations of choice? Readers and church members unconsciously accept Warren's use of paraphrases as God's Word when he quotes nearly a thousand biblical texts. This is especially true when fewer church members now bring their Bibles to church or are even encouraged to do so. In other words, getting into the Word individually has become a lost art in many contemporary churches.

For years, of course, many teachers and preachers in all churches have been looking for texts that support their personal views—they are true eisegetes. But Warren and similar seeker-friendly pastors are doing something novel in this area, today, and getting away with it. They have creative thoughts or a particular message—on which they build an entire book or movement—and then they find a Bible translation or paraphrase that would seem to support their idea or claim, even if that particular translation has distorted the biblical passage.[3]

The average church member or reader of *PDL* believes that Warren and others are actually using the Bible as authority, but few will ever check the quoted passage for its accuracy and its context. All this reminds me of 2 Peter 3:16, where the apostle warns of some who "twist" or "torture" [literal translations] the Scriptures.

How should church members be protected? Do what the Bereans did—

---

2. *PDL,* 325.

3. Warren makes a strong point in wanting to make "the Bible accessible to unbelievers. . . . Since God's Word is 'the Word of life,' we must do everything we can do to bring the unchurched into contact with it and help them feel comfortable using it. There are several things you can do to relieve anxiety and spark interest in the Bible among the unchurched. *Read Scripture from a newer translation.* With all the wonderful translations and paraphrases available today, there is no legitimate reason for complicating the Good News with four-hundred-year-old English."—*PDC,* 297. What Warren misses is the basic principle that we must use translations and paraphrases that rightly represent the Greek and Hebrew Testaments.

they "searched the Scriptures daily to find out whether these things were so" (Acts 17:11).

The reality is that most listeners or readers do not take the time to look up Warren's proof texts, either in the book's endnotes or in the Bible. For most readers, if texts are quoted in the book, that's the end of it. They don't know when illegitimate "twists" are made. What would definitely help both Warren and his readers and hearers would be to make clear that when they read *The Message* or *The Living Bible*, for example, these paraphrases are only the paraphraser's opinions. If we called these versions commentaries, it would be more honest.

We noted earlier that pragmatism opens the door to weak and flawed biblical teachings. Pragmatism is the notion that the worth of a thing is determined and tested by practical consequences. In other words, pragmatism looks to the world's marketing methods or poll results for its value, rather than to New Testament mandates. For pragmatists, if something works (that is, if it brings people into the church), it's OK! The Bible's intent is not a priority for pragmatists!

However, let no one misunderstand. There is no question that Rick Warren is Bible-based; in his book he uses almost a thousand scriptural quotations from fifteen different translations and paraphrases. And he tells us why! "First, no matter how wonderful a translation is, it has limitations. . . . Obviously, nuances and shades of meaning can be missed, so it is always helpful to compare translations."

So far, so good!

He then emphasizes that he "deliberately used paraphrases in order to help you see God's truth in new, *fresh* ways." This is where his use of Scripture falls apart. Paraphrases, especially, are primarily subjective impressions of what the paraphraser thinks the Bible says. The only way to determine whether the paraphrase is legitimate is to compare it with the New Testament Greek or Old Testament Hebrew. No other way!

I reviewed Warren's nearly one thousand Bible quotations in *PDL*. For me, the majority of the texts were used acceptably. That is, regardless of translation or paraphrase, Warren seemed to faithfully reflect the biblical meaning of the texts quoted about 95 percent of the time. I found this refreshing and constructive. But what the author did with the remaining 5 percent is another matter!

Warren has many critics. The Internet, as well as many books and articles, attack his use of Scripture, some claiming that every third page of his books is full of error! From my observation, these critics can be classified as

(1) those who are verbal inerrantists, that is, they do not believe that biblical writers made mistakes of any kind; (2) those who are attached to one translation, such as the King James Version, above all others and to whom a multitude of translations and paraphrases are anathema; and (3) those who are Calvinists and are not comfortable with Warren's emphasis on free will.

As you will see, I do not fall within any of these three groups. I believe in thought inspiration; that is, I believe God revealed His messages over a period of sixteen hundred years to men and women with very different writing skills and powers of perception. They were God's penmen, not His pen. I believe that *all* translations, to some extent, reflect the bias of the translator; they all did their best *with the presuppositions* that guided their pen.

The only way to test the accuracy of a translation is to read the text in the Hebrew or Greek. Regarding the Calvinist-Wesleyan debate, I personally accept the biblical position that God's grace calls for man's response, which can be freely given or rejected.

A few examples are given below of what I consider to be misuse of biblical texts by Warren in *PDL*. These fall into three categories: (1) quoting only part of the text and omitting the rest that would alter his point; (2) looking for texts that use his favorite words, such as *purpose* and *plans,* without first considering whether the use he makes of the text fairly reflects its biblical meaning—in other words, looking for texts to prove his point rather than exegeting the texts in order to discover the true meaning; and (3) lifting texts completely out of their original context, leading to faulty conclusions. Keep in mind, too, that earlier I stated that, in my opinion, Warren uses biblical texts responsibly in his books in the vast majority of cases.

In Appendix D we will go through *PDL*, examining its faulty use of Bible texts chapter by chapter. But for now, we will examine a sampling of those texts under the three categories just mentioned.

1. Texts that are quoted only partially, where the full text would contradict Warren's reason for using the text.

"I have labored to no purpose; I have spent my strength in vain and for nothing" (Isaiah 49:4, NIV). PDL, 30 (chapter 3).

Here is an example of not reading all the text. Isaiah is responding to God with some regret that it seems he does not have much to show for his preaching, but he finishes his sentence with a ringing affirmation of confidence that his "just reward is with the LORD, and my work with my God"—which is just the opposite of the way Warren is using this text.

"What is your life?" (James 4:14b, NIV). PDL, 41 (chapter 5).

Warren uses this text to build his own question: "How do you see your life?" He goes on to use this text as a springboard for his own teaching message—that we should have our own "life metaphor." But he does not read on to note that James answers this question differently than Warren would choose: "It [your life] is even a vapor that appears for a little time and then vanishes away."

"The LORD is pleased only with those who worship him and trust his love" (Psalm 147:11, CEV). PDL, 64 (chapter 8).

This is a true statement, but it is not what the psalmist is saying. The word here translated "worship" should be translated "fear." Of course God is pleased when we worship Him, but this text is saying something quite different.

"It is not good for man to be alone" (Genesis 2:18). PDL, 130 (chapter 17).

In the second half of this verse—that Warren does not quote—God states the reason why Adam and all men should not be alone; Adam needed a "helper," a female helper! Warren redirects this text to suggest that the solution to man's loneliness is church community. God's reason seems better.

2. Texts that contain the words purpose or plan are used without considering whether they accurately reflect the point being made.

"It's in Christ that we find out who we are and what we are living for. Long before we first heard of Christ and got our hopes up, he had his eye on us, had designs on us for glorious living, part of the overall purpose he is working out in everything and everyone" (Ephesians 1:11, Msg). PDL, 20 (chapter 1).

This paraphrase seems to be tailor-made for *PDL.* But when we read the whole context of verses 3 through 12, we discover an entirely different direction. Paul is saying nothing in these verses about discovering our purposes through a relationship with Christ. He is speaking about God's purpose for us—that we have been made heirs of God through no merit of our own. That is God's purpose, not ours.

"You, LORD, give perfect peace to those who keep their purpose firm and put their trust in you" (Isaiah 26:3, TEV). PDL, 32 (chapter 3).

I think Warren must have used concordances to find texts that contain the word *purpose* regardless of the text's meaning. This text promises peace to those "whose mind is stayed on God," not especially to those who "keep their purpose firm."

Warren writes, Joshua *"surrendered his plans to the Angel before the battle of Jericho" PDL,* 82 (chapter 10). Joshua 5:13-15.

The text says that Joshua "fell on his face . . . and worshiped, and said to Him, 'What does my Lord say to His servant?' Then the Commander of the LORD's army said to Joshua, 'Take your sandal off your foot, for the place where you stand is holy.' And Joshua did so." The text contains no reference to Joshua "surrendering" his plans—just a willingness to listen to counsel.

3. Texts lifted out of context, thus leading to faulty conclusions.

"God decided to give us life through the word of truth so we might be the most important of all the things he made" (James 1:18, NCV). PDL, 24 (chapter 2).

This translation completely overlooks the intent of the New Testament word *firstfruits* by giving it the meaning "most important." (For how the New Testament uses the word *firstfruits* see Romans 8:23; 16:5; 1 Corinthians 15:20, 23; Revelation 14:4). This text refers in no way to the "importance" of a certain group today, but to James's contemporaries—the first of those now called "Christians."

"I have carried you since you were born; I have taken care of you from your birth. Even when you are old, I will be the same. Even when your hair has turned gray, I will take care of you. I made you and will take care of you" (Isaiah 46:3, 4, NCV). PDL, 25 (chapter 2).

This may be a comfortable verse to some, but in context, God is talking to Israel—not to mankind in general, nor to believers in the church today. This text does not say (as Warren uses it) that God made anyone of us today in order to show how much He loves us.

"I know what I am planning for you. . . . 'I have good plans for you, not plans to hurt you. I will give you hope and a good future' " (Jeremiah 29:11, NCV). PDL, 31 (chapter 3).

This text has been a great motto for many and is one of Warren's favorites. He quotes it several times in *PDL.* But this verse is not a promise that wonderful changes will happen in our lives once we believe our purposes. In this text, God is promising Israel a future after its captivity in Babylon.

"Stop quarreling with God! If you agree with him, you will have peace at last, and things will go well for you" (Job 22:21, NLT). PDL, 82 (chapter 10).

This is Eliphaz speaking, of whom God said later: "My wrath is aroused against you and your two friends, for you have not spoken of Me what is right, as My servant Job has" (Job 42:7). Eliphaz was dead wrong in using these words against Job. He was sure that Job must have sinned greatly in order to be so afflicted, but Job remonstrated that he did not sin and therefore did not bring all these calamities on himself. Context is everything!

Conclusion

Does all this make any difference when our author means well? Many readers have maneuvered through *PDL* and *PDC* and have found excellent motivational thoughts.

Without question, everything that Warren writes is not wrong. I have found many pages to be refreshing and, in some respects, exceptional advice in areas such as fellowshiping with friends or visitors and noting that God calls His faithful followers, His friends.

The irony is that although Warren places a great emphasis on his biblical resources, why doesn't he prove his points by using proper biblical support instead of using unfortunate—often twisted—translations or paraphrases? His use of Scriptures suggests to the reader that Warren begins with his presuppositions—his main themes—and then looks in his array of fifteen translations and paraphrases for certain words that he can extract to support his main themes, regardless of the texts' original meanings.

Some may ask, "What's the big deal? There is so much good in Warren's books, what does it matter that he misuses Scripture here and there? No one is perfect, right?"

But it should not go without notice that everybody who professes Christianity claims to believe in the Bible! Each group or church or denomination uses its favorite translation to support its uniqueness. I am not referring to differences of opinion regarding a text here and there; I am most concerned with faulty methodology. Warren's method, for example, is to work with a presupposed philosophy and then search for texts that seem most likely to support his main themes.

But even more troubling, possibly, is the fact that large segments in all churches today either don't see the problem or don't feel that it matters that much. After all, *tolerance* is the key word these days. And if an author says things about God that are satisfying and can make one feel good about himself—what's the big deal?

The big deal is truth! *Truth matters!*

EIGHT

Philosophical Contexts Cause Concern

*W*arren's *epistemology seems upside down.*

Without depreciating Warren's intent and personal commitment to Jesus Christ, which is obvious to me, it also seems obvious that he views the Scriptures through the eyes of his own experience and, thus, his own presuppositions. Conversely, he does not seem to view his experience through the eyes of Scripture. For the most part, Warren uses the Bible to say what he wants it to say. He is not alone. Warren surely isn't the first preacher or teacher to do so, and many of his detractors are doing the same thing!

But that process reveals his epistemology—the basis and foundation of how one develops his understanding of truth. Everybody has his or her own epistemology—his or her own way of determining how to find truth. Only when a reader grasps an author's epistemology (that is, his method of finding and teaching truth) will that reader really understand how to judge the author's message.

Earlier, in chapter 3, we noted Warren's pragmatic methodology in marketing his message and in measuring success. His foundational question seems to be, Does it work?

In looking at Warren's methodology, we must look for the philosophy and worldview that steer his phenomenal, worldwide movement. We need to realize—as it seems most of his followers do not—that any philosophy and worldview not built boldly on the fullness of the New Testament gospel limits the legitimacy of how one applies biblical texts.

From one standpoint, Warren's pragmatic principles determine in a systematic way how he will proceed in developing his message. That is, he starts with the vision that he wants to create. That vision is then defined

71

and measured in terms of exit outcomes. Warren's vision is spelled out in his purpose for himself and the purposes he outlines for his followers. And the measure of success is how well the purposes can be measured—most often by growth and income, etc.

We will now examine some of the philosophical roots that nourish Warren's thinking and methodology. He speaks freely of his indebtedness, for example, to Robert Schuller's model of church growth.[1] But not so freely to the charges that Warren has many roots among New Age enthusiasts and other thinkers not noted for their biblical principles.[2]

Warren followed Robert Schuller's model of church growth, but not his message

In chapter 1, we noted that Warren and his wife, Kay, during his last year at Southwestern Theological Seminary drove west to visit Robert Schuller's Institute for Church Growth. For Kay, this venture into a nontraditional ministry scared her to death. But Schuller won them over. Warren said, "We were captivated by his positive appeal to nonbelievers. I never looked back."[3]

Much has been made of Warren's supposed connection or indebtedness to Robert Schuller, much of it pure fantasy from my point of view. That Schuller was Warren's mentor is based on a *Larry King Live* program (March 14, 2005) that described Schuller as Warren's mentor. Schuller made no attempt to correct that statement. Warren has called this statement the "most overblown" thing he has ever had to contend with. Many have repeated this "mentor" comment and that Warren has attended Schuller's pastoral training classes many times. All these statements are groundless.[4]

Warren maintains that Schuller has stepped far outside the borders of New Testament Christianity with his religious pluralism, his use of Transcendental Meditation, and his particular emphasis on "positive thinking." Warren has written Schuller about his disappointment with the guest speakers Schuller invites to his Crystal Cathedral. He especially condemned Schuller for giving his pulpit to Stephen Covey, a leading Mormon, and to a Muslim—to which Schuller responded that these

---

1. Warren reflects Schuller's methods but not his message.
2. See chapter 11, "Use of New Age Leaders."
3. Tim Stafford, "A Regular Purpose-Driven Guy," *Christianity Today*, November 18, 2002.
4. Richard Abanes, op. cit., 99.

individuals worship the same God that "we" worship. And Warren replied, "No, we don't!"[5]

But Warren does give Schuller credit for the creative ways in which he has developed his nontraditional church that eventually became the Crystal Cathedral and for some of Schuller's ideas regarding how to reach the unchurched. In 1980, among other questions, Warren asked, "Why do you think most people don't attend church?" That was one of Schuller's questions back in 1955 when he was starting out, and for Warren, that is a basic question.

Warren is condemned for connections to New Age principles

This charge must be handled with care. Warren would respond that he uses well-known writers and public figures as did Paul in his sermon before the Areopagus when he quoted well-known Greek writers (see Acts 17). Warren does it, he says, for the same reason Paul did—to get the attention of those in the general public who will give him points for recognizing these opinions.[6] The question remains, How much of the beliefs of these quoted men and women does Warren imbibe? When he makes these connections without regard for their theological beliefs, he surely sets himself up for questions.[7] More on this in chapter 11.

Though he denies the connection, Warren is strongly criticized for his pop-psychology

Yes, Warren does use phrases that are endemic in what many call psychobabble.[8] But we should be careful with flippant labels. For instance, Warren writes in *PDL* that "most conflict is rooted in unmet needs."[9] Immediately many think of Carl Rogers, Lester Crabb, Sigmund Freud, and others. (As a matter of fact, even these three notables differ on what is meant by "unmet needs.")

But shared words or phrases or overlapping terms do not always mean direct connections. It may be true that the Bible never says that "conflict is rooted in unmet needs," as some have condemned Warren for saying. But

---

5. Ibid., 104.

6. Among those whom Warren quotes or refers to are Mother Teresa, Brother Lawrence, John Main, Madame Guyon, and Henry Nouwen—all Roman Catholics.

7. See chapter 11, "Use of New Age Leaders."

8. See *PDL*, 27, 28, 63, 102, 103, 154, 245, 246, 247, 248, 249, 254, 273, and 275 for examples.

9. *PDL*, 154.

they should read further in *PDL*—such as the very next sentence, where Warren continues: "Some of these needs can only be met by God. . . . *No one* can meet all our needs except God." In the next paragraph, Warren quotes James 4:1, 2 and then writes, "Instead of looking to God, we look to others to make us happy and then get angry when they fail us. God says, 'Why don't you come to me first?' " I give this as one example of the unfair shots some have taken at Warren regarding pop-psychology. But there are other instances in which Warren employs phrases that do seem to crop up frequently among those who enjoy modern psychological jargon.

I read *PDL* carefully, and I conclude—with Warren—that *PDL* is an antiself-help book.[10] He is straightforward: "It is not about finding the right career, achieving your dreams, or planning your life. It is not about how to cram more activities into an overloaded schedule. Actually, it will teach you how to do *less* in life—by focusing on what matters most. It is about becoming what *God* created you to be."

Warren looks at a diversity of writers to support his principles

Indeed, Warren refers to Aldous Huxley, George Bernard Shaw, St. John of the Cross, and Mother Teresa—and his critics ask whether these individuals were born-again Christians who would believe in Paul's gospel.

When Warren misuses Ephesians 4:6 by quoting the New Century Version, many think of Robert Schuller and Bernie Siegel—and then of their connection with New Age gurus, Theosophists, and Shirley MacLaine! But to connect Warren with such figures as Helena Blavatsky (1831–1891) and Alice Bailey (1880–1949) simply because of their affiliation with other individuals whom he freely and publicly endorses leads us unnecessarily into murkiness. Present-day channelers of a "new gospel" teach that humanity is in peril and that their "Christ" or "Master" can explain how his new gospel will unify the world's major religions and bring peace to the world. For such individuals, we are not "sinners" because we are all part of the one body of Christ and the body of God. Their new gospel teaches that when we reach our "God potential" or "Christ within," we are supernaturally activated and thus are part of the "one body" of God that includes all mankind. Some of Warren's opponents link all this with his use of Ephesians 4:6 and his liberal endorsements of those who push this line of thought further than he does at this time.[11]

From another angle, some of Warren's detractors accuse him of teaching pantheism—that God is in every thing and that human beings are

10. Ibid., 19.

11. More about this in chapter 11, "Use of New Age Leaders."

gods. But have they read such comments by Warren as this clear statement? "Let me be absolutely clear: You will never become God, or even *a* god. That prideful lie is Satan's oldest temptation. Satan promised Adam and Eve that if they followed his advice, *'ye shall be as gods.'* Many religions and New Age philosophies still promote this old lie that we are divine or can become gods."[12]

Some who don't read carefully believe that when Warren uses texts such as Ephesians 4:6, he is promoting New Age thinking—that God is everywhere and in everything. But it seems to me that Warren is only emphasizing what Paul was emphasizing—that God is immanent, that He can dwell within men and women through His Holy Spirit, and that He is omnipresent. Though God is everywhere, *He is not everything nor is He in everything,* for that indeed would be pantheism.

---

12. *PDL,* 172.

NINE

Weaknesses of Assumptions

It appears that Rick Warren has been willing to face the challenge of balancing the demands of biblical authority with the demands of pragmatism. In a way, every thoughtful Christian leader must carefully consider that balance or risk losing either relevancy or the authority of truth. Without truth, relevancy quickly becomes meaningless—and dangerous.

For most readers of *PDL*, Warren has done a good job of joining an "orthodox" gospel (the gospel as generally believed by most Protestants) with innovative, nontraditional methods. In chapter 12, however, we will examine what I believe are several aspects of his "orthodox" gospel that are alien to the teachings of the Old and New Testament.

In this chapter, let's examine some of the main thoughts in *PDL* that many consider to be Warren's slippery assumptions:

▸ In the first few chapters of *PDL*, Warren suggests that *we come to Christ because we lack a sense of purpose.* But is that the message of Scripture? Luke 15 describes in three unforgettable parables *how God comes* to men and women, opening our eyes to our need to be forgiven and to be empowered to live as grateful sons and daughters. All this Warren will not deny.[1] But he steers his readers into thinking that we initially come to Christ in order to receive a number of benefits—fulfillment, self-esteem, an improved marriage, a thrilling lifestyle, or purpose. The need for freedom from sin and

---

1. "The Good News is that when we trust God's grace to save us through what Jesus did, our sins are forgiven, we get a purpose for living, and we are promised a future home in heaven."—*PDL*, 294. The subtle omission here is that the good news offers more than forgiveness—power to overcome the sins for which we ask forgiveness is as important as is forgiveness itself in the gospel ellipse.

the gift of eternal salvation seems overshadowed by his emphasis on satisfying our "felt" needs.

▸ *Christians need to think like unbelievers.* In other words, Christians need to put themselves in the shoes of unbelievers and present messages that are relevant to their "felt" needs. But this assumption is valid only when believers really remember what it was like before they made Jesus Lord of their lives. Jesus, however, goes straight to the heart of the matter—He spoke to mankind's "deepest" needs. That didn't mean that Jesus was abrupt and didn't take into account the differing levels of perception and sophistication of His hearers—He speaks to real needs graciously and with keen appeal to all levels of society. From another viewpoint, it seems obvious that preachers should use a different method in speaking to unbelievers than they would use in weekly worship services—as Warren himself does.[2]

But after saying that, we need to consider whether the early Christian church defined its target audience by taking a poll or by using some other form of social marketing. Hardly! Neither did the apostles work from the generally accepted premise that churches with similar sociological backgrounds grow more quickly because "like attracts like." The book of Acts seems to contradict modern marketing techniques. Churches sprang up everywhere—Gentiles and Jews, rich and poor, learned and unschooled—in response to the message of a crucified Lord who offered all men and women freedom from sin, changed lives, and an advent hope.

Os Guinness writes, "Scripture and history are . . . clear: Without maintaining critical tension, the principle of identification is a recipe for compromise and capitulation. It is no accident that the charge of being 'all things to all people' has become a popular synonym for compromise."[3]

Some of that compromise omits or mutes truths that the preacher personally believes or may write about on other occasions but that are not clearly revealed in his books such as *PDL.*

▸ *Messages should be governed by "felt" needs.* Here, again, some forget that Warren works with twin goals—he separates his messages for unbelievers from those for believers. However, it would be easier to track Warren in books such as *PDL* if, when beginning where his audience is, he would end the sermon or chapter with words that

---

2. *PDC,* 294, 295.

3. Os Guinness, *Dining with the Devil* (Grand Rapids, Mich.: Baker Book House, 1993), 28.

God has decisively spoken—without using only parts of verses to make his points.

God does reveal Himself to men and women according to a sinner's needs—that was Christ's only method. But Guinness observes that His method seems to be turned upside down in much modern marketing of the gospel: "When the audience and not the message is sovereign, the good news of Jesus Christ is no longer the end, but just the means. As a result, when megachurch pastors seek to mold a message to their 'market' of constituents' needs, their preaching omits key components. Gone are the hard sayings of Jesus. Gone is the teaching on sin, self-denial, sacrifice, suffering, judgment, hell. With all its need-meeting emphases, there is little in the church-growth movement that stands crosswise to the world."[4]

The apostle Paul had only one driving purpose: to be faithful to the truth about God that he dug out of the Old Testament (the only Bible he had) and that was given him through the ministration of the Holy Spirit (see Galatians 1:10–12; 2 Timothy 1:11–13; 4:1–4). His faithfulness to the truth determined how and when he spoke to real needs as well as "felt" needs.

Again Guinness seems to spotlight the issues: "The . . . problem with the modern use of need is that, endlessly engineered and marketed, an obsession with need results in consumer indifference to *specific, genuine, real* needs. People skilled in learning to meet the needs that the professional elites identify become deaf to their own true needs—their needs as God, not the world, defines them."[5]

Of course, no preacher or marketer can get an audience if the intended audience doesn't perceive that he is dealing with its "felt" needs. Every wise preacher replicates our Lord's approach to "felt needs"—Jesus was known very quickly as One who understood such felt needs as poverty, sickness, hopelessness, hypocrisy, and fear. And He responded appropriately. People everywhere heard Him gladly.

But Guinness wants modern preachers to continue following our Lord's example of using "felt" needs as the door through which to bring solutions and remedies to the audience's "real" needs. To stop with "felt" needs could leave the audience with a false sense of assurance.

▶ *Success equals numeric results.* Warren suggests "we should never criticize any method that God is blessing."[6] But the corollary to this

---

4. Ibid., 78.

5. Ibid., 67.

6. *PDC*, 156

thinking is that if the numbers plateau or stagnate, something unhealthy must be going on—God must not be blessing!

Think of our Lord's ministry. Obviously, numerical growth can take place for wrong reasons. In John 6 we see the classic development of a growth movement that thinks Jesus is the answer to its "felt" needs. But suddenly numerical growth turns into a plateau—and worse—for Christ's earthly ministry. After seeing incredible signs of His divinity, after hearing what Jesus considered to be their real needs, "From that time many of His disciples went back and walked with Him no more" (verse 66).

When one thinks about the expansion of Christianity, especially since Constantine and his magnificent improvement of church numbers by forcing his army into a wholesale "baptism," only a blind and deaf person would think that the growth of Christianity, apart from a commitment to gospel purity and genuine Christian order and life, is evidence of God's blessing.[7]

▶ *PDL's audience includes both believers and unbelievers.* But the author does not maintain a distinction between the two. Promises that apply only to believers are stated as if they apply to both. Unbelievers can become deceived and believe they are saved, when they have not heard the gospel that does save. Much of the expansion of Christianity, in the past and today, has been at the expense of gospel purity and Christian integrity.

---

7. I was astounded when H. B. London, a vice president of the *Focus on the Family* organization said, "Nearly every pastor is a salesmen or a marketer . . . we have a philosophy to sell. The best marketers and best salesmen will have more converts, will have more people, will take in more money."

TEN

Comments Cause Concern

When one reads *PDL* or *PDC* it is hard to ignore subtle distortions, half-truths, conflicting messages, or instances of pragmatic permissiveness. The premise seems to be, If it works, that is, if it brings people into the church, it's OK.

Then when Warren emphasizes, "God loves variety," one is impressed to be lenient. He has so many good points, but they seem mixed up with so many confusing and theologically weak points that it is hard to keep it all straight. The *PDL* reader finds a great point, and then Warren throws in a quote from Mother Teresa or Aldous Huxley or Bernie Siegel—and the mind reels. We want to believe that God has a "smiley" face, but we also believe that we should not ignore His justice.

It seems to me that one rule every writer or speaker should have etched into his mind is this: It is important to be clearly understood but far more important to keep from being misunderstood.

Rick Warren has taken the world by storm because of his enormous ability to speak to the common man or woman. He speaks to his or her "felt" needs and spells out many irrefutable principles of a healthy, growing church. But his detractors have a point: It is not necessarily what he says that troubles them—it's what he leaves out, ignores, or doesn't choose to emphasize in areas that need further explanation. In other words, Warren is selective toward whatever drives his message—such as presuppositions that he may or may not be aware of.

For example, how should we understand Warren's rule for church growth that tells us to "never criticize what God is blessing,"[1] implying that

---

1. *PDC*, 62.

church growth and changed lives prove God's delight in our human methods? Doesn't this rule seem to cancel the biblical call to be alert and to discern deception (see 1 Thessalonians 5:21; 2 Timothy 2:15)? Surely, no one whose teaching is beyond biblical accountability can be God's anointed.

You can imagine what many readers will think when they read that "the *last* thing many believers need today is to go to another Bible study."[2] George Barna has researched the American mind, especially those who call themselves "born-again."[3] His conclusions are deafening. When asked about specific questions, "born-again" Christians are dreadfully illiterate when it comes to core Bible truths. They may believe that God loves them and that they should love one another—but life habits are often not changed.[4]

In the judgment, according to Warren, "God won't ask about your religious

---

2. *PDL*, 231.

3. " 'Born again Christians' were defined in these surveys as people who said they have made a personal commitment to Jesus Christ that is still important in their life today and who also indicated they believe that when they die they will go to Heaven because they had confessed their sins and had accepted Jesus Christ as their Savior." Barna then separated "born-again" Christians from those who had a biblical worldview: "A biblical worldview was defined as believing that absolute moral truths exist; that such truth is defined by the Bible; and firm belief in six specific religious views. Those views were that Jesus Christ lived a sinless life; God is the all-powerful and all-knowing Creator of the universe and He stills rules it today; salvation is a gift from God and cannot be earned; Satan is real; a Christian has a responsibility to share their faith in Christ with other people; and the Bible is accurate in all of its teachings."

4. Another analysis: "People's views on morally acceptable behavior are deeply impacted by their worldview. Upon comparing the perspectives of those who have a biblical worldview with those ['born-again Christians'] who do not, the former group were 31 times less likely to accept cohabitation (2% versus 62%, respectively); 18 times less likely to endorse drunkenness (2% versus 36%); 15 times less likely to condone gay sex (2% versus 31%); 12 times less likely to accept profanity (3% versus 37%); and 11 times less likely to describe adultery as morally acceptable (4% versus 44%). In addition, less than one-half of one percent of those with a biblical worldview said voluntary exposure to pornography was morally acceptable (compared to 39% of other adults), and a similarly miniscule proportion endorsed abortion (compared to 46% of adults who lack a biblical worldview). Among the more intriguing lifestyle differences were a lesser propensity for those with a biblical worldview to gamble (they were eight times less likely to buy lottery tickets and 17 times less likely to place bets); to get drunk (three times less likely); and to view pornography (two times less common). They were also twice as likely to have discussed spiritual matters with other people in the past month and twice as likely to have fasted for religious reasons during the preceding month. While one out of every eight adults who lack a biblical worldview had sexual relations with someone other than their spouse during the prior month, less than one out of every 100 individuals who have such a worldview had done so."—"A Biblical Worldview Has a Radical Effect on a Person's Life," December 1, 2003, <www.barna.org/FlexPage.aspx?Page=BarnaUpdate&BarnaUpdateID=154>. See also Barna, *Think Like Jesus*, 19–30.

background or doctrinal views. The only thing that will matter is, did you accept what Jesus did for you and did you learn to love and trust him?"[5] Is that safe counsel? Each person will have his own way of answering those questions if he hasn't taken Paul's advice to young Timothy: "As I urged you . . . remain in Ephesus that you may charge some that they teach no other doctrine." "Till I come, give attention to reading, to exhortation, to doctrine" (1 Timothy 1:3; 4:13).

It seems perplexing that Warren mutes the importance of doctrine with his emphasis on "what Jesus did for you"! Is this always a safe approach to follow? What about the church member who just won the lottery? Perhaps Mormons and Jehovah's Witnesses should take great comfort in Warren's advice. In this counsel, is he including the Mormon Jesus, who is Lucifer's brother? Or the Jehovah's Witnesses's Jesus, who is merely an exalted angel? Or the Jesus celebrated in the Roman Catholic eucharist? Do these issues matter?

Warren endorses Christ's counsel that we should not "criticize, compare, or judge each other . . .

"Whenever I judge another believer, four things instantly happen: I lose fellowship with God, I expose my own pride and insecurity, I set myself up to be judged by God, and I harm the fellowship of the church."[6] But that is not all the counsel that biblical writers urge. Obviously we should not judge hypocritically (see Matthew 7) or on the basis of personal preference in matters not commanded in Scripture (see Romans 14). But what about judging on the basis of biblical truth when someone comes preaching "another Jesus whom we have not preached, or if you receive a different spirit which you have not received, or a different gospel which you have not accepted" (2 Corinthians 11:4)?

What about following the Bereans who "were more fair-minded than those in Thessalonica, in that they received the word with all readiness, and searched the Scriptures daily to find out whether these things were so" (Acts 17:11; see also John 7:24; 1 Corinthians 2:15; 14:29; 1 John 4:1)?

Warren refers to "many studies" that reveal that "the average person possesses from 500 to 700 different skills and abilities—far more than you realize." And that "your brain can store 100 trillion facts."[7] It would be helpful if Warren could cite some references.

---

5. *PDL*, 34.

6. *PDL*, 164.

7. *PDL*, 242.

In outlining how temptation works, Warren states that "temptation starts when Satan suggests (with a thought) that you give in to an evil desire."[8] The apostle James said, "But each one is tempted when he is drawn away by his own desires and enticed. Then, when desire has conceived, it gives birth to sin" (1:14, 15). How does Warren know that Satan can directly plant a thought in our minds? Does not Satan use external visual and aural stimuli to tempt us to satisfy sinful personal, internal desires?

"What God wants most . . . is a relationship,"[9] writes Warren. Yes, but Warren makes it sound so easy by not emphasizing that this abiding relationship comes after repentance and genuine conversion—not before.

Of course, believers are part of God's family and should cultivate the graces of community and restored fellowship. But in Warren's emphasis on fellowship, there seems to be a lack of emphasis on personal holiness, separation from evil, and genuine obedience to God's explicit will. New Testament writers are much concerned about personal holiness and the purity of the church. Sometimes this demands separation or a word of reproof and rebuke, which leads to broken fellowship and disharmony.

What happens when a genuine pastor or a sincere church member believes that he or she must counsel a member who is treading on the margins of Christian living—and that person calls him or her "judgmental" or "unloving" or "legalistic"? What happens when a person says, "Don't judge me; you don't know my motives"? Or "I'm sincere in my actions, and that is all that matters"? Yet the alert church leader knows that motives and actions are as important to God as character and good works. Christ's final judgment proves that one's works, motives, and character truly matter to God. Surely believers should be taught to be "sincere and without offense till the day of Christ" (Philippians 1:10).

I think Warren would strengthen his message if he would include New Testament counsel to watch out for false doctrine—a command that permeates Paul's advice to Timothy. It would deflect some of Warren's critics who believe he minimizes the need for doctrinal purity by stressing the importance of love and unity above anything that would cause strife or division. Warren seems to believe that love and unity should take precedence over doctrine and purity in the church—despite the fact that the Bible links true, biblical, agape love with obedience to the commandments of God (see John 7:24; 14:15; 1 John 2:3–5).

Sincerity and warm fellowship is not the test of truth. The awful words

8. *PDL*, 203.

9. *PDL*, 70.

of Jesus to those very active church members who are doing "many wonders" throughout the world must not be forgotten: "I never knew you; depart from Me, you who practice lawlessness!" (Matthew 7:23). In other words, "I never knew you to be what you said you were!"

"God wants you to be yourself,"[10] Warren declares. Of course this is true, but without significant explanation it reminds us of Tammy Faye Bakker who said, "I got to be me!" For the past forty years people have been told to look for the "real me," as if they were pealing an onion to see what is inside! This kind of language fits New Age psychobabble and sells big time with unregenerate "seekers."

Warren makes a strong point when he says that those who have had "painful experiences" can be a great comfort to others with similar experiences. But then he writes that "Paul understood this truth, so he was honest about his bouts with depression"[11] and quotes 2 Corinthians 1:8–10, LB, as evidence for his statement. But this text does not support the idea that Paul experienced clinical or psychological "bouts of depression" and "deep insecurity." Here again, Warren is forcing humanistic psychological principles on a biblical text. He doesn't seem to have read on in 2 Corinthians to really catch Paul's positive, triumphant spirit—for instance, chapter 4!

PDL's insights on worship are creative. When Warren says "real worship is all about—*falling in love with Jesus*,"[12] all kinds of images come to mind. How does one know who Jesus really is? Especially when Warren has told us that doctrines don't matter.[13] We must know more about Jesus than the fact that He told parables and died on the cross for sinners. Where did Jesus come from? Why did He come to earth? Will He ever come back? If so, how and when? What did He say about the Ten Commandments? The Christian world that "loves Jesus" has all kinds of different answers to these questions—and these answers create all kinds of worship patterns and life behaviors. Emphasizing that loving Jesus is all there is to worship can open up a flood of man-centered subjectivism.

Jesus said that we are to worship God "in spirit and truth"; David stated we are to worship Him "in the beauty of holiness" (John 4:24; Psalm 29:2). Warren makes a strong point when he writes that worship should bring pleasure to God.[14] But that is what many pagans thought they were doing

---

10. *PDL*, 103.

11. *PDL*, 247.

12. *PDL*, 67.

13. *PDL*, 34.

14. *PDL*, 64.

with their human sacrifices and self-immolations. Somewhere it must be made clear that worshiping God "in truth" is more than a subjective falling in love with Jesus. It is well known that the religious emotion of the unregenerate soul is almost exactly the same as genuine spiritual emotion—or, for that matter, as the infatuating "love" of the opposite sex that can substitute the name of one's lover in many modern choruses about Jesus. Believers should derive their theology of worship from the Bible, not from fellow believers who feel at home in our modern culture with its love for the casual, all the while drawing worship methodologies from the modern "beat."

In other words, does worship in the twenty-first century reflect the adoration of holiness, or does it reflect the expectations of those who have become accustomed to believing that everyone's opinion is as good as anyone else's?

Think of Aaron while his brother Moses was meeting God on Mount Sinai. The Israelites felt the awesomeness of the occasion, and to show their piety and excitement they induced Aaron and other religious leaders to produce a "seeker-friendly" worship service (see Exodus 32:15–26).

The Israelites were not accustomed to holiness, but they were used to "feeling" their religion. Catching the rhythm, Aaron forged a golden calf to represent Jehovah who had brought them out of Egypt (see verse 4). They set aside a special day for worship; they brought their offerings and food for the potluck. And "they rose up to play" (verses 5, 6). All this in the name of worship! They worshiped in "spirit" but not in "truth." Something more is expected of genuine believers than worshiping in the way that pleases them most.

Another area where Warren walks on quicksand is his appeal for us to practice "the presence of God."[15] From my reading of *PDL* I think the outrage of many against the book is unfounded. Yes, Warren does counsel his readers to develop a habit of thinking about God throughout the day and night. He even suggests using visual reminders to keep before us that " '*God is with me and for me right now!*' "[16]

I do something very similar throughout the day and at night when I awaken. It is not a mystical form of devotion or an example of contemplative religion. I call it "experiential Christianity."

What troubles many, however, is Warren's support in his books and public meetings for well-known mystics such as Richard Foster, Thomas

---

15. *PDL*, 89.

16. Ibid.

Merton, Henri Nouwen, and Brennan Manning, who advocate New Age–type "contemplative prayer" ideas and whom Warren quotes in *PDL*.

It seems to me that Warren is trying to practice the presence of God while avoiding the mental kind of contemplation that opens up all kinds of "spiritual" excursions and meditations that lead to various paths—either getting away from life as far as possible in some quiet cave or participating in spiritual retreats with others that at times anesthetize moral clarity. A warning from Warren would be helpful here. The only test of spiritual meditation is whether it helps to transform struggling sinners into willing, cheerful, transformed men and women who "walk just as He walked" (1 John 2:6).

One of the best-known features of Saddleback's program is its music. Warren refers often to that three-by-five card that he distributed to his starting group in the earliest days of his ministry, asking people to "write down the call letters of the radio station you listen to." He makes a point that the people who returned the cards were church people—not unbelievers. What response did he get back? "I didn't have one person who said, 'I listen to organ music.' Not one. . . . So, we made a strategic decision that we are unapologetically a contemporary music church. And right after we made that decision and stopped trying to please everybody, Saddleback exploded with growth. . . . I'll be honest with you, we are loud. We are really, really loud on a weekend service. . . . I say, 'We're not gonna turn it down.' Now the reason why is baby boomers want to feel the music, not just hear it. . . . God loves variety!"[17]

In *PDL*, Warren writes that "God loves all kinds of music because he invented it all—fast and slow, loud and soft, old and new. You probably don't like it all, but God does!"[18]

How can anyone claim that God invented all kinds of music? Or, how can Warren prove that "God loves all kinds of music"? Something seems to be wrong when we view much of today's music and then say, "God invented it." It doesn't take much research to discover where much of the music for the last half century in America came from. The throbbing beat of hard rock? Or the hypnotic tones of New Age music? Is God the source of such music? It seems, rather, that the world has made Warren's musical choices for him.

The test of Saddleback's program seems to lie in seeing numerical growth as the evidence of successful Christian witnessing. Numbers are one way to judge a program, but what happened to judging teachers or

17. "Building a Purpose-Driven Church" (seminar), January, 1998.

18. *PDL*, 65.

preachers by what they teach? After all, the Mormon church is one of the fastest growing churches in the world; does this mean that God is blessing that outreach?

One of Warren's helpful chapters is his emphasis on the importance of worship. He lists three excellent tests: worship must be accurate ("Worship must be based on the truth of Scripture."[19]); worship must be authentic ("When we worship, God looks past our words to see the attitude of our hearts."[20]); worship must be thoughtful ("Jesus' command to *love God with all your mind* is repeated four times in the New Testament"[21]).

But then Warren quotes a friend who listed nine different ways to love God or draw near to Him—and summarizes with "there is no 'one-size-fits-all' approach to worship. . . . God wants you to be yourself." Then to throw the reader off even further from his own three points, Warren quotes Peterson's *The Message* paraphrase of John 4:23—" *'That's the kind of people the Father is out looking for: those who are simply and honestly* themselves *before him in their worship'* "—making the whole subject misty and subjective. The real meaning of Christ's words is, "But the hour is coming, and now is, when the true worshipers will worship the Father in spirit and truth; for the Father is seeking such to worship Him" (John 4:23, NKJV).

Seeking the Lord "in spirit and truth" is far different from worshiping "simply and honestly." The modern interest in "spirituality" is founded on the heady belief that *everyone* is "spiritual" and we all must find our spirituality one way or another, "simply and honestly." All are climbing the same mountain, but on different paths. Just be honest with your deepest thoughts, and you will find God.

Warren may not put it in those words, but when he says that we are all on the "same team," one wonders where such thoughts on worship are leading him.

Anther concern that many have is Warren's "salvation prayer": "Wherever you are reading this, I invite you to bow your head and quietly whisper the prayer that will change your eternity: *'Jesus, I believe in you and I receive you.'* Go ahead.

"If you sincerely meant that prayer, congratulations! Welcome to the family of God!"[22]

19. *PDL*, 101.

20. Ibid.

21. Ibid., 103.

22. *PDL*, 58, 59.

Who can criticize that prayer? Don't we all want as many people as possible to "change" their future and eternity? Of course! But if any should pray that prayer with little or no awareness of a Holy God, or the unholy power of sin—with little or no awareness of what the Cross means, with little or no sense of the great gulf that genuine repentance must cross in a changed life, with no sense of how the Holy Spirit will be one's only protection in the hour of temptation—then surely there is real trouble ahead for the struggling believer. And for the church that welcomes such into the family of God.

In fact, about the best that one can say is that such a prayer has saved that person from purposeless living—not from the clutches of sin.

A measure of Warren's popularity and demand is the fact that he has been asked to contribute a monthly column to the *Ladies Home Journal.* In the March 2005 issue, his column is titled "Learn to Love Yourself." Remember, the opening words of his first chapter in *PDL* are "It's not about you."[23]

In this column, he tells his readers that "to truly love yourself, you need to know the five truths that form the basis of a healthy self-image." Here are his five truths:

▶ *"Accept Yourself.* God accepts you unconditionally, and in his view we are all precious and priceless. . . .

▶ *"Love Yourself.* God really does love me without strings attached. . . .

▶ *"Be True to Yourself.* Discover, accept and enjoy your unique 'shape' [a reference to Warren's S.H.A.P.E. program]. Be content with them [your weaknesses].

▶ *"Forgive Yourself.* God doesn't expect perfection but He does insist on honesty. . . .

▶ *"Believe Yourself.* Start affirming the truth about yourself!"

Does any of this sound like the gospel? Or is it pop-psychology? Let's look at his first affirmation. Where in the Bible do we find that God "accepts" us unconditionally? It's true that He *loves* us unconditionally, but we are unacceptable to God in our natural state. However, we are *made* acceptable "in Christ," with all that Paul means by that phrase.

Where in the Bible are we told to "love ourselves"? We are told to love God with all our heart, soul, and mind and to love others, as we already do ourselves (see Matthew 22:37–40; Ephesians 5:28, 29). In fact, the only

23. *PDL,* 17.

Bible text that speaks of "self love" connects it with the evil of the last days (see 2 Timothy 3:2).

Where in the Bible do we find that we should tell unbelievers that it is OK to accept themselves when they may be dead in their sins (see Ephesians 2:1)? Such counsel may be soothing, but does it point them to Jesus, who indeed will make them "true" to themselves?

Where in the Bible do we find a hint about forgiving ourselves? We are called to "repent" and "confess" our sins to Him, and *He will surely forgive*. But we don't have the ability or authority to "forgive" ourselves. God invites us to *accept* forgiveness, to believe that our guilt is removed and that the future is brighter than the past.

Where in the Bible are we to believe in ourselves? Yes, we are to believe—but *on the Lord Jesus* (see Acts 16:31).

These may seem like quibbles. It's easy to see what Warren is trying to do in this column. But as a gospel minister, does he hit the mark or not? This column is an example of one of the themes in *PDL*—doctrine doesn't matter, just believe in Jesus (whatever that may mean). This kind of human motivation gives reason to many to wonder about the biblical orientation of Warren's program.[24]

My intent in this chapter is to point out where some of Warren's comments open up the possibility that he has not said everything clearly enough to avoid being misunderstood. As all writers must, he probably should forthrightly restate some of what he has said in these areas to avoid any misunderstanding.

---

24. I am indebted to Gary Gilley in *This Little Church Went to Market* (Webster, N.Y.: Evangelical Press, 2005), 108, 109.

ELEVEN

Use of New Age Leaders

One of the constant challenges to public figures is the problem of guilt by association or affiliation. Many are condemned unfairly; others get what they deserve. But associations and affiliations do matter!

If I accepted an invitation to be the keynote speaker at a Wicca convention or at a national Spiritualist convention, you would say, correctly, that I had either lost my mind or didn't care much about my relationship with Jesus Christ. I am sure that any confidence in me by fellow Christians would quickly erode. And rightly so! Reputations are won or lost by our associations.

Association and *affiliation*—two words that trouble many regarding Warren's connections to many New Agers or to those in the new spiritualism movement.

Let's look at some of Rick Warren's references.

Bernie Siegel, M.D.

"Hope is as essential to your life as air and water. You need hope to cope. Dr. Bernie Siegel found he could predict which of his cancer patients would go into remission by asking, 'Do you want to live to be one hundred?' Those with a deep sense of life purpose answered yes and were the ones most likely to survive."[1]

Bernie Siegel, a Connecticut physician, authored *Love, Medicine & Miracles,* in which he described this remarkable experience:

"In June 1978, my practice of medicine changed as a result of an

---

1. *PDL,* 31.

91

unexpected experience I had at a teaching seminar. Oncologist O. Carl Simonton and psychologist Stephanie Matthews (then Simonton's wife) gave a workshop—Psychological Factors, Stress, and Cancer—at the Elmcrest Institute in Portland, Connecticut.

"The Simontons taught us how to meditate. At one point they led us in a directed meditation to find and meet an inner guide. I approached this exercise with all the skepticism one expects from a mechanistic doctor. Still, I sat down, closed my eyes, and followed directions. I didn't believe it would work, but if it did I expected to see Jesus or Moses. Who else would dare appear inside a surgeon's head?

"Instead I met George, a bearded, long-haired young man wearing an immaculate flowing white gown and a skullcap. It was an incredible awakening for me, because I hadn't expected something to happen. . . .

"George was spontaneous, aware of my feelings, and an excellent adviser. He gave me honest answers, some of which I didn't like at first. . . .

"All I know is that he has been my invaluable companion ever since his first appearance. My life is much easier now, because he does the hard work."[2]

In 1995, Siegel personally endorsed Robert Schuller's book *Prayer: My Soul's Adventure with God*, as found on the opening page: "This is a beautiful book of value to all people. . . . Robert Schuller's newest book reaches beyond religion and information to what we all need—spirituality, inspiration and understanding. Read it and live a life with meaning."[3]

Siegel's modern pantheism is reflected in two of his books, *Prescriptions for Living* and *How To Live Between Office Visits*. Sample assertions: "God is in everyone and everything."[4] "God is all."[5] Warren opens himself to the charge that he agrees with Siegel when he uses the NCV version of Ephesians 4:6: "He [God] rules everything and is everywhere and is in everything."

To best understand this verse that seems to lend support for pantheistic thoughts, we must read it in context (the pronoun "you" is in some Greek texts and not in others): "One God and Father of all, who is above all, and through all, and in you all" (Ephesians 4:6). Even if we eliminate the pronoun "you," the parallelism with the two preceding phrases does

2. Siegel, *Love, Medicine & Miracles* (New York: Harper-Collins Publishers, 1998), 19, 20.

3. Schuller, *Prayer: My Soul's Adventure with God* (Nashville: Thomas Nelson, 1995).

4. Siegel, *Prescriptions for Living* (New York: Harper/Collins Publishers, 1998) 107.

5. Siegel, *How To Live Between Office Visits* (New York: Harper/Collins Publishers, 1993) 180.

no violence to Paul's contextual meaning in chapter 4. But to use this text *apart* from Paul's context fits well with New Age teachings of God's immanence—that God is "in" everyone and everything—which is completely contrary to biblical teaching.

So what is Paul's context? In Ephesians, chapter four, Paul is writing to the "saints which are at Ephesus, and faithful in Christ Jesus" (Ephesians 1:1). He is not writing to everyone in the world. His target audience are those who, like the apostles, "are His [God's] witnesses" (Acts 5:32). Thus, in context, Ephesians 4:6 is not saying that God "is in everything." It is saying that He is "in" believers. The clarion call of New Agers is that we are all one, which is getting close to accepting the mantra that God is yourself. But, the only time that men and women are one is when they are "one in Christ Jesus" (Galatians 3:28).

All this does not deny the biblical truth that God indeed is speaking to all men and women, everywhere and at all times. God does work through the Holy Spirit in speaking to the consciences of everyone, past and present (see Romans 2:14–16). But God lives within those who choose to "abide" in Him (see John 15). He stands at the door and knocks and if anyone "opens the door" He "will come in to him" (Revelation 3:20). Isaiah said it clearly:

> "For thus says the High and Lofty One
> Who inhabits eternity, whose name is Holy;
> 'I dwell in the high and holy place,
> With him who has a contrite and humble spirit" (Isaiah 57:15).

The High and Lofty One is not the same as His creation—but He does dwell in those who are contrite and humble.

The point I am making is that by selecting Siegel and other New Age teachers for their supporting thoughts, with no explanation of who these well-known people are, Warren opens the door for confusion and legitimate concerns.

Robert Schuller

Although Warren has tried often to distance himself from Schuller, a quick review of *PDL* shows a number of "coincidences" that warrant further inspection. Here are a few:

Warren: "Hope is as essential to your life as air and water. You need hope to cope."[6] Twenty years earlier, Schuller wrote, "Our very survival 'as

---

6. *PDL*, 31.

a species depends on hope. And without hope we will lose the faith that we can cope.' "[7]

Warren: "If you have felt hopeless, hold on! Wonderful changes are going to happen in your life as you begin to live it on purpose. God says, *'I know what I am planning for you. . . . "I have good plans for you, not plans to hurt you. I will give you hope and a good future"'* (Jeremiah 29:11, NCV)."[8] Sixteen years earlier, Schuller, after quoting the same text, said, "This Bible verse says plainly that God has a plan and a dream and it includes you. You were born for a purpose."[9] Both uses of the text take these words out of context. (These uses of Jeremiah 29:11 are not at all what Jeremiah meant!)

Warren: "What is the driving force in your life?"[10] Twenty-four years earlier, Schuller wrote, "The Eternal Creative Force of the universe we call God can surge within your being to give you self-belief, self-esteem, self-love, self-confidence! Without it—you're sunk, with it—you're invincible."[11]

The significance of these connections is recognized by anyone who is acquainted with New Age terminology—"force" is a key New Age concept. Confusion arises when Christians accept language without any warning about New Age implications leading swiftly into the new spirituality. This is called overlapping terminology.

We should at least ask Warren what he means by *force.* Is it the same as "May the Force be with you"? Utter this famous line in today's world, and there's no mistaking that you're referring to the driving Force behind the *Star Wars* world of exploding planets and intergalactic wars. In the words of the character Obi-wan Kenobi, a Jedi knight, "The Force is what gives the Jedi his power. It's an energy field created by all living things. It surrounds us and penetrates us. It binds the galaxy together."

Here again is the *overlapping* of words that go back to Eastern religions, such as Taoism.

In his first sermon, given on March 30, 1980, in a trial run a week before his first public sermon, Easter Sunday, April 6, 1980, Warren outlined his vision for Saddleback, a vision that he said God had given to him. His

---

7. *Self-Esteem: The New Reformation* (Waco, Tex.: Word Books, 1982), 19.

8. *PDL,* 31.

9. *Be Happy You Are Loved* (Nashville: Thomas Nelson Publishers, 1986).

10. *PDL,* 27.

11. *Discover Your Possibilities* (New York: Ballantine Books, 1978), 3.

Saddleback vision was given in seven "dreams" that have been remarkably fulfilled in the twenty-five years since 1980.[12]

In 1974, Schuller wrote that "dreaming" is the first step in his formula of "Eight Steps of Mountain-Moving Faith."[13] In 1982, Schuller wrote, referring to the Lord's invitation, " 'Follow me.' What does that mean? It means daring to dream a great dream."[14]

He also wrote, "I am not fully forgiven until I allow God to write his new dream for my life on the blackboard of my mind, and I dare to believe, 'I am; therefore, I can. I am a child of God. I am somebody. God has a great plan to redeem society. He needs me and wants to use me.' "[15] "I must accept the dream God gives me and develop its inherent possibilities."[16]

In Warren's October 27, 2003, email message noted earlier, he wrote, "This weekend, I'll begin a series of five messages on God's dream to use you globally—to literally use YOU to change the world! I'll unveil our Global P.E.A.C.E. plan, and how God has uniquely prepared you for this moment of destiny. . . . The Global Peace Plan IS GOING TO HAPPEN."

In 1978, Schuller wrote, "Pray, seek God's guidance and what's going to happen? You'll get a dream to pursue. . . . Find a dream. Once you've got that dream and you know it's God's dream for your life, then be daring. Dare to say it. Let the redeemed of the Lord say so. Announce to the world that it's going to happen."[17]

Why didn't Warren take this golden opportunity to indeed show that he is not indebted to Schuller's dream and its remarkable resemblance to his five-step P.E.A.C.E. Plan nor to the eerie resemblance in Neale Donald Walsch's Five-step Peace Plan?

Neale Donald Walsch

Warren never refers to Walsch in either *PDL* and *PDC*, but frequent "coincidences" do occur.

Warren: "Before you were born, God planted *this moment* in your life. It is no accident that you are holding this book. God *longs* for you to discover

---

12. *PDC*, 43. On this page, all seven dreams are announced with some specificity.

13. *Move Ahead With Possibility Thinking* (Old Tappan, N.J.: Fleming H. Revell, 1967), 188.

14. *Self-Esteem*, 119.

15. Ibid., 104.

16. Ibid., 75.

17. *Discover Your Possibilities*, 100.

the life he created you to live—here on earth, and forever in eternity."[18]

Walsch: "This book has arrived in your life at the right and perfect time. . . . Everything happens in perfect order, and the arrival of this book in your life is no exception."[19]

Walsch, a depressed and disillusioned former radio talk show host, wrote an angry letter to God. He was shocked when "God" seemed to answer him through an inner voice. He transcribed all these "answers" and later published them in his first book, *Conversations with God: Book I.* It immediately became a bestseller. Walsch directly challenges everyone to accept the new gospel of the new spirituality that "We are all One."[20]

Walsch praised Robert Schuller in his 2002 book *The New Revelations: A Conversation with God*[21] by passing on that his "God" used Schuller to help make their case for world peace based on the "self-esteem" principles of new spirituality.

Walsch's Five Steps to Peace (using the word *Peace* as an acronym, as does Warren) are

"*P*ERMIT ourselves to acknowledge that some of our old beliefs about God and about Life are no longer working.

"*E*XPLORE the possibility that there is something we do not understand about God and about Life, the understanding of which could change everything.

"*A*NNOUNCE that we are willing for new understandings of God and Life to now be brought forth, understandings that could produce a new way of life on this planet.

"*C*OURAGEOUSLY examine these new understandings and, if they align with our personal inner truth and knowing, to enlarge our belief system to include them.

"*E*XPRESS our lives as a demonstration of our highest beliefs, rather than a denial of them."[22]

---

18. *PDL*, dedicatory page.

19. *Conversations with God: An Uncommon Dialogue, Book 2* (Charlottesville, Va.: Hampton Roads Publishing, 1997), 1.

20. *Conversations with God: An Uncommon Dialogue, Book 1* (New York: G. P. Putnam's Sons, 1996), 1, 2.

21. Walsch, *The New Revelations: A Conversation with God* (New York: Atria Books, 2002), 281.

22. Conversations with God Web site <www.cwg.org/5stepstopeace.pdf>.

It seems more than coincidence that both Warren and Walsch claim to be inspired by God in developing their P.E.A.C.E. plans. Walsch writes, "The universe does nothing by accident. . . . You can change the course of human history. This is not an exaggeration."[23]

Warren writes, "You are not a part of Saddleback Church by accident. . . . I say this without fear of exaggeration—God is going to use you, and all of us together at Saddleback, to change history."[24]

One would think that Warren, with what he considers to be a biblically based, five-step P.E.A.C.E. Plan, would take this magnificent opportunity to show how unbiblical Walsch's plan is.

Eugene Peterson

I reluctantly include Peterson in this list, but not because his paraphrase of the Bible is Warren's favorite in *PDL*. In fact, five of the six scriptures in just the first chapter of *PDL* come from Peterson's *The Message*. Among the many questionable paraphrases (not translations) Warren uses from *The Message* is Colossians 1:16: "For everything, absolutely everything, above and below, visible and invisible. . . *everything* got started in him and finds its purpose in him." It takes a lot of imagination to read that into what Paul is really saying in this verse! But I can see why Warren chose Peterson's paraphrase above more faithful translations—he liked Peterson's gratuitous use of the word *purpose.*

But there is something even more inappropriate and alarming in this paraphrase of Colossians 1:16—the phrase "*above and below*" instead of "that are in heaven and that are on earth." What is so interesting about Warren's use of this verse containing this phrase—"*above and below*"? This rendition is almost identical to the phrase Peterson used in translating a certain line in the Lord's Prayer:

> "Our father in heaven,
> Reveal who you are,
> Set the world right;
> Do what's best—as above, so below. . . ."

The phrase "*as above, so below*" is a common occultic New Age term. Just "google" the words "as above, so below," and you'll find many references to mystical, Eastern, New Age, and magical sources. For example: "This phrase comes from the beginning of *The Emerald Tablet* and embraces the

---

23. *Tomorrow's God: Our Greatest Spiritual Challenge* (New York: Atria Books, 2004), ix.

24. Saddleback Church email, October 27, 2003, containing the announcement of Warren's Five-Step Global P.E.A.C.E. Plan.

entire system of tradition and modern magic that was inscribed upon the tables in cryptic wording by *Hermes Trismegistus.* The significance of this phrase is that it is believed to hold the key to all mysteries. All systems of magic are claimed to function by this formula: 'That which is above is the same as that which is below.' . . . The universe is the same as God. God is the same as man.'"[25]

Another Web site says: "This ancient phrase, 'As above, so below' describes the Oneness of All That is."[26]

What is the point? Peterson has a way of coming up with dreamy, imaginative paraphrases of biblical texts. His treatment of the Lord's Prayer and Colossians 1:16, which Warren uses on the first page of the first chapter of *PDL,* lends some credence to the charge that Peterson, and perhaps Warren, are blind to the rising development of modern forms of spiritualism or the impact of the new spiritualism in the near future.

This phrase surely would confuse any former New Ager who might read *PDL.* Such paraphrases obscure the truth and set one up for deception in time to come. When Christian leaders such as Warren use the same overlapping words as do New Agers in their messages, they need to speak out forcefully, making it clear that they have a gospel *radically* different from that taught by the New Age philosophy. Otherwise, their readers and others will be greatly deceived when forces and groups already in place make their move.

Does the Christian church generally have any idea what is going on— that modern spiritualism in the form of rampant New Age teachings and those of its country cousin—new spirituality—is marching through Christian churches today? Churches that do not see the problem of overlapping language will find that confusion only opens the door to greater wonders that the powers behind the new spirituality are ready to unleash.[27]

After the horror of September 11, 2001, I became aware of a book titled *From the Ashes: A Spiritual Response to the Attack on America.*[28] Articles by Billy Graham, Bruce Wilkinson, Charles Colson, Max Lucado, Bill Hybels, and Rick Warren were mixed with others by prominent New Age

---

25. <www.themystica.org/mystica/articles/a/below_above.html>.

26. <theosophy.org/tlodocs/AsAboveSoBelow.htm>.

27. This mystical appeal to a "higher power" is exactly what "drove" those evil terrorists into New York's Twin Towers (September 11, 2001) and that keeps motivating men and women to blow themselves up with hundreds of others in restaurants, buses, and hotels in Baghdad, Bali, Tel Aviv, London, and Amman.

28. (Emmaus, Penn.: Rodale Press), 2001.

leaders such as Neale Donald Walsch, the Dalai Lama, and Starhawk the Wiccan.

What is most interesting is that the New Agers were challenging the Christian leaders, in light of September 11, 2001, to accept and preach the new gospel that "We are all One."

Of course Walsch claims that the Bible supports the idea that "We are all One." He wrote

> "We must change ourselves. We must change the beliefs upon which our behaviors are based. We must create a different reality, build a new society. . . . We must do so with new spiritual truths. We must preach a new gospel, its healing message summarized in two sentences:
>
> "We are all one. Ours is not a better way, ours is merely another way.
>
> "This fifteen-word message, delivered from every lectern and pulpit, from every rostrum and platform, could change everything overnight. I challenge every priest, every ministry, every rabbi and religious cleric to preach this."[29]

I have no idea how many copies of this book were read or sold. But I do know that this is the kind of "peace" message for which terrified men and women everywhere were sighing following September 11. After all, when and where will the next terror attack happen?

What was needed in *From the Ashes* was a response from every Christian contributor that would dismantle the false hope of the New Agers. How? Rick Warren could have given a clear, unambiguous biblical statement that men and women are not divine and that the only "oneness" we can hope for is to find our "oneness" with God through Jesus Christ. He could have made it clear that God alone has spelled out a lasting peace plan for this world.

Ken Blanchard

One of the most interesting additions to Warren's growing team is Ken Blanchard. In a November 2003 sermon at Saddleback Church, Rick Warren announced, "Ken [Blanchard, famous for his leadership conferences and his book *One Minute Manager*] has signed on to help with the Peace Plan, and he's going to be helping train us in leadership and in how to train others to be leaders all around the world."[30]

Ken Blanchard is recognized worldwide for his management seminars,

29. Ibid., 21.

30. <www.saddlebackfamily.com/peace/Services/110203_high.asx>

especially in Christian organizations, and has much to offer Warren with his organizing skills.

This news shocked those who know that Blanchard frequently aligns himself with New Age and mystical leaders and movements. The record is extensive regarding his beliefs in the benefits of mantra meditation, yoga, and Buddhist principles.

Many books with New Age content carry Blanchard's endorsements. In the foreword to *What Would Buddha Do at Work?* Blanchard wrote, "Buddha points to the path and invites us to begin our journey to enlightenment. I . . . invite you to begin your journey to enlightened work."[31]

It remains to be seen who influences whom the most as time goes on. But let there be no mistake: Much that Rick Warren has written in *PDL* has indeed warmed the hearts of millions. In the next chapter, let's look at some of those concepts that have warmed my own heart in spite of the cloudy haze that also permeates the book.

---

31. Franz Metcalf, B. J. Gallagher Hateley (New York: McGraw Hill, 2002). Blanchard's endorsements can be found on Deepak Chopra's *Seven Spiritual Laws of Success*, Marshall Goldsmith's *The Corporate Mystic*, Jim Ballard's *Mind Like Water*, Ellen Tadd's *Death and Letting Go*, Tim Laurence's *The Hoffman Process*, Jack Canfield's *Success Principles*, and Marc Lesser's *Z.B.A.: Zen of Business Administration—How Zen Practice Can Transform Your Work and Your Life.*

TWELVE

Saddleback's Doctrinal Statement Compared With Adventist Beliefs

The Saddleback Church's Web site lists the following doctrines.[1] I found them void of theological mumbo jumbo, easy for anyone to understand. Although I am tempted to add to them, I am sure that Rick Warren and his associates could do the same. But they wanted brevity. Where I sense that Saddleback's doctrinal statements are misleading or contrary to what Adventists believe, I will respectfully state these differences.

"ABOUT GOD

"God is the Creator and Ruler of the universe. He has eternally existed in three persons: the Father, the Son and the Holy Spirit. These three are co-equal and are one God."

In its brevity, I don't see how any Christian would have trouble with this statement.

"ABOUT MAN

"Man is made in the spiritual image of God, to be like Him in character. He is the supreme object of God's creation. Although man has tremendous potential for good, he is marred by an attitude of disobedience toward God called 'sin.' This attitude separates man from God."

This statement is surely true. It would be interesting to know what Saddleback thinks about *when* sin "happens" in humans—whether because of birth or by conscious decisions as the child grows. And exactly *what* sin is—can specific acts be sins if men and women are not aware of their responsibility?

---

1. See Appendix C: Saddleback's Doctrinal Statements.

"ABOUT ETERNITY

"Man was created to exist forever. He will either exist eternally separated from God by sin, or in union with God through forgiveness and salvation. To be eternally separated from God is Hell. To be eternally in union with Him is eternal life. Heaven and Hell are places of eternal existence."

Here is one of Saddleback's fundamental deficits—its understanding of the nature of mankind. Certainly, human beings were created to live forever—but that gift was conditional as the episode in Eden tragically reminds us. Although not precisely stated, Saddleback believes that humans have immortal souls, a belief without biblical foundation.[2] To be eternally separated from God is surely hell, but not an ever-burning, conscious hell. Adventists and other Christians accept the biblical position that hell's punishment lasts forever, but not its punishing—the duration is not the issue, but its lasting effect (see Matthew 10:28; Revelation 20:9).

"ABOUT JESUS CHRIST

"Jesus Christ is the Son of God. He is co-equal with the Father. Jesus lived a sinless human life and offered Himself as the perfect sacrifice for the sins of all men by dying on a cross. He arose from the dead after three days to demonstrate His power over sin and death. He ascended to Heaven's glory and will return again to earth to reign as King of kings, and Lord of lords."

Nothing is said about the kind of human being Jesus became for thirty-three years. Christian history is loaded with different opinions about the humanity of Jesus. What is He doing now as our High Priest? And what determines when He will return?

"ABOUT SALVATION

"Salvation is a gift from God to man. Man can never make up for his sin by self-improvement or good works. Only by trusting in Jesus Christ as God's offer of forgiveness can man be saved from sin's penalty. Eternal life begins the moment one receives Jesus Christ into his life by faith."

If a few words were added to this statement, it would show the difference confession and repentance make in relation to "God's offer of forgiveness." And God offers more than forgiveness; He offers to take away sin from our lives, here and now, not waiting until the resurrection. Yes, "eternal life" indeed begins the moment one "receives Jesus," here and now, but not in the sense that it can never be lost—as we will discuss later.

2. *PDL*, 37.

Many pastors and scholars have trouble with Warren's prayer for salvation.[3] They feel that "accepting Jesus" involves more than merely an emotional response. To base salvation on simply saying "Jesus, I believe in You and I receive You" seems to be a door to great misunderstanding. Many churches have their own understanding of who Jesus is. Those who wish more from Warren on this point would like him to welcome eager people into learning more about the kind of life that genuine believers should live before he tells them "Welcome to the family of God!" My understanding is that this prayer may be Warren's first step for the eager seeker and should be greatly encouraged—but it should lead immediately into doctrinal studies so that the "seeker" will find the New Testament Jesus, a journey that is not emphasized in *PDL*. The next steps should link the head with the heart so that a deep commitment is made regarding what is involved in becoming a eyes-wide-open follower of our Lord and a member of the family of God.

"ABOUT ETERNAL SECURITY

"Because God gives man eternal life through Jesus Christ, the believer is secure in salvation for eternity. Salvation is maintained by the grace and power of God, not by the self-effort of the Christian. It is the grace and keeping power of God that gives this security."

The doctrine of irresistible grace is rooted in Calvinism. Often it is referred to as "once saved, always saved." Yes, the Saddleback statement gives 100 percent credit to God for His "keeping power," but Warren overlooks key New Testament texts regarding the conditions that determine how far God can go to keep us from falling (see Jude 24). Of course, the argument is that those who apostatize never did really give their lives to Jesus. But that takes away any solid assurance that one's decision for Christ is truly genuine. And where is man's responsibility in developing a character that God can entrust with eternal life? Does God promise eternal life to those who merely call themselves "believers"? (See Matthew 7:21–23.)

Paul often reminds his readers that salvation is conditional "if you hold fast that word which I preached" (1 Corinthians 15:2; see also Hebrews 10:26–36).

At times in *PDL* we read exhortations such as "There's a Grand Designer behind everything. Your life is not a result of random chance, fate, or luck. There is a master plan. History is *His story*. God is pulling the strings. *We* make mistakes, but God never does. God *cannot* make a

---

3. *PDL*, 58.

mistake—because he is God."[4] This is one of the places where Warren's Calvinism and Arminianism blend and lack clarification.

"ABOUT THE HOLY SPIRIT

"The Holy Spirit is equal with the Father and the Son as God. He is present in the world to make men aware of their need for Jesus Christ. He also lives in every Christian from the moment of salvation. He provides the Christian with power for living, understanding of spiritual truth, and guidance in doing what is right. The Christian seeks to live under His control daily."

This could not be stated better or more clearly in the few words that are used. Following this teaching to its conclusion would force Warren to restate his understanding of "eternal security."

"ABOUT THE BIBLE

"The Bible is God's word to all men. It was written by human authors, under the supernatural guidance of the Holy Spirit. It is the supreme source of truth for Christian beliefs and living. Because it is inspired by God, it is truth without any mixture of error."

Many Christians would agree with this statement. But much depends on what one means by "without any mixture of error." Does Saddleback mean that biblical writers never made mistakes—such as Matthew's miscue in Matthew 27:9, when he wrote *Jeremiah* instead of *Zechariah*? Or, what was the actual wording of the sign placed above Christ on the cross (see Matthew 27:37; Mark 15:26; Luke 23:38; John 19:19)?

Summary

Other than the two explicit deficits mentioned—eternal security and immortal soul issues—what seems to trouble many generally is not what is said in *PDL* but what is left unsaid. In our next chapter, we will be more specific by outlining what Seventh-day Adventists believe, especially when compared to Saddleback's doctrinal beliefs.

---

4. *PDL*, 195. Emphasis in text.

THIRTEEN

What Adventists Can Contribute— Part 1: The Great Controversy Theme

Adventists are a very inclusive people. We are a worldwide family, one of the strongest-knit church groups in the world. Diversity is the most apt description of what one sees when one of our quinquennial General Conference sessions is held somewhere in the world with delegates from almost every country on the planet.

Since the mid-nineteenth century, millions of Catholics, Methodists, Baptists, Presbyterians, charismatics, Hindus, Muslims, Buddhists, etc. have joined together in response to the presentation of the everlasting gospel (Revelation 14:6). This gospel is the simple unfolding of the kind of God who is running the universe and what He plans to do with all of us on planet Earth. Adventist doors are open, day and night, to those seeking clarity and comfort in a world that seems to become more erratic by the day.

Open secret

What is the open secret of the advancing Adventist presence throughout the world? The answer lies in the precision and passion of what is termed the great controversy theme (GCT). It is the mother lode of Adventist theology.[1] Rick Warren gives several clues that he would be one of the first to recognize the fruitful contribution that the GCT could make to his Purpose Driven movement. Warren's emphasis on God being our Friend puts him in a rare theological class.[2] In fact, most of his

---

1. I am indebted to Dale Martin for this incisive analogy.

2. "God wants to be your best friend. Your relationship to God has many different aspects: God is your Creator and Maker, Lord and Master, Judge, Redeemer, Father, Savior, and much more. But the most shocking truth is this: Almighty God yearns to be your Friend!" *PDL*, 85.

detractors work from a very different picture of God, and that picture determines their theology.

The GCT is about the kind of God who created and runs the universe. So much of the Christian and non-Christian world sees God as a taskmaster who needs to be appeased in some way. Going to this or that "holy" place; offering up children in "sacred" ceremonies; living in a monastery or cave, as far away from normal life as possible; heavy-duty offerings of money or extreme self-sacrifice—and much more—all to please a God that must be placated in order to get His attention and favor.

But that is not the God that Jesus came to reveal. Listen to His last words to His disciples a few hours before He was shackled by Roman soldiers: " 'No longer do I call you servants, for a servant does not know what his master is doing; but I have called you friends, for all things that I heard from My Father I have made known to you' " (John 15:15).

Our heavenly Father, our Lord Jesus, and the Holy Spirit are our "Friends"! Not the Cosmic Cop, not the Exacting Bookkeeper, not the Harsh and Severe Judge! In fact, if Warren would emphasize all this, he would stand head and shoulders over most of his detractors who think of God in terms of someone who must be approached gingerly and through others—such as Mary or the saints—to get favorable attention from the Father.

But Jesus removed this veil that hides the face of the Father, even from most Christians: "In that day you will ask in My name, and I do not say to you that I shall pray the Father for you; for the Father Himself loves you, because you have believed that I came forth from God" (John 16:26, 27).

If asked which they would rather see first following the resurrection—Jesus or the Father—most Christians would almost always say, "Jesus." Why is that? Somehow, Christ's words—one of the basic truths of the GCT—have not been made clear!

Let Paul help us: "But God has shown us how much he loves us—it was while we were still sinners that Christ died for us! . . . We were God's enemies, but he made us his friends through the death of his Son. Now that we are God's friends, how much more will we be saved by Christ's life! But that is not all; we rejoice because of what God has done through our Lord Jesus Christ, who has now made us God's friends" (Romans 5:8–11, TEV).

And further:

"When anyone is joined to Christ, he is a new being; the old is gone, the new has come. All this is done by God, who through Christ changed us from enemies into his friends and gave us the task of making others his friends also. Our message is that God was making all mankind his friends through Christ. God did not keep an account of their sins, and he has given us the message which tells how he makes them his friends.

"Here we are, then, speaking for Christ, as though God himself were making his appeal through us. We plead on Christ's behalf: let God change you from enemies into his friends!" (2 Corinthians 5:17–20, TEV).

They are our Friends!

Men and women and children everywhere need to know what God—the Father, the Son, and the Holy Spirit—is really like. The Members of the Godhead are our Friends! This fact lies at the heart of the GCT and the everlasting gospel (see Revelation 14:6). This fact is precisely what Satan wants to obscure. For him, everything hangs on picturing God as distant and severe. Jesus came to destroy this picture that has well-nigh enshrouded the world with its darkness. He came to give us good reasons to trust our heavenly Father as a wonderfully loving and infinitely gracious God of the universe. He came to "glorify" the Father (see John 17:4).

And that is what the Bible is all about—the fact that God can be trusted and that He is not the kind of person that Satan has made Him out to be. From Genesis to Revelation, this cosmic struggle is on display. It is not only a philosophical clash of good versus bad, or right versus wrong; this controversy roars every day in the lives of men and women. Fundamentally, it is a battle for the loyalties of human beings in all lands at all times.

The controversy began in heaven (see Revelation 12:7) and ends in heaven with the mighty chorus of the redeemed when the universe hears "the mighty voice of a great multitude in heaven, crying, 'Hallelujah! Salvation and glory and power belong to our God, for his judgments are true and just'" (Revelation 19:1, 2, RSV; 15:3).

In this mighty affirmation lies a clue as to what the conflict has been about. We hear the echoes of Satan's charges that God has been unfair, that He is severe and arbitrary. The great controversy ends only when God's created intelligences throughout the universe are convinced that He is worth loving and deserving of trust.

Bible is the theater

The Bible is the theater wherein we observe (1) the antagonist at work stalking his victims like a roaring lion (see 1 Peter 5:8), relentlessly subverting God's government, and (2) the infinitely patient, gracious God telling His side of the conflict.

Satan has been very successful in convincing men and women that God has been unfair in making loyalty a matter of willing obedience. How would, or should, God respond to rebellion? How would He forgive a rebel? By putting into effect what we call the "plan of salvation."

For thousands of years throughout Old Testament times, God had been explaining to men and women that He could be trusted—that He didn't have to be appeased with all kinds of human effort. Then, when He thought the "fullness of the time had come" (Galatians 4:4), God personally came to tell His side of the controversy. He came into the ugly arena called earth. Why did He come? To reveal (1) the truth about the way God chooses to run the universe (John 1:1–3, 14), and (2) the truth about men and women and how they can be released from sin's bondage. Jesus was Exhibit A.

God's Exhibit B was to show the universe that Jesus succeeded in telling these two truths. How would He do that? By working through men and women who caught our Lord's messages. Through faith—the joining of fact and feeling—these new loyalists would bring a new dynamic to the human race, "for it is the power of God to salvation for everyone who believes [has faith]" (Romans 1:16). This good news promised that "the God of peace will crush Satan under your feet shortly" (16:20).

These thoughts lead us to recognize why God now needed men and women of faith as witnesses that what Jesus did as our Example, as well as what He did as our atoning Sacrifice, nails Satan against the wall of universal scrutiny. In other words, through the march of loyal men and women, and before God brings down the curtains on the great controversy, all this will be made clear to those who seek truth in the end of time.

Today, men and women need to hear answers to the big picture: Can God be trusted? Does He care about the misery and disasters that are piling up with exponential rapidity? Can He really alter neural paths so that addicts of all descriptions can overcome these internal demons? In short, will the power of the gospel really work today as it did in Paul's day? Will the gospel truly restore men and women into reflections of Christ so that they are safe to save? Can they be trusted with an eternal life in which God has promised that sin will never arise again?

We now can understand more clearly why the purpose of the gospel has so much to do with helping God settle the great controversy with Satan. Did God place an impossible burden upon His followers when He exhorted them to walk as Jesus walked? (See 1 John 2:6; cf. Ephesians 5:1, 2; Philippians 1:1–5; 1 Peter 1:15, 16.) Was God asking too much when He predicted that in the end time His loyalists would "keep the commandments of God and the faith of Jesus" (Revelation 14:12; 12:17)?

In Revelation 14:15, God painted the last of the last days in terms of the global harvest that is "fully ripe" (RSV). That is when the wheat and the tares, the loyalists and rebels, are fully revealed for the universe to see and evaluate.

In summary, the main issue in the great controversy has been whether God or Satan had the blueprint for a safe, secure, loving universe built on mutual trust of all parties.

When the last words are said, the universe will have all the evidence needed for the vindication of God's character and government (see Revelation 15:3, 4; 19:1, 2). Not only will the faithful of earth help to vindicate God's character, but so will Satan and his loyalists—they will have demonstrated that rebellion against truth is always self-defeating and self-destructive, for the "wages of sin is death" (Romans 6:23) just as God said in the beginning (see Genesis 2:17)!

Now we will quickly review how the great controversy theme (GCT) organizes the thinking of Adventists as they read the big picture from Genesis to Revelation.

The great controversy theme organizes Adventist thinking

The GCT is the organizing, biblical principle of what has come to be known as the distinctive message of the Seventh-day Adventist Church. It provides the glue of coherency to all of its teachings—theology, health (health maintenance plus the prevention and cure of disease), education, missiology, ecclesiology, social relations, environmental stewardship, etc.

The uniqueness of Adventist thinking is not some particular element of its theology; rather, it lies in an overall understanding of the Bible's central message. This distinctive totality focuses on the person of Jesus Christ and how this focus affects the destiny of humanity—and of the universe.

The main issue in the great controversy is who can best run the universe—God's plan as expressed in His awesome gift of freedom fleshed out in His unambiguous commandments or Satan's theory of individual self-determination. Satan has charged that God is unfair, unforgiving, arbitrary, and supremely selfish.

God's defense has been both passive and active. Passive in that He has allowed time to proceed so that Satan's principles could be seen for all their suicidal destructiveness; active in that He has revealed His character and trustworthiness in many ways so that all inhabitants throughout the universe as well as on earth could make up their minds as to who has been right and wrong in the controversy.

The essence of God's response to Satan's charges is the way He forgives and empowers men and women to overcome Satan's temptations. In a few words, the purpose of the gospel is to restore humanity to the image of God (see Romans 8:29). Not merely forgiveness, but restoration—to restore what had been lost by sin; to bring men and women back to their original state, step by step.

This germinal seed (the restoration of the image of God in the redeemed) from which grows the unbendable, central trunk and the many coherent branches of the GCT, affects all Adventist teachings. It becomes the litmus test in measuring all other attempts to describe the New Testament gospel.

When one attempts to attach alien doctrinal branches to the GCT trunk, alarms and whistles should go off somewhere in the church body. Some of those attempts to add doctrines contrary to the main principle of the GCT are recognized when theologians begin to refer to paradoxes and tensions that we have to live with. It creates the fog of pluralism and easily becomes a patchwork theology.

However, when Adventists let the Bible be seen within the big picture without importing definitions grounded in other theological systems, a remarkable simplicity and consistency happens—it is the coherency of the GCT.

The GCT explains why Jesus came and why He died

Jesus came to reveal what God is like (see Hebrews 1:1–4; John 1:1–3, 14) and what man may become with His help (see John 15:8; 17:8; Revelation 3:21).

According to the New Testament, Jesus was born and joined the human race as all baby boys are born. He came (1) to "taste [the second] death for everyone" (Hebrews 2:9); (2) to join humanity "as the children have partaken of flesh and blood, He Himself likewise shared in the same" (Hebrews 2:14); (3) to become a human being, not only to have a human form but to become a human being in "all things" (Hebrews 2:17; "in every respect," RSV); (4) so that He could qualify as humanity's "merciful and faithful High Priest" because "He Himself has suffered, being tempted, [thus] He is able to aid those who are tempted" (Hebrews 2:17, 18); so that all believers would have the confidence that "we do not have a High Priest who cannot sympathize with our weaknesses, but was in all points tempted as we are, yet without sin"; so that all believers could "come boldly to the throne of grace, that we may obtain mercy and find grace to help in time of need" (Hebrews 4:15, 16).

This understanding of Jesus' humanity has been supported by some of the most distinguished scholars in the history of Christianity. It is the cornerstone of the GCT. Knowing who Jesus is and why He came simplifies the biblical message. When John tells us to "walk just as He walked" (1 John 2:6), we know that he is not merely writing poetry—he is telling us how to live the Christian life if we want to sit down with Him with the Father in the earth made new (see Revelation 3:21). When Peter pleads with us to follow Jesus as our "Example" (1 Peter 2:21), he is not asking for the impossible. Why? Because Jesus has already shown us the way in the same flesh all humanity shares (see Hebrews 2:14, 17; 4:14–16).

If we do not allow the New Testament to guide our thinking, we have opened the door to all kinds of speculation, such as (1) the immaculate conception of His mother Mary or (2) a Jesus who could not sin and came only to die, or (3) a Jesus who had a body that was weakened after thousands of years of sin but a mind that could not be truly tempted from within and without as all men and women.

Again, in terms of the GCT, why did He die? The everlasting gospel is clear—He died for our sins. When He died, He had my name—and yours—on His mind. But the GCT says there was more! The life and death of Jesus helped to answer the charges and lies of Satan (see Revelation 12:4) and showed that God was self-denying and unselfish and did care very much for His created intelligences. Further, He died to show the universe what the second death (see Revelation 20:14) would be like for the willing disobedient. In other words, God was not the kind of person that Satan had made Him out to be!

The GCT explains where Jesus is now and what He is doing as our High Priest

Paul tells us that we should "consider" the High Priesthood of Jesus "who has passed through the heavens, Jesus the Son of God" (Hebrews 3:1; 4:14; 8:1). Why? Because "we do not have a High Priest who cannot sympathize [an understanding born out of the same life experiences] with our weaknesses [moral and physical that predispose to sin], but was in all points tempted as we are, yet without sin" (Hebrews 4:15, 16).

Rick Warren is close to these precious thoughts in his focus on the close relationship God wants with believers. But he remains stuck on only one side, or focus, in the ellipse of truth (which we discuss later in this chapter) and doesn't seem to see the other side that fills out the ellipse.

Warren writes gracefully, "If God never did anything else for you, he would still deserve your continual praise for the rest of your life because of what Jesus did for you on the cross. *God's Son died for you!* This is the greatest reason for worship."[3]

But he has it only half right. How much more "reason for worship" would Saddleback members have if they would take Paul's advice and follow Jesus into His high priestly ministry!

Because Warren is only half right, using only one half of the ellipse of truth,[4] focusing only on Christ's death, he permits himself to fall into the trap of a limited gospel. The limited gospel looks at the Cross as Christ's "finished work," and overlooks the fact that the Cross was Christ's *sacrificial* atonement and that His cleansing work as our High Priest completes His work in preparing a people for eternity. Warren doesn't yet see that one of the truths of the gospel is that man's restoration—not only our Lord's forgiveness—*determines his destiny.* This is one of the major weaknesses in Warren's whole program—he doesn't yet see the eternal implications of restored believers whom Jesus has invested with the opportunity to help settle the great controversy. And it is our Lord's high priestly ministry in conjunction with the Holy Spirit that dramatizes how His priesthood makes available the grace to help us overcome in our hour of need (see Hebrews 4:16).

But there is more to the importance of our Lord's high priesthood today. Why? Because it is reflecting the purpose of Aaron's priesthood that God initiated for the spiritual life of the Israelites. The sanctuary service was the everlasting gospel in miniature, its meaning better understood after the life and death of Jesus.

The sanctuary service's contributions, however, did not end when Jesus died. The Day of Atonement teaches us something awesome about how God deals with sin, now and at the end of the world. The high priesthood of Jesus is now fulfilling the intent of the earthly Day of Atonement—the cleansing of the sanctuary once and for all. What does that mean?

The "cleansing" refers to the removal of sin, symbolically and literally, in the lives of God's loyalists. Where does our Lord's priesthood figure in all this? As our High Priest, He understands from personal experience what His loyalists go through and knows exactly what they need—"mercy [forgiveness] and grace [power] to help in time of need" (Hebrews 4:16).

---

3. *PDL,* 112.

4. See the opposite page for a quick summary of the ellipse of truth. Leroy Moore in describing this essential quality of "truth" uses the analogy of the paradox wherein both "sides" of the paradox must be properly unified. Another analogy my friend Ron Frey suggests is that both wheels on the car axle must be going at the same time to get forward motion—emphasizing one or the other is self-defeating.

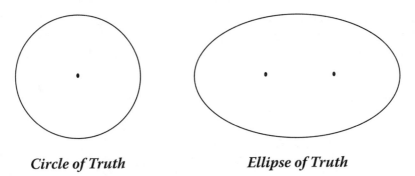

Circle of Truth   **Ellipse of Truth**

A circle has one focus (center); an ellipse has two focuses (foci)

1. In an ellipse, if the two foci separate from each other, we eventually get something like a hot dog. If they get too close to each other, we have made a circle.

2. Either way, we no longer have a true ellipse; machinery that uses the ellipse principle would suddenly not work if the two foci were moved either closer or farther away.

3. A real ellipse needs both foci—with equal emphasis on each—or it ceases to be an ellipse. For example, if we want a glass of water, we don't ask for hydrogen. Or for oxygen. To get water, we must have H_2O; that is, both hydrogen and oxygen are needed in the water ellipse. We can't have one without the other and still have water!

4. Theological truths always use the elliptical pattern. For example, God is one focus of the ellipse, and man is the other. In a way, as far as we are concerned, we can't have one without the other.

5. For example, the ellipse of salvation needs grace and faith; if we want salvation, we can't have grace without faith and vice versa.

6. The ellipse of the gospel can be expressed by joining pardon and power. Pardon, without the power to overcome the sin for which we want pardon, is only a partial gospel and thus is not what God intended.

7. When we want to understand Christ's role in our salvation, we note that He is both our Substitute and our Example—we don't have one without the other.

8. When we want to understand Christ's work as our Savior, we see Him on the cross, and we see Him as our High Priest—we don't have one without the other.

One of these days, Jesus will determine that His loyalists in the last days have truly listened to the good news, and, as High Priest, He will declare

His duties are over and that "he who is unjust, let him be unjust still; he who is filthy, let him be filthy still; he who is righteous, let him be righteous still; he who is holy, let him be holy still" (Revelation 22:11). The end is truly near.

The GCT explains the job description of the Christian church

Before Jesus ascended, He laid out the job description for the Christian church in His incredibly moving prayer: "As You sent Me into the world, I also have sent them into the world" (John 17:18; see also 20:21).[5] Could it be that, in some important aspects, the plan of salvation depends on His disciples' doing faithfully what He did so faithfully? And if they do not, they would be His followers in name only (see Matthew 7:21–23)!

Just hours before the Cross, Jesus was putting Missionary Plan C into action.[6] Adam and Eve failed God's Missionary Plan A when they backed out of the Garden. Missionary Plan B failed when Israel missed its opportunity to be God's faithful messengers in telling the truth about Him and how He wants to restore the moral image in His loyalists.

Paul never ceased to wonder at this awesome responsibility that Jesus had given to His growing church—Missionary Plan C. The Christian church is Christ's instrument to tell the truth about God in such a way that He would be glorified by the faithfulness of His followers that "we who first trusted in Christ should be to the praise of His glory" (Ephesians 1:12); "you were sealed with the Holy Spirit of promise, who is the guarantee of our inheritance until the redemption of the purchased possession, to the praise of His glory" (verses 13, 14); "to the intent that now the manifold wisdom of God might be made known *by the church* to the principalities and powers in the heavenly places, according to the eternal purpose which He accomplished in Christ Jesus our Lord" (Ephesians 3:10, 11; emphasis supplied); "being filled with the fruits of righteousness which are by Jesus Christ, to the glory and praise of God" (Philippians 1:11).

This emphasis on God's loyalists as vindicators of His mighty plan for man's salvation is not something new to New Testament Christians. God told the prophet Ezekiel how Israel had brought dishonor to His name and failed to fulfill its mission:

---

5. Our Lord's use of *as* is most significant. He would be outlining an impossible task for Christians to share His mission if He did not share with all men and women the same human "equipment" (Hebrews 2:14, 17; 4:14–16).

6. I am using Missionary Plans A, B, and C as another way of emphasizing how God is using willing inhabitants of this world as His emissaries to tell His side of the great controversy.

"But when they came to the nations, wherever they came, they profaned my holy name, in that men said of them, 'These are the people of the LORD, and yet they had to go out of his land.' But I had concern for my holy name, which the house of Israel caused to be profaned among the nations to which they came.

"Therefore . . . It is not for your sake, O house of Israel, that I am about to act, but for the sake of my holy name, which you have profaned among the nations. . . . And I will vindicate the holiness of my great name, which has been profaned among the nations. . . . and the nations will know that I am the LORD . . . when through you I vindicate my holiness before their eyes" (Ezekiel 36:20–23, RSV).

Our Lord's life and death were one phase of the vindication of God that lies at the heart of the great controversy. The second phase of vindicating the name—the character—of God would be lived out through the work of grace in the lives of loyal Christians. We all pray, reciting the Lord's Prayer, "Hallowed be Thy name." But tragically, those who claim the name of the Lord but not His power and character will hear those dreadful words: "I never knew you; depart from Me, you who practice lawlessness" (Matthew 7:23). Christians today should never think that they have heard our Lord's words too much!

Becoming members of the family of God involves more than a simple prayer for acceptance.[7] New members must hear the same message that the Ephesians heard when Paul wrote, "You should no longer walk as the rest of the Gentiles walk, in the futility of their mind. . . . that you put off, concerning your former conduct, the old man which grows corrupt according to the deceitful lusts, and be renewed in the spirit of your mind, and that you put on the new man which was created according to God, in righteousness and true holiness" (4:17–24).

Paul reminded early Christians that they were destined to be God's demonstration—to both the inhabitants of earth and the universe—that His plan and power work as promised. Further, Paul is emphatic that their witness to God's name and glory helps determine the future of that universe: "The whole creation is on tiptoe to see the wonderful sight of the sons of God coming into their own" (Romans 8:19, Phillips). What a remarkable prediction—that God will give to ordinary men and women the

---

7. "People are breezing through those wide, comfortable, inviting gates with all their baggage, their self-needs, their self-esteem, and their desire for fulfillment and self-satisfaction. And the most horrible thing about it is they think they're going to heaven. . . . Listening to a seeker-sensitive evangelical preacher today, we're likely to think it's easy to be a Christian. Just say these little words, pray this little prayer, and poof! you're in the club."—John MacArthur, Jr., *Hard to Believe* (Nashville: Thomas Nelson Publishers, 2003), 12, 13.

dignity and privilege of participating in reversing all that Satan and sin have done on planet Earth.

The GCT reveals the ellipse of salvation that saves us from confusion in understanding the plan of salvation

All truths, biblical or otherwise, are expressed within the ellipse of truth (see page 105). For example, we get water because of the ellipse principle. Water does not exist unless the circles of hydrogen and oxygen are re-formed into an ellipse. If one should ask, Which is more important in the formation of water, hydrogen or oxygen? The answer would be, Both are equally important if you want a glass of water. Understanding the ellipse makes the question silly.

In theology, truth is the sum total of its objective and subjective elements: One focus is on God's revelation and His gracious appeals and offers to sinners; the other focus is on the human response. Salvation truth thus binds together the objective will of God (His commandments, etc.) and the subjective Yes of a responsible ("response-able") person. Even as water cannot be divided into hydrogen and oxygen and remain water, so the will of God and the faith response of His loyalists cannot be divided and yet remain "salvation." It is silly to ask which side of the ellipse is more important.

Let's look at this theologically:

▸ An overemphasis on *justification* (the objective) leads to human passivity, with faith becoming primarily a matter of saying "Yes" to a doctrinal statement. This often leads to a *careless* use of such phrases as "Jesus paid it all." Or, "The atonement was completed on the cross."

▸ An overemphasis on *sanctification* (the subjective) leads to warm feelings or cool reason or good works as the test of faith. This often leads a person to *minimize* the primary authority of God and to make predominant such words as "It's not truth for me unless I feel it!" Or people may place primary weight on visual "evidence" such as faith healers, glossolalia (speaking in tongues), charismatic speakers, hugging, or even laughter in religious meetings. Or, on the quiet satisfaction that they have dutifully "kept" the commandments.

▸ An overemphasis on objective justification tends to make imputed righteousness the most important element in salvation.

▸ An overemphasis on subjective sanctification (imparted righteousness) tends to make a person a target for religious feeling or human reasoning.

▶ Overemphasizing Christ's ministry on the Cross tends to eclipse (1) the essential importance of Christ's ministry as our High Priest and (2) the essential work of the Holy Spirit in developing Christlike characters.

In other words, to emphasize only one focal point of the ellipse is to distort truth. Even though each focus in the ellipse emphasizes truth worth dying for, arguments will never end until a person accepts the total picture of the truths by keeping both foci in play. This understanding of truth is as inescapable as the joining of hydrogen and oxygen to make water.[8]

Another insight that the ellipse of truth contributes is that it saves us from three errors within Christianity—predestination, universalism, and legalism. When we understand that in the great controversy God made man in His own image (see Genesis 1:27)—two persons interacting with the ability to say yes and no—we can better understand the core truth in the relationship between grace (God's part) and faith (man's part).

Throughout the Old and New Testaments God is pleading for man's free and willing response to His grace. Nowhere in the Bible do we see God threatening people who have no ability to respond because He has already decided their destiny. To think otherwise is to play into Satan's hands when he accuses God of being severe, harsh, and unfair.

On the other hand, to make God out to be so loving that He will find a way to save everyone forever is to, again, miss the point in the great controversy. Truth is at stake! Who can run the universe best, God or Satan? Is

---

8. David P. Gushee, professor of moral philosophy, Union University, nailed this issue well in "Our Missing Moral Compass" (*Christianity Today*, November 2005). "If one labors in the vineyards of most sectors of American evangelical life, it does not take long before one notices the staggering moral sloppiness that frequently characterizes us. It's not just that Christians are sinners, too, and that we mess up like everyone else does. . . .

"The problem goes deeper, to the way in which we have understood the very structure and meaning of the Christian experience. For many of us, Christianity is primarily a *faith*, that is, a body of beliefs to which we assent. Or it is primarily an *experience*, that is, a repertoire of inspiring, encouraging, or even ecstatic states entered into through worship and prayer. Or it is an *event*, that is, a one-time moment of conversion in which we 'walk the aisle,' profess our faith publicly, and join the church, guaranteeing ourselves a heavenly mansion when we die.

". . . We are indeed morally sloppy, and I think it is because we have embraced truncated versions of the Christian faith that have trained us to be this way. . . .

"Christianity is more than an event, an experience, or a set of beliefs. It is a way of life characterized by moral seriousness and the quest for holiness."

the universe predictable? Is the law of cause and effect only a philosophical issue? Will God be able to find men and women who will freely trust Him, believing that His way of love and responsibility is the best way to live, either on earth or in heaven? In other words, only men and women who are on track, developing habit patterns of saying yes to God and no to self-centered ways, will be entrusted with eternal life. After all, why import rebels and start wars in heaven all over again? The freedom of choice is God's greatest gift to created intelligences!

The gospel ellipse warns against legalism. It is hard to know what is more self-defeating—legalism or license. Both are surely contemporary problems in all churches. But legalism is a problem that affects those who are honestly trying to "do what's right."

Legalism is pathological—it is a spiritual disease that everyone must treat. Its pathogenesis lies in a misunderstanding of the character of God. The only sure vaccine is to get the character of God right! We don't have to get His attention by impressing Him with greater offerings or more "work"—even laudatory work. He already loves us and cares for us as the most doting parent would. Nothing pleases God more than genuine trust and a spontaneous desire on our part to live our lives the way He lives His life.

The history of religion is full of men and women in all cultures and in all times past and present who have done extraordinary things to get God's favor, to please Him by going to "holy" places or "giving up" something precious.

But Christianity adds it own twist in trying to "please" God. For instance, the question that everyone should ask is, Am I giving this offering to impress God or to honor Him? The virus of legalism is always present when the everlasting gospel is not understood—when church members either are confused in thinking that they can be saved by their own merits or confused in thinking that they can be saved in their sins. They both want salvation *without* character development. The legalist, crippled and dwarfed in religious growth, has not yet understood the meaning of faith—that powerful New Testament word that describes one's total appreciation for Christ's grace of pardon and power. Genuine faith fulfills the purpose of the everlasting gospel; it claims God's promises that He will transform us from self-centered rebels to happy, willing loyalists. Faith is a spiritual transaction from start to finish—from struggling sinners to those who are mature in Christ. No way do men and women of faith try to impress God with anything they think or do; they simply want to honor Him by what they think and do. Legalism dies when we realize that commandment keeping is imperative but possible only by the living, healing power of the Holy Spirit whom we trust to fulfill our Lord's promises. *That* is the life of faith!

The GCT explains the divine co-op plan in the plan of salvation

Obviously, the first question is, How can this work of witnessing to the world be done in such a way that God can declare that Satan's awful experiment is over? After all, God has only rebels to work with!

So, how does God change rebels into willing loyalists? By His grace! By forgiving us and by empowering us—the two hands of grace. Theologians call this double gift the righteousness that comes from God through, and by means of, our faith (see Ephesians 2:8; Philippians 3:9).

Genuine faith is man's part in this marvelous co-op plan of salvation; grace is God's part. Without faith, grace is frustrated; without grace, faith is meaningless.

Unfortunately, these two words—*grace* and *faith*—have been the most controversial words in Christian history. On one side, those who stress grace but reduce faith into a passive response end up saying "the right words" as the way to find assurance. On the other side, those who de-emphasize the authority of God and stress faith as "relevance, feeling, and reason" soon end up with "truth that makes sense to me." For them, all personal opinions are as good as any other because we are all heading in the right direction.

Grace and faith cooperate as much as two sides of the same pane of glass are needed or as much as hydrogen and oxygen are needed to produce water.

The GCT explains why the return of Jesus has been delayed

Warren sets himself apart from most Christian preachers, even Evangelicals, when he writes, "What we *do* know for sure is this: Jesus will not return until everyone God wants to hear the Good News has heard it. Jesus said, *'The Good News about God's kingdom will be preached in all the world, to every nation. Then the end will come.'* If you want Jesus to come back sooner, focus on fulfilling your mission, not figuring out prophecy."[9] In other words, Warren believes that faithful Christians can hasten or delay the return of Jesus and thus agrees with Peter when he wrote that Christians in the end time are "looking for and hastening the coming of the day of God" (2 Peter 3:12).

---

9. *PDL*, 286.

But notice Warren's overriding theory of predestination: "Jesus will not return until *everyone God wants to hear* the Good News has heard it" (emphasis supplied). This touch of predestination seems to quietly permeate *PDL*. Thus, only those who have been elected by God can think of Him *"smiling* at your birth."[10] However, on other occasions Warren definitely empathizes that "God has given us a free will."[11] Something is missing in all this that can be cured only by understanding the big picture of the GCT.

Warren is half right (in a way)—every nation in the world will hear the good news before Jesus comes. The problem is twofold—(1) how do we define the good news? and (2) what kind of Christians are indeed *witnesses* to the good news? As we have already noted, the good news that hastens the return of Jesus is the everlasting gospel, not the limited gospel so prevalent in the Christian world today. And the kind of Christian witness that will accompany this gospel is described in Revelation 14:12 as "those who keep the commandments of God and the faith of Jesus."

That is why Adventists are unique with their end-time message; they put the spotlight on the global impact of genuine Christians and not primarily on the state of the world. *That* is exactly opposite from all the emphasis on the end of the world and the return of Jesus that one sees in books, magazines, films, and TV sermons everywhere.

But this Adventist uniqueness is exactly what Jesus was emphasizing in Matthew 24 and 25. In referring to " 'wars and rumors of wars,' " Jesus said, " 'see that you are not troubled . . . the end is not yet' " (Matthew 24:6). He went on: " 'For nation will rise against nation, and kingdom against kingdom. And there will be famines, pestilences, and earthquakes in various places.' " But " 'all these are the beginning of sorrows,' " not particular signs of the end of the world (verses 7, 8).

Our Lord's unambiguous answer is in verse 14: " 'And this gospel of the kingdom will be preached in all the world as a witness to all the nations, and then the end will come.' " Then he went on to warn that " 'false christs and false prophets will arise and show great signs and wonders, so as to deceive, if possible, even the elect' " (verse 24, compare Revelation 13:13, 14). This emphasis on "false christs and false prophets" surely is relevant in the twenty-first century!

---

10. *PDL*, 63. Warren writes, "Before God created you, he decided what role he wanted you to play on earth. He planned exactly how he wanted you to serve him, and then he shaped you for those tasks. You are the way you are because you were made for a specific ministry."—*PDL*, 234.

11. *From the Ashes*, 130.

One of the clearest messages regarding the world just before Jesus returns was our Lord's comparison of Noah's day with the last generation: " 'But as the days of Noah were, so also will the coming of the Son of Man be' " (verse 37). No secret rapture here nor a great end-time focus on the State of Israel! Just as Noah preached the truth about righteousness for many years before the Flood (see 2 Peter 2:5), so God will have a people preaching the everlasting gospel that prepares people for translation or the quiet sleep awaiting the resurrection (see 1 Thessalonians 4:14). Both worlds, Noah's and ours, will be troubled with unspeakable wickedness, and "evil continually" (Genesis 6:5).

Before finishing His sermon, Jesus painted four snapshots of those who will be the faithful witnesses "to all the nations, and then the end will come" (Matthew 24:14). The first is the faithful servant to whom his master entrusts the responsibility to give "food in due season" and "blessed is that servant whom his master, when he comes, will find so doing" (verses 45, 46). God's witnesses will be faithfully dispensing the good biblical food—as did their Master more than two thousand years ago.

The second picture is that of the five wise virgins who had prepared themselves for the possible delay in the return of the bridegroom: "But while the bridegroom was delayed, they all slumbered and slept" (Matthew 25:5). All the bridesmaids had their lamps. They all had the theory of truth; they all were waiting for the return of the bridegroom. But only the wise possessed light gained through knowing Him; only they knew that the Spirit alone could transform the words of the Bible into the habits of their hearts.

Here Jesus was emphasizing that even Bible information is not enough to prepare church members for the Advent. What did the wise bridesmaids know that made the difference? The truth about God—not only a list of doctrines. They knew through experience how He will save men and women from their sins and prepare them to live forever. Through experience they learned that God can be trusted to fulfill His promises. The light that separated the wise from the unwise was the character of God shining through them in their everyday duties.

The next snapshot tells us how we become these trustworthy and wise servants in God's household and in His bridal party. By learning the lessons of the business owner who entrusts his assets to his employees while he goes to "a far country" (Matthew 25:14). This parable shows us what it means to watch for our Lord's return.

We all will render an account for the way we have lived our lives. The issue is whether we have rightly represented our Employer with the capabilities and opportunities that we have. No one will have an excuse. The divine-human co-op plan could not be better presented—God gives the opportunities to match our capabilities; we give back to Him the blessings we have passed on to others.

The important lesson to learn is that our *first duty to God and others is self-development*—we owe it to God and to our fellowmen.[12] If we are not growing daily, increasing our capabilities and usefulness at every opportunity, we are not fulfilling God's purpose for our lives. Self-development is the only way we can be ready for service if our goal is to serve God with our improved physical, mental, social, and financial skills. God waits for those who have let the Spirit do His work of preparing them to truly be ready when others need them. Our concern for self-development to improve our usefulness for others is light years away from self-absorption. A self-absorbed person has other motives for self-development such as the desire to be number one or the richest person in the family or the most attractive person in the office.

But there is one more snapshot that Jesus is painting for us—that of the sheep and the goats. If Jesus had stopped with the first three portraits, some might think that Christian maturity is primarily knowing the truth or doing "good" works. This is what the five foolish church members waiting for the second coming of our Lord and the self-serving, talent-burying employees learned too late.

What Christ showed us so graphically in the parable about the difference between the sheep and the goats is not how much or little they knew or did with their opportunities. The difference is found in one principle—the law of loving service. This is the turning point in the judgment. Such loving bridesmaids and faithful employees will reflect the glory of their Lord's own earthly experience. In many cases, they may not know much theology, but they have coveted opportunities to serve, to lift the distressed, to cheer the downhearted, to help right the wrongs done to those who have been mistreated. But the self-absorbed—no matter how much doctrinal truth they may know—and the self-indulgent who become unconscious of these opportunities—have permitted Satan to blind them.

"Those who keep the commandments of God and the faith of Jesus" (Revelation 14:12) have learned how to love both God and their fellowmen. Not impulsively, but as a spontaneous habit—when the impulse to help and bless others springs constantly from within. Light shines through their lives; they "glorify" God as Jesus did.

---

12. White, *Christ's Object Lessons*, 329.

The GCT explains why habits of mind and body are determining
where we will be when Christ returns

Adventists accept the Bible seriously. God will wait for the maturing of Christian character in a significant number of people as the chief condition determining end-time events.

In Mark 4, Jesus explains the nature of the kingdom of God in terms of His harvest principle: " 'The kingdom of God is as if a man should scatter seed on the ground, and should sleep by night and rise by day, and the seed should sprout and grow, he himself does not know how. For the earth yields crops by itself: first the blade, then the head, after that the full grain in the head. But when the grain ripens, immediately he puts in the sickle, because the harvest has come' " (Mark 4:26–29).

When Jesus was describing to John on Patmos the nature and timing of His second advent, He re-emphasized His harvest principle as the key to understanding why all heaven waits for a delayed harvest down in the twenty-first century: "And I looked, and behold, a white cloud, and on the cloud sat One like the Son of Man, having on His head a golden crown, and in His hand a sharp sickle. And another angel came out of the temple, crying with a loud voice to Him who sat on the cloud, 'Thrust in Your sickle and reap, for the time has come for You to reap, for the harvest of the earth is ripe' ["fully ripe," RSV]. So He who sat on the cloud thrust in His sickle on the earth, and the earth was reaped" (Revelation 14:14–16).

In both chapters, Jesus compared His second coming to an earthly harvest. We learn that the goals of the kingdom of God and the field of grain are the same: Neither is ready to harvest unless the seed has matured. No other goal makes sense.

So the first lesson we learn from the Lord's analogy is that even as the wise farmer must wait for his seed to mature, so Jesus chooses to wait until the gospel seed has produced a significant group of mature Christians in the last generation.

Another interesting parallel: Farmers and prophets have several things in common, the chief of which is that both engage in conditional prophecies. Farmers know that they must keep their eyes on their corn rather than on the seed catalog's promise and the kitchen calendar. No one harvests a premature crop. Wise farmers wait, for that is what being a farmer is all about.

Similarly, our Lord is saying to His church that the delay in this world's harvest has not been due to a change of mind on the part of the divine Husbandman. As far as God is concerned, the harvest could have—and should have—ripened years ago. We now live in the time of the delayed harvest. The fruit, the Christian witness that reproduces the character of Jesus, has not yet matured. Thus, the purpose of planting the gospel seed has not yet been achieved.

The bottom line: We don't blame God for His delay, and we don't focus on wars, pestilence, earthquakes, and famines to see if they are awful enough for God to lose patience with this rebellious world.

The harvest principle in no way limits God's sovereignty. To the contrary, it only adds to His majesty as One who is infinitely patient, merciful, and forbearing for the sake of the universe. He ordained that Jesus would return when earth's harvest is ripe. Not before, and not one day too late! The delay only confirms the nature of the great controversy.

God doesn't need anything proved to Him. But He is concerned that the principles of both His government and that of His adversary, Satan, should develop fully so that there will never again be a doubt in any created being's mind whether God's ways are just and merciful. Never again will the question arise anywhere in the universe as to whether God can be trusted!

The Christian witness in the end time has a central role to play in the final display of God's case before the universe. They silence once and for all the eternal differences between God's government of love and law, on one hand, and, on the other, that of selfish, arrogant greed and force—the central point in the cosmic controversy.

That time, when the full harvest of these contrasting principles is on display, is not predetermined by an arbitrary celestial clock that forces God to act before His purposes are fulfilled. That would conflict with His character that Satan has been trying to distort. God never forces; He waits for His purposes to ripen.

In Revelation 7, we learn that God will withhold judgment on this earth—check the hand of Satan who is anxious to ravage the earth—"till we have sealed the servants of our God on their foreheads" (verse 3). God will not close probation for the world until His professed followers vindicate His character, prove that His way of life can be lived on earth, and proclaim a credible witness to all nations.

Those last-day loyalists finally prove that the faith of Jesus indeed makes commandment keepers (see Revelation 14:12), and they will be sealed with God's approval "on their foreheads." What does this mean?

Revelation 14 tells us that those who have God's name "written on their foreheads" are the ones who follow the Lamb wherever He goes. These were redeemed from men, being first-fruits to God and to the Lamb. And in their mouth was found no guile, for they are without fault before the throne of God" (verses1–5).

That surely describes the ripened harvest for which the gospel seed has been planted! These two chapters are telling us that God will not close this world's probation until all living at a given time have had a fair opportunity to see the difference between those who truly keep His commandments and those who do not.

Those who choose to not "follow the Lamb wherever He goes," who choose not to join those who "keep the commandments of God and the faith of Jesus," will get their way: God will leave them alone!

Those who are left alone by God are the ripened tares—the wheat and the tares mature together. God knows when both groups have matured. No man or devil can delay God's harvest when the conditions have been fulfilled, when the harvest is "fully ripe." The GCT is on full display—God's loyalists are on full display and Satan's followers are on full display.

Why did Jesus want us to keep our eyes on what He expects from His church, rather than on the world, when we are looking for clues as to the nearness of His return (see Matthew 24, 25)? For this reason: to place un-due emphasis on world conditions (which are always in turmoil) as the chief signs of the end of the world is similar to a farmer saying, "I oiled my combine; it must be time to harvest the wheat." Or, "It looks like a bad thunderstorm coming; it must be time to pick my corn." There is as much relationship between a thunderstorm and picking ripe corn as between distress in the world and the readiness of the church for the Advent.

Conclusion

Rick Warren sees only a faint glimmer of the big picture that we call the great controversy theme. Yet, many elements of his Purpose-Driven min-istry suggest that he stands at the door of full appreciation for the God he calls his Friend.[13]

---

13. *PDL*, 85.

FOURTEEN

What Adventists Can Contribute— Part 2: The Everlasting Gospel

The everlasting gospel has been the good news since God gave that message of hope to Adam and Eve in the Garden after sin entered (see Genesis 3:15). It became even clearer when Jesus came to planet Earth and explained much more about how God thinks and acts. Paul, the New Testament church's foremost theologian, was part of those heroic early Christians who were turning "the world upside down" with the everlasting gospel (Acts 17:6). He personally witnessed to the fact that he was "not ashamed of the gospel of Christ, for it is the power of God to salvation for everyone who believes [has faith]. . . . For in it the righteousness of God is revealed from faith to faith, as it is written, *'The just shall live by faith'*" (Romans 1:16, 17, emphasis in original).

The New Testament gospel distorted through the centuries

Sadly, this gospel has been wrenched and diluted through the centuries. The chief culprit was the blending of Greek philosophies with the gospel until it became almost impossible to find people who remembered "the full gospel."

Good men and women argued, and even fought over, different interpretations of the New Testament gospel. Most saw clearly only parts of this gospel. Luther shocked his world with the rediscovery of faith in a personal Lord, breaking away from the limited gospel of Romanism. Calvin, contemporary with Luther, saw that the sovereignty of God was more important than the sovereignty of the church. Zwingli, another contemporary, saw the gospel differently than both Luther and Calvin. Wesley stood on a higher mountain and saw clearly the divine-human co-op plan in the plan of salvation—a much fuller gospel.

But even Wesley did not see the fullness of the everlasting gospel. His misunderstanding of the nature of man and what happens after death muted his grasp of what God was waiting for regarding the end of the world. Thus, along with the other valiant Reformers, Wesley was setting up his followers for the delusions and confusion of last-day spiritualism.

In the rise of the Seventh-day Adventist Church, Lutherans, Presbyterians, Methodists, Baptists, Catholics, and many other Christians found the fullness of the everlasting gospel—just what God promised (see Revelation 14:6). This new movement caught a fresh view of the purpose of the gospel, that it would lead men and women to glorify God—" 'Fear God and give glory to Him, for the hour of His judgment has come' " (Revelation 14:7).

Recovery of the fullness of the gospel

The *fullness of the everlasting gospel* includes Christ's substitutionary death on the cross and His high priestly ministry in heaven, the truth about what happens after death, the profound connection between the law of God and a maturing Christian experience, the truth about when Jesus returns, and how God finally ends the great controversy.

In recovering the fullness of the gospel, something very important had been reclaimed—the happy connection between grace and faith—the simple formula for the New Testament explanation of righteousness by faith. Only with this formula worked out in the lives of willing loyalists will the purpose of the gospel and the overarching goal of the GCT be reached— the restoration of rebels who become joyful, willingly obedient sons and daughters of the family of God. Only when the phrase *righteousness by faith* becomes the formula for changed, transformed, Christ-reflecting lives that will vindicate God's enduring patience and His trustworthy promises will the everlasting gospel be truly preached.

Understanding of the nature of man saves from many delusions

One of the acute deficits in *PDL* is not apparent in a fast read, except for isolated statements. But Saddleback's statement of doctrines unfolds Warren's anthropology—what he understands the nature of man to be: "Man was created to exist forever. He will either exist eternally separated from God by sin, or in union with God through forgiveness and salvation. To be eternally separated from God is Hell. To be eternally in union with Him is eternal life. Heaven and Hell are places of eternal existence."[1]

---

1. See Appendix C: Saddleback's Doctrinal Statements.

Warren holds to the teaching that man has an immortal soul—that he was "created to exist forever,"[2] that "he will either exist eternally separated from God . . . or in union with God." Hell, for Warren, is an eternal existence. His ambivalent doctrine of predestination mingled with his emphasis on free will presents not only an incomplete gospel but a very distorted and wrong picture of God.

What do I mean? We discussed predestination earlier—a strange doctrine that invaded the Christian church most dramatically by Augustine, who argued that holiness is the *result* of election, not its *source*. Both Luther and Calvin were Augustinian in respect to predestination, especially Calvin, who derived his understanding of predestination from his doctrine of the sovereignty of God, which, in turn, supported his doctrine of assurance (irresistible grace).

Warren's beliefs in regard to the immortal soul and eternal hell link him with the deficiencies in Calvinism, which, in turn, did not forsake these Roman Catholic doctrines that had ruled Christian thought for centuries. The problem is that the notion of an immortal soul is based purely on Greek philosophy and a few mistranslated or misunderstood biblical texts.

But saying all this does not diminish the power of this error. Thinking that people go directly to heaven or hell at their death creates all kinds of emotional responses—all unnecessary. It sets up people everywhere to be unaware of the devilish intentions of spiritualism of all kinds.[3] One of the attractions of the many-faceted New Age appeal is the modern emphasis on "spirituality"—a certain kind of connection with the "spirit" world, most often referring to a connection with the individual's understanding of God. All this is without biblical foundation.

Another deficit in accepting this age-old notion that men and women do not really die but live on in some kind of afterlife is that the death of Christ is not fully appreciated. Those who believe in the immortality of the soul automatically deprive themselves of understanding that Christ *actually died* on Calvary.

Of course most Christians recognize that Christ died the first death

---

2. See *PDL*, 37.

3. On December 14, 2005, a Eugene, Oregon, woman told police that she killed her seventeen-month-old daughter to protect the baby from spirits. The mother confessed to suffocating her baby with her hand. She admitted that she had been practicing various forms of spiritualism. She told a friend that "she had some deities that she was taking care of and she hadn't been taking care of them, so she was really afraid" for her daughter.—Associated Press, *Monterey Herald*.

(like the rest of mankind) and was buried and then resurrected on Sunday morning. But they miss the breathtaking thought that Jesus actually died the *second* death that lies ahead for all sinners (see Revelation 20:14). We can understand this when we let Paul's words sink in: "The wages of sin is death" (Romans 6:23)—not the death that Adam and Eve and the rest of humanity have experienced, but the everlasting death.

Paul said that Jesus "died for our sins" (1 Corinthians 15:3); He must "taste death for everyone" (Hebrews 2:9). Paul is not speaking of our *first* death because all of us die that death, which the Bible calls only a sleep (see 1 Thessalonians 4:15–17; Luke 8:52; John 11:13; Acts 7:60).

But when Jesus died, He suffered the second death for everyone so that no man or woman would ever have to suffer eternal death for themselves. All may have to experience the first death, "the sleep of death" (if Jesus does not come soon), but this death is not the "wages of sin" that the Bible talks about. Jesus experienced ultimate death for "all men" (Titus 2:11) as our Savior. No one since Creation has ever died the second death except Jesus! Everyone else has merely gone to sleep.

If someone argues that Jesus did not suffer the "lake of fire" that John described in Revelation 20:14, we should pause and remember Gethsemane as well as the Cross. Reading Revelation 20:11–15, we get a slight glimpse of this dreadful moment when the books of heaven are opened. The full story of every person who made a habit of rejecting the voice of the Holy Spirit, as He repeatedly appealed to them will be open to all.

Self-condemnation will be more awful than anyone can imagine today. Hearing the Spirit again; looking at Jesus, their Savior whom many personally rejected; realizing how selfish and hurtful, cruel and insensitive, they were—words can not describe the horror of realizing what they have lost and rejected! It will be identical to the horror that Jesus felt in Gethsemane, where He was shut out from the light of His Father's presence. So dreadful were these hours alone, really alone, that Jesus cried out, "My soul is exceedingly sorrowful, even to death" (Matthew 26:38). Sin appeared so dreadful to Him that He was tempted to fear He would be shut away from His Father forever! The gulf was so black, so deep, that He shuddered; He was suffering the consequences of our sins. He saw what was yet ahead for every man or woman who turned off the voice of the Holy Spirit to their soul. Beyond words, Jesus trembled at the thought of separation from His Father.

He looked around, and no one on earth understood what He was going through. Not even close! It seemed His thirty-three years were a failure.

He looked up, and the heavens were unresponsive. He was paying the price for every human soul—the "wages of sin" was just such a death as He was experiencing! "For He [God] made Him [Jesus] who knew no sin to be sin for us" (2 Corinthians 5:21).

Jesus underwent superhuman agony; blood oozed from his pores. He fell dying to the ground. He could do no more for the universe. Shuddering under this mysterious dread, He "tasted death for everyone." Then the angel came and helped him back from that eternal abyss—only to face it all over again on Friday morning! Why?

So that humanity could see and record that awful day for men and women everywhere for all time to come. The Gethsemane horror echoed on Calvary: *"My God, why have You forsaken Me?"* (Matthew 27:46, emphasis in original).

For three hours, from high noon to three o'clock in the afternoon, the "mantle of God" enshrouded Calvary. Mel Gibson's movie *The Passion of the Christ,* missed the whole point—the "blood" was only the marker of the second death that Jesus was experiencing for us all. His mental torture was beyond human ability to describe—except it was the foretaste of what awaits all the willingly disobedient.

No, Jesus didn't die from the pain of the nails in his hands and feet. He died of a broken heart, thinking of those who would face their own God-forsaken moments in the *second* death. This is the death of all deaths. This is the horror and dread of those who see the "books" opened (Revelation 20:12). Horror-stricken people will either rise up under Satan to fight their way into the New Jerusalem or flee from the face of their Lord; both will know what it means to be God-forsaken. The lake of fire will end the awfulness of a wasted life.

The wages of sin is the self-inflicted result of a life lived in contradiction to the conscience of all men and women, which bears witness to the voice of God (see Romans 2:15).

I could hope that Rick Warren would somehow come face to face with these profound facts that lie at the heart of the good news. Not only would his followers begin to grasp the depth of our Lord's substitutionary death, they would be alert to the age-old deception that human beings don't really die when they pass on at the end of their days on earth.

Thus they would be aware of the devilish appeal of spiritualism. At the same time, they could be looking forward to the return of Jesus when He will link up the living and those sleeping in death at the resurrection of the faithful (see 1 Thessalonians 4:13–18).

The law of God reveals His character and is our hedge against sin

At the heart of the GCT is the question of whether God is fair in creating intelligences that can think and choose—and then allowing them to receive the consequences of their choices. This freedom was God's greatest gift to His created beings throughout the universe. Freedom is the atmosphere in which love flourishes. The ability to choose one's highest desires and the ability to pursue one's personal potential is an atmosphere that only an incredibly loving person would provide. Freedom and genuine love coexist like the two sides of a windowpane—we can't have one without the other.

But nothing in the Bible even hints that the ability to say no is part of God's design for this universe; *no* is simply the dark side of freedom. Yes, a lover, even God, can be rejected! How else to understand the Lover's lament: "How can I give you up, Ephraim? How can I hand you over, Israel?" (Hosea 11:8).

How would any created being know, in advance, the rewards of saying yes to God rather than no? Even in the Garden of Eden, our first parents were warned of the dark cloud of evil in the universe (see Genesis 2:16, 17). They soon discovered the dark side of evil—disobedience and the consequences. They walked through the protective "hedge" that God and angels had erected.

Ever since, men and women have had to recognize that God's commands, expressed in many ways, are divine hedges against discovering the awful consequences of misusing freedom.

The early Hebrews were hit between the eyes with God's own voice and finger regarding how best to make life's choices and stay healthy, happy, and holy. The Ten Commandments are surely unambiguous (see Exodus 20:1–20). Whenever they breached the "hedge," they paid dearly, both as a nation and individually.

Jesus reflected and amplified the divine hedge

In His beatitudes, and on other occasions, Jesus showed how the brief statements of God's principles on Sinai have deeper meanings—that outward behavior should match the heart's desire to obey God's laws—and that if not, dire consequences will follow, both in this life and in the final judgment.

Paul strongly upheld God's laws to both Jew and Gentile (see Romans 2:13–16; 6:15–23; 7:12, 22; 8:4). And John, in so many ways, echoes Paul (1 John 3:4–9, 24; 5:3).

I didn't find references to the high expectation and possibility of keeping God's laws in the writings of Rick Warren. Yes, he does emphasize obedience, in a way. He writes

"**I must choose to obey God in faith.** Every time you trust God's wisdom and do whatever he says, even when you don't understand it, you deepen your friendship with God. We don't normally think of obedience as a characteristic of friendship; that's reserved for relationships with a parent or the boss or a superior officer, not a friend. However, Jesus made it clear that obedience is a condition of intimacy with God. He said, '*You are my friends if you do what I command.*' "[4]

But *PDL* does not dwell on the biblical specifics of what is to be obeyed. Obedience to what? Warren's church members are left to themselves to figure out what the laws of God mean to them. That is scary!

The seventh-day Sabbath—God's way to keep us focused

The Bible is full of how God's loyalists proved themselves to be God's friends, especially in regard to the seventh-day Sabbath. In the middle of the Ten Commandments, the core of our relationship with God and others is His "command" to " 'remember the Sabbath day to keep it holy. Six days you shall labor and do all your work, but the seventh day is the Sabbath of the LORD your God' " (Exodus 20:8–10).

God gave special attention to the seventh day, the Sabbath, as part of Creation week—He "blessed the seventh day and sanctified it" (Genesis 2:3). Before any "chosen" people existed, the Sabbath was a significant part of time—holy time for God's earthly friends.

Linking the Creation story with His lifework, Jesus tied Himself personally to the seventh-day Sabbath. He said, " 'The Sabbath was made for man, and not man for the Sabbath. Therefore the Son of Man is also Lord of the Sabbath' " (Mark 2:27, 28). If anyone has any doubt as to which day of the week is still our Lord's Sabbath today, we need only remember that Jesus was crucified on Friday, rested in the tomb "on the Sabbath according to the commandment," and arose on the "first day of the week" (see Luke 23:54–56; 24:1).

Why does God want us to "remember the Sabbath to keep it holy"? Because every seven days we remember that He—Father, Jesus, and the Holy Spirit—joined in creating men and women. We are not merely higher up on the food chain after hundreds of millions of evolutionary years. And we remember Him as our Re-Creator, our Redeemer who lived and died for us.

4. *PDL*, 95.

It is so easy for all of us in this busy, modern turmoil called living to forget that He is the only One who can give us the peace we need to be better parents, co-workers, children, and neighbors. The Sabbath is an invitation to shut out the world's agenda for twenty-four hours; in it God provides the mental, physical, emotional, spiritual, and even the financial strength to fulfill our responsibilities. And all through the week we are to "remember" that Sabbath is coming! What a perfect plan God has devised no matter where we are on planet Earth!

When we forget to "remember," we quickly become victims of our own self-importance; our relationships with others become so self-centered that the glue of respect and love dries up.

The Sabbath is God's service station where we can be tuned up with a fresh glimpse of His goodness and promises. Families become "restored." All of us find new reasons for being honest with God and with others. Our vision of what matters most is sharpened every seventh day. What a gift of time and promise!

Warren surely would add a new level to his magnificent appeals for worship to be "authentic," "thoughtful," and "practical"[5] if he would help his followers to "remember the Sabbath day to keep it holy. Six days you shall labor and do all your work, but the seventh day is the Sabbath of the LORD your God" (Exodus 20:8–10). What greater motivation for worship would a person have than to honor God every seventh day by remembering He is the Creator who has built a hedge around His loyalists to keep them from destroying themselves in sinful, self-inflicting practices?

The seventh-day Sabbath an end-time issue

Adventists see the unique significance of the Sabbath as a worldwide issue in the end time. As we have seen earlier, God's loyalists in the last generation are described as those "who keep the commandments of God and the faith of Jesus" (Revelation 14:12). That thought alone heightens the respect and urgency of honoring the seventh-day Sabbath. When the Sabbath becomes a worldwide issue, everyone will have to make some kind of decision regarding God's appeal to remember and respect His holy day. Adventists have always believed that most of God's faithful are still in other religious bodies;[6] these faithful ones, living up to the light they have, will recognize the implications of last-day events and respond to "another voice from heaven saying, 'Come out of her, my

---

5. *PDL*, 100–105.

6. "The great body of Christ's true followers are still to be found in their communion." —*The Great Controversy*, 390. See also pp. 283, 449.

people, lest you share in her sins, and lest you receive of her plagues' " (Revelation 18:4).

To put it another way, "Sundaykeeping is not yet the mark of the beast, and will not be until the decree goes forth causing men to worship this idol sabbath. The time will come when this day will be the test, but that time has not come yet."[7]

The everlasting gospel—specific, precise, and unambiguous

The everlasting gospel does not confuse

▸ *confession with repentance.* Confession is insincere and meaningless without a sincere desire to trust God's promise to change those sinful thoughts and habits that one is confessing.

▸ *repentance with obedience.* When repentance is no more than being sorry for one's sins, nothing has been gained except a false assurance that all is well.

▸ *obedience with legalism.* The loyally obedient are happy to honor God in how they think, act, or feel; loyal legalists think, act, and feel in order to impress God. The first senses the joy and wisdom in doing God's will; the legalist may do the same things but out of duty more than joy. The joyfully obedient hears both the words and the music; the devoted legalist hears only the words.

▸ *commitment with character transformation.* Committing oneself to the "believer's prayer" and accepting the fact that Jesus died for sinners is only the beginning of the Christian walk. Young Christians must realize that the purpose of the gospel is to change lives so that they are safe to save—and that is a daily process of permitting the Holy Spirit to work out God's will in one's life.

The everlasting gospel does not split the ellipse of salvation. It does not make circles out of either side of the gospel ellipse. For example, it does not separate spirit from truth.

In righteousness by faith, the gospel does not separate justification and sanctification; it keeps them in proper relationship even as water does not separate hydrogen from oxygen. We can't have one without the other.

In the mission of Jesus, we must not separate roles but keep each role in proper relationship—one cannot exist without the other:

---

7. Ellen White Comments, *Seventh-day Adventist Bible Commentary,* vol. 7, 977.

▶ Christ as Sacrifice and Christ as High Priest

▶ Christ as Redeemer and Christ as Ruler

▶ Christ as Substitute and Christ as Example

▶ Christ as Savior and Holy Spirit as our Powerful Friend

▶ Christ's work without and Spirit's work within

▶ Christ's free gift of pardon and the free gift of His attributes in developing character

The divine-human plan of salvation does not separate aspects of redemption but keeps each aspect in proper relationship:

▶ God's authority and human response

▶ grace and faith

▶ law and gospel

▶ God's work and man's work

▶ prayer for pardon and prayer for divine power

▶ repentance and reformation

▶ faith and works

▶ believing in Christ and abiding in Him

The everlasting gospel can be looked at from many angles, but the result is always the same: God's plan to save men and women from their sinful habits and transform them into people who can be trusted with eternal life will be the story that will never end throughout eternity.

Other intelligent beings on other worlds will never get enough of listening to the stories of Adam and Eve down to the last of the last generation who were on tiptoe listening for the trumpets and waiting for the eastern sky to brighten as never before.

The joy of it all will be the quiet realization that rebellion will never arise again. The unfallen angels and inhabitants of other worlds will have abundant reason to never allow a shadow of a doubt to ever arise again about God's goodness and fairness. And the redeemed, in cooperation with the Spirit, will have settled the whole rebellion question forever. Their neural pathways are solidly settled into habits of trust and joy and willing obedience—they have lived out the Lord's Prayer that God's will should be done in their lives on earth as it is done joyfully, enthusiastically, and compliantly in heaven.

FIFTEEN

Adventists Have an End-Time Urgency

Adventists are convinced that we are living in the end times. This studied conviction rests on several lines of study:

The longest time prophecy of the Bible—the 2,300-year prophecy of Daniel 8 and 9—began in 457 B.C. and ended in A.D. 1844. This prophecy demolishes the 7-year gap that is associated with the rapture theory. How is that? Because it foretells exactly when that last 7 years of the 490 years (the years that the angel Gabriel detailed to Daniel) would take place and when the Crucifixion would occur. This amazing 2,300-year prophecy can be nailed down as certainly as the A.D. 31 date ("the middle of the week," Daniel 9:27) for Christ's death on the cross.

The rest of the 2,300-year prophecy, the 1,810 years, ended in 1844. (So much of course was happening in the years just proceeding 1844 that enhance what was to happen in 1844—but that is a story for another book.)

To keep this simple, during the 1840s the Adventist movement arose, composed of men and women from many Christian denominations. Their primary message and responsibility was based on Revelation 14—to proclaim to the world the fullness of the everlasting gospel and the message that Jesus was now ready to return. His loyalists, with precision and passion, were to clearly alert men and women throughout the world that God was preparing a people to be translated. They were described as "those who keep the commandments of God and the faith of Jesus" (Revelation 14:12).

The next line of thought pointing to the nearness of the end times focuses on world events such as "natural" disasters, international conflicts, pestilences, etc. Are these events worse today than in the past? It depends on how we look at the evidence. Most experts would say that natural disasters occur in cycles and that when one lives in one of these cycles, disasters always seem to be "the worst ever." But is there something different about disasters of the twenty-first century—some call them "megacatastrophes"?

I say yes, and I describe it in terms of the exponential curve. Draw a line that slopes increasingly upward in contrast to a line representing a straight, upward slant. When the curve begins to turn straight up, something dramatic is about to happen. For example, think of interest on your bank account. If you receive 8 percent interest on $100,000, you can draw a straight line to represent the simple interest—the amount of simple interest you will earn over a period of time. The line would begin with $8,000 the first year, a total of $16,000 the second year, etc. In ten years you would have earned $80,000 interest and still have your $100,000 (that is, you own $180,000). In thirty years, you would own a total of $340,000.

But if you were earning *compound interest* at 8 percent, you would not have a predicted straight line of $8,000 interest per year, but a line that would slope up continually. At the end of the second year, your interest would be $16,640—not $16,000. At the end of the third year, the interest would be $25,971—not $24,000. At the end of four years, the interest would be $36,048—not $32,000. And after thirty years, you would have a total of $1,006,266 including interest and your original $100,000. Compare this with the total of $340,000 with simple interest.

How does this "curve" relate to the various types of disasters in recent years? All the awful catastrophes of the past will be repeated but in exponential rapidity. Very much like the mother's labor in childbirth! Most women remember—ten minutes apart, then five, then two—and you had better be in the hospital! Each birth pang gets more intense.

The steepening slope of last-day events began, slowly at first, in the early 1980s. Can anyone deny that hurricanes, floods, famines, pestilences, national debt, personal debt, bankruptcies, moral degradation, fantastic surveillance technology, depletion of water aquifers, global pollution, energy consumption, etc., are increasing with astonishing speed?

Most people live with the sense that everything is out of control compared to the life we lived even twenty-five years ago. There seems to be no way to turn back the clock. The escalator, either down or up, seems to go faster every day with every news broadcast. And everyone has the lurking feeling that he can't get off that escalator.

The sense of escalation is heightened when the latest disaster is wired into our living rooms through CNN or FOX News in living color. Instantly, we are fed the reporter's hype, and this constant feed gives us the feeling that it is happening more rapidly, that we are surrounded with distress.

Everyone on planet Earth is involved in these rapidly developing end-time events that the Bible has predicted. The gospel going to all the world seems to be suddenly accelerating. The Internet has embraced the world! And events will speed up rapidly, especially under the "loud" cry of the fourth angel and his earthly counterparts.

The winds now held by those angels in Revelation 7 seem to be loosening (we haven't seen anything yet!), waiting for God's loyalists to catch on as to why Jesus has delayed His return.

"These wonderful manifestations will be more and more frequent and terrible just before the second coming of Christ and the end of the world, as signs of its speedy destruction."[1]

Rick Warren's followers would be most grateful if he would delve deeper into biblical prophecies relating to end-time events. One of these days, they may surely wonder why they were not told!

---

1.   Ellen White, *Patriarchs and Prophets*, 109

SIXTEEN

Counterfeits in the End Time—Part 1: Accommodation Leading to Spiritualism

If you were Satan, you surely would think up ways to deceive, delude, and confuse men and women the world over during the end time. Counterfeit truths would probably be your chief instrument of deception. *But counterfeits are not unlike the truth.* The whole point of counterfeits is to mislead those looking for truth; they will appear to be truth itself!

That is what is so subtle about counterfeits. The tease begins with "There is so much good in what he says. . . ." We all have heard this argument since childhood.

Try to think like Satan, who is furious with God's loyalists in the end time "who keep the commandments of God and have the testimony of Jesus Christ" (Revelation 12:17).

▸ When Satan sees that God's people are finally responding to the biblical prediction that there will be a growing worldwide movement encircling the world with a message that is precise and passionate—*Imitate it with counterfeit movements that will successfully appeal to "felt" needs more than to "real and deeper needs"—movements that promise eternal life without character transformation.*

▸ When Satan sees God's loyalists looking forward to seeing their loved ones in the resurrection when Jesus returns—*Do one better; help a confused world "see" and "hear" their loved ones now, not later.*

▸ When God's loyalists are persuading many to keep holy the seventh-day Sabbath, "according to the commandment" (Luke 23:56)—*Give a confused world a more convenient day, Sunday, to mark its worship worldwide.*

▶ When God's loyalists are persuading many that the only peace plan that will solve this world's international problems of war, famine, pestilence, AIDS, etc., is the everlasting gospel and the soon return of Jesus—*Present alternate peace plans that will promise "peace in our time," a dramatic, unforeseen plan that will unite the world under "one mind" (Revelation 17:13).*

Let's now review these very real counterfeits as they are playing out before our eyes today. Adventists discern in last-day events—such as remarkable revivals and church growth and other religious phenomena—those concepts that will speed along a worldwide movement that will unite Protestants and Catholics. What is the catalyst? Under the unparalleled economic pressures and disasters of unprecedented fury in the end times, this religious union will establish a national Sunday law that will be duplicated worldwide. The consequences will be enormous!

Underneath it all is the main issue in the end time: the proclamation of the "everlasting gospel" (Revelation 14:6) that reveals those cosmic forces—both good and bad—aligned with global groups on planet Earth. These global groups, in turn, will force the question as to who best represents the God of the universe. How people respond to unprecedented issues in the end times will depend on how they respect freedom and God's plan to redeem people who can be entrusted with eternal life.

Counterfeit movements will appeal to "felt" needs more than "real and deeper" needs

As we have discussed in earlier chapters, the astonishing phenomenon of the last thirty years or so—at least within American Christianity—has been the shift from denominationalism to congregationalism and the supermarket approach. This has been accompanied by a corresponding shift from religion to spirituality—a definition that is determined by the seeker rather than Scripture.

Others see this simply as a replay of the history of truth, one that has been replicated many times—for example, the church in Old Testament times accommodated itself to the spirit and systems of its time and ended up in Babylonian captivity. We can track the same path with the leading Protestant movements originating in the Reformation. Or in what happened to Lutheranism in the 1930s when it was lured into an alliance with German nationalism and then with Adolf Hitler's Nazism. The parallels are many, and *every* church has had to regret these accommodations and alliances with passing political and philosophical leaders.

Today we are witnessing the same replay among the Evangelicals since the 1950s and 1960s when they were once known for distinctly expressed beliefs and clear mission statements. Mimicking popular culture, accommodating to so-called "felt" needs, always ends up in theological impotence—as some Evangelical voices are regretting.[1]

What happens when even Bible-based churches move from religion to spirituality? The process is predictable. Church groups become more individualistic and mute their identification with a corporate body. They are increasingly syncretistic rather than discriminating. After all, if God is working with individuals, how can anyone use the "authority card" to tell us what is right and wrong? "I know what is right for me," becomes the mantra.

Another appeal that is widely promoted in the shift from religion to spirituality is the emphasis on "Give me Jesus, not religion." Or "It's all about Jesus." For many, this is the acceptable way to smooth over doctrinal differences, and it is a very heady plea! To say that encouraging one another is more important than being doctrinally correct sets up the world for "the one mind" in the end time (Revelation 17:13).

In the messages of these congregationalist-tending churches one does not hear the strongest, clearest truths about who God is. Rick Warren may say, "It is not about you. . . . you must begin with God."[2] Yet, his picture of God is framed in ambiguity—certain wonderful facets of God's character are persuasively described, but other equally important aspects are either muted or never discussed.

Why have Evangelicals, with their megachurches[3] and paradigm churches,[4] slipped into accommodation and adaptation in attracting their audiences? Because these make it easier to draw a crowd! Because people generally

---

1. "The fact is that while we may be able to market the church, we cannot market Christ, the gospel, Christian character, or meaning in life. The church can offer handy childcare to weary parents, intellectual stimulation to the restless video generation, a feeling of family to the lonely and dispossessed—and, indeed lots of people come to churches for these reasons. But neither Christ nor his truth can be marketed by appealing to consumer interest, because the premise of all marketing is that the consumer's need is sovereign, that the customer is always right and this is precisely what the gospel insists cannot be the case."—David Wells, *God in the Waste Land* (Grand Rapids, Mich.: Eerdmans, 1994), 82. Dr. David Wells is the Andrew Mutch Distinguished Professor of Historical and Systematic Theology at Gordon-Conwell Theological Seminary, South Hamilton, Massachusetts.

2. *PDL*, 17.

3. Churches with attendance of two thousand or more are called megachurches.

4. Willow Creek Community Church under Bill Hybels or Saddleback Valley Community Church under Rick Warren are considered "paradigm" churches.

are ready for anything that will fill their perceived spiritual needs! And because it is hard to argue that accommodation and adaptation do not produce results—big results, just as marketers can prove with their calculators!

Bonhoeffer did not accommodate

One of the best examples of a Christian leader who refused to bow to the popularity of his time is Dietrich Bonhoeffer, the Lutheran pastor in the 1930s who refused to go the easy way of accommodation. He saw clearly that Lutheranism's emphasis on a limited gospel did not prepare the German people for the challenges to come. "Cheap grace" was his characterization of a gospel that did not include an equal emphasis on character transformation.[5] He was appalled at Protestant capitulation to National Socialism. He rejected the arguments of his church leaders (which seemed so logical). He flatly declared his allegiance to Jesus Christ—to His authority that was far more important than the authority of Adolf Hitler. Bonhoeffer brought much encouragement to a loyal few who were willing to stand up for their clear-headed devotion to Jesus—and many of them paid for this commitment with their lives. Bonhoeffer was strangled slowly. Loyalty to Scripture meant more than loyalty to his age. He understood the difference between "felt" needs and "real" needs.

Bonhoeffer's experience is being replayed in every church member's life today. The appeal, the personal reward, of accommodating to what seems "successful" and convenient beckons everyone. Especially when we realize that one of Satan's most successful counterfeits is to mimic genuine spiritual revival.

> "The Spirit and power of God will be poured out upon His children. At that time many will separate themselves from those churches in which the love of this world has supplanted love for God and His word. Many, both of ministers and people, will gladly accept those great truths which God has caused to be proclaimed at this time to prepare a people for the Lord's second coming. The enemy of souls desires to hinder this work; and before the time for such a movement shall come, he will endeavor to prevent it *by introducing a counterfeit.* In those churches which he can bring under his deceptive power he will make it appear that God's special blessing is poured out; there will be manifest what is thought to be great religious interest. Multitudes will exult that God is working marvelously for them, when the work is that of

---

5. Dietrich Bonhoeffer is best remembered by his analysis of "cheap grace" that laid at the bottom of the Protestant capitulation to National Socialism. The same analysis strikes at the core of most of the weakness in Christian churches today. See *The Cost of Discipleship* (New York: The Macmillan Company, 1949, with many reprintings).

another spirit. Under a religious guise, Satan will seek to extend his influence over the Christian world.

"In many of the revivals which have occurred during the last half century, the same influences have been at work, to a greater or less degree, that will be manifest in the more extensive movements of the future. There is an emotional excitement, a mingling of the true with the false, that is well adapted to mislead. Yet none need be deceived. In the light of God's word it is not difficult to determine the nature of these movements. Wherever men neglect the testimony of the Bible, turning away from those plain, soul-testing truths which require self-denial and renunciation of the world, there we may be sure that God's blessing is not bestowed."[6]

In other words, God's loyalists in the last days will have to think carefully about how faithful they are to their message—the everlasting gospel framed by the great controversy theme. Loyalists will move in the direction of corporate fellowship and away from congregational goals. They will teach their congregations, both seekers and church members, the complete picture of God as revealed in the life and teachings of Jesus (and *not just some* of what Jesus said and did). For seekers, it will be step by step; for church members, it will be "for the edifying of the body of Christ, till we all come to the unity of the faith and the knowledge of the Son of God, to a perfect man, to the measure of the stature of the fullness of Christ" (Ephesians 4:12, 13).[7]

Seventh-day Adventists should listen carefully to these perceptive words:

"Popular revivals are too often carried by appeals to the imagination, by exciting the emotions, by gratifying the love for what is new and startling. Converts thus gained have little desire to listen to Bible truth, little interest in the testimony of prophets and apostles. Unless a religious service has something of a sensational character, it has no attractions for them. A message which appeals to unimpassioned reason awakens no response. The plain warnings of God's word, relating directly to their eternal interests, are unheeded."[8]

---

6. *The Great Controversy*, 464 (emphasis supplied).

7. As Os Guinness put it: "In an age when comfort and convenience are unspoken articles of our modern bill of rights, the Christian faith is not a license to entitlement, a prescription for an easy-going spirituality, or a how-to manual for self-improvement. The cross of Jesus runs crosswise to all our human ways of thinking. A rediscovery of the hard and the unpopular themes of the gospel will therefore be such a rediscovery of the whole gospel that the result may lead to reformation and revival."—*Prophetic Untimeliness* (Grand Rapids, Mich.: Baker Books, 2005), 100.

8. *The Great Controversy*, 463.

146 · TRUTH MATTERS

Counterfeit gospels will satisfy "felt" needs without providing "real" needs

It sounds impossible! How could something so simple in the Bible become the most confused and debated subject in the history of the Christian church? How could the simple formula set forth in the words of Jesus and those of the apostles become so misinterpreted that almost every division in Christianity will fight over their interpretation of this simple question: How do rebels become willing, loyal followers of Jesus? What is so complicated about the following verses, which are only a sampling[9] of the New Testament?

▸ *Angel of the Lord to Mary:* "... you shall call His name JESUS, for He will save His people from their sins" (Matthew 1:21).

▸ *Jesus to Mary:* "Neither do I condemn you, go and sin no more" (John 8:11).

▸ *Paul before Felix:* "Now as he reasoned about righteousness, self-control, and the judgment to come, Felix was afraid" (Acts 24:25).

▸ *Paul before Agrippa:* "... to open their eyes and to turn them from darkness to light, and from the power of Satan to God, that they may receive forgiveness of sins and an inheritance among those who are sanctified by faith in Me" (Acts 26:18).

▸ *Paul in Romans:* "For I am not ashamed of the gospel of Christ, for it is the power of God to salvation for everyone who believes [has faith], for the Jew first and also for the Greek" (1:16).

▸ *Paul in Romans:* "... who 'will render to each one according to his deeds': eternal life to those who by patient continuance in doing good seek for glory, honor, and immortality" (2:6, 7).

▸ *Paul in Romans:* "... that the righteous requirement of the law might be fulfilled in us who do not walk according to the flesh but according to the Spirit" (8:4).

What we have in these texts is the gospel formula, perhaps best expressed in Ephesians 2:8–10—grace plus faith equals salvation. "The grace of God that brings salvation has appeared to all men" (Titus 2:11). By faith, grace reaches its goal. In other words, without grace, no faith; without faith, no grace—as far as anyone's salvation is concerned.

---

9. For a longer sampling of New Testament texts that spell out the clear, unambiguous understanding of Jesus and apostolic writers, see Appendix E: A Sampling of New Testament Texts That Spell Out the Everlasting Gospel.

Faith is the response of yes to God from a responsible person. Faith is constantly learning and growing (see Romans 1:17), but it is always walking into the light of truth. Faith is the response of appreciation, trust, and obedience—and far more than only knowledge.

Muting the response of faith

The problem for the last two thousand years is that many—including Calvinists and many Evangelicals today—have focused on grace and muted the response of faith. Others have focused on faith without recognizing what God's grace wants to do for sinners. When faith becomes mere warm feeling, or cold reason, or mental acceptance of historical facts, or whatever "seems right for me," faith slips into relativism—in which everyone's opinion is as good as anyone else's. This is how most people think today.[10]

The truth of the gospel is expressed best in the ellipse of the gospel. Grace and faith are the two foci in the ellipse of the gospel—you can't have the gospel by focusing on grace alone or on faith alone. Grace comes to us with two hands—the hand of pardon, and the hand of power. Faith joyfully accepts the pardon and relies completely on the power to live a life that overcomes any sin or temptation that turns up. Grace and faith working together is described in the sampling of New Testament texts noted above. Faith is the joyful response that says yes to whatever God has said Christians should do in choosing to abide in Christ.

Preparing people for translation

Now what does this have to do with a counterfeit gospel that is so prevalent in these end times? The purpose of the everlasting gospel that will mark the worldwide movement predicted in Revelation 14:6 is to prepare people for translation—living people ready for the return of Jesus. The mark of this gospel is that its believers are claiming the grace of pardon

---

10. Zane Hodges and Charles C. Ryrie are two examples of Evangelicals who speak boldly regarding "faith" being no more than believing the facts of the gospel. In reading Hodges's *Absolutely Free!* (Grand Rapids, Mich.: Zondervan, 1989) and Ryrie's *Balancing the Christian Life* (Chicago: Moody, 1969), one finds clear statements that submission to Christ's supreme authority as Lord is not germane to the saving transaction because the death of Christ and His resurrection is the complete gospel—nothing else must be believed for salvation. Repentance is not essential to the gospel message and not related to saving faith. Heaven is guaranteed to believers, but Christian victory is not. "Calling on the Lord" means appealing to Him, not submitting to Him. All those who claim Christ as Savior, even those involved in serious or prolonged sin, should be assured that they belong to God come what may. Evangelicals are embroiled in the Lordship/no Lordship controversy, and John F. MacArthur, Jr., has outlined this in *Faith Works* (Dallas: Word Publishing, 1993).

and power in their lives, permitting the Holy Spirit to restore in them the image of their Maker (see Romans 8:29).

Loyal believers are clear about the formula of salvation: God's grace and their faith will produce the kind of lives that God is waiting to seal (see Revelation 7:1–3; 14:15). They are letting the Lord prepare them for His wedding (see Revelation 19:7, 8).

The counterfeit gospel emphasizes the grace of forgiveness while contending that character transformation has nothing essential to do with one's salvation. The emphasis on faith is primarily focused on a blurred understanding of commitment. For those in Warren's empire, faith is above all else a sense that God accepts them unconditionally as they "love and trust God's Son, Jesus."[11]

But this language is foreign to the New Testament regarding how a person "comes to Jesus." Nowhere does the New Testament teach that God *accepts* men and women unconditionally, though He *loves* them unconditionally. The Scriptures, however, emphasize that the repenting sinner has a whole new look at grace as both pardon and power as a result of Calvary; faith is his new insight and hold on these mighty truths.

The bottom line of the New Testament gospel is that the righteousness that God wants to give to His followers comes with two hands, not one: "Our only ground of hope is in the righteousness of Christ imputed to us, and in that wrought by His Spirit working in and through us."[12]

Relation to counterfeits in the end time

What does all this have to do with counterfeits in the end time? A thoughtful writer wrote, "Satan can present a counterfeit so closely resembling the truth that it deceives those who are willing to be deceived, who desire to shun the self-denial and sacrifice demanded by the truth; but it is impossible for him to hold under his power one soul who honestly desires, at whatever cost, to know the truth."[13]

Ellen White nailed this counterfeit gospel as she observed it developing in her day with its new cloak:

"There is a spurious experience prevailing everywhere. Many are continually saying, 'All that we have to do is to believe in Christ.' They claim that faith is all we need. In its fullest sense, this is true; but they do not

---

11. *PDL*, 37.

12. *Steps to Christ*, 63.

13. *The Great Controversy*, 528.

take it in the fullest sense. To believe in Jesus is to take Him as our redeemer and our pattern. If we abide in him and he abides in us, we are partakers of his divine nature, and are doers of his word. The love of Jesus in the heart will lead to obedience to all his commandments. But the love that goes no farther than the lips, is a delusion; it will not save any soul. Many reject the truths of the Bible, while they profess great love for Jesus; but the apostle John declares, 'He that saith, I know him, and keepeth not his commandments, is a liar, and the truth is not in him.' While Jesus has done all in the way of merit, we ourselves have something to do in the way of complying with the conditions. 'If ye love me,' said our Saviour, 'keep my commandments.'"[14]

A counterfeit gospel will become a worldwide movement capturing the attention and praise of the media, in print or TV. It will be a limited gospel, a gospel of convenience that will satisfy modern "felt" needs. The consequence of a counterfeit limited gospel so prevalent today, especially in the seeker-friendly churches, is a church full of people enjoying the grace of forgiveness but with no clear grasp of the grace of power that will indeed make them into overcomers. Two of the chief reasons for this limited understanding of the grace of power (see Hebrews 4:16) are a cloudy understanding of why the commandments of God are essential to salvation and why Jesus is our High Priest.

Here we return to an emphasis we have discussed before. We should recognize the relationship between a distorted understanding of the relationship of the laws of God and the limited gospel. We have had our clear warning: "A wrong conception of the character, the perpetuity, and the obligation of the divine law has led to errors in relation to conversion and sanctification, and has resulted in lowering the standard of piety in the church. Here is to be found the secret of the lack of the Spirit and power of God in the revivals of our time."[15]

Tolerance, an enemy of truth

How does this wrong conception affect the everlasting gospel? It destroys the ellipse of salvation. It unlinks what the Bible never separates. It separates the "conversion" experience from "growth of grace" (sanctification). These two inseparable steps form the biblical formula by which faith cooperates with grace in reconciling men and women to God. This reconciling means bringing the repentant into "accord with the principles of His law."[16]

---

14. *Historical Sketches of the Foreign Missions of the Seventh-day Adventists* (1886), 188, 189; see *The Great Controversy*, 464.

15. *The Great Controversy*, 465.

16. Ibid., 467.

We live in a time when the law of God has been attacked or ignored for many reasons, but probably the one reason in our day that seems especially to dim its importance is the amazing emphasis on tolerance being more important than truth. The modern sense that everyone is climbing up the same mountain but from different sides seems like a spiritual tsunami sweeping both young and old.

The time is coming in the United States when tolerance (everyone's opinion as valid as anyone else's) and pluralism (the majority accepting the prevailing notion of tolerance)[17] will prevail over traditional convictions that rest on the principles of Protestantism and a republican form of government. One opinion will be perceived as good as another, and whatever the majority wants at any given time will be the law of the people. We call that the tyranny of the majority.

On the Phil Donahue show, Norman Vincent Peale, probably the best known Protestant preacher in the middle of the twentieth century, announced, "It's not necessary to be born again. You have your own way to God; I have mine. I found eternal peace in a Shinto shrine. . . . God is everywhere."

Phil Donahue was so shocked that he actually came to the defense of Christianity: "But you're a Christian minister, and you're supposed to tell me that Christ is the way and the truth and the life, aren't you?"

Peale replied, "Christ is one of the ways. God is everywhere."[18]

Note these statements that surely hit the target of truth today: "Wherever the divine precepts are rejected, sin ceases to appear sinful or righteousness desirable."[19] "The doctrine that men are released from obedience to God's requirements has weakened the force of moral obligation and opened the floodgates of iniquity upon the world."[20]

---

17. The danger of pluralism in religious matters is obvious. Many Christian leaders are blatantly announcing that there are many roads to heaven, Jesus being one Guide along with Buddha, etc. What may be truth for you, they say, may not be truth for somebody else—so we shouldn't be too hasty in condemning one another. What we used to think about doctrine is not meaningful today—just give us Jesus, not doctrine! "If it tastes good, eat it; if it feels good, do it" seems to be the guiding light for so many. Tolerance trumps truth because loving one another (which means accepting one another's beliefs as equally valid), they say, is more relevant and necessary today than dividing families, neighborhoods, and nations over appeals to someone's opinion regarding absolute truths.

18. Dave Hunt, "Revival or Apostasy," *The Berean Call,* October 1997.

19. *The Great Controversy,* 584.

20. Ibid., 585.

We are witnessing today the unfolding of a prediction made at the end of the nineteenth century: "Men hang with admiration upon the lips of eloquence while it teaches that the transgressor shall not die, that salvation may be secured without obedience to the law of God. . . . The existing confusion of conflicting creeds and sects is fitly represented by the term 'Babylon,' which prophecy (Revelation 14:8; 18:2) applies to the world-loving churches of the last days."[21]

Counterfeit movements will identify in some way with spiritualism

Attempts to communicate with the dead are as old as human history.[22] Believing that men and women live on somewhere after passing into the grave is based on the notion that they have an immortal soul, whether that term is used or not. Think of the Egyptians, the Norse, and American Indians! One way or another, they all were spiritualists—they believed in the spirit world.

But Christians should know better. Jesus said that the dead are only sleeping (see John 11:11–14), and Paul said that they would be awakened when Jesus returned (see 1 Thessalonians 4:13–17).

In the last days, spiritualism will be a worldwide issue. John predicted that "spirits of demons, performing signs, which go out to the kings of the earth and of the whole world, to gather them to the battle of the great day of God Almighty. . . . called . . . Armageddon" (Revelation 16:14–16).

What sets the stage for this remarkable event? The union between all those on earth who believe in the idea of an immortal soul. They will be thrilled with the "performing signs" that will overwhelm their eyes, ears, and sense of touch.

What have Adventists believed for more than 150 years? That those laid to rest in grassy plots or buried in the depths of the sea are now sleeping (see Luke 8:52; John 11:11–14; Acts 7:60; 1 Corinthians 15:6); that they know nothing during this sleep (see Ecclesiastes 9:5; Psalm 146:3, 4).

> "History is to be repeated. I could specify what will be in the near future, but the time is not yet. The forms of the dead will appear, through the cunning device of Satan, and many will link up with the one who loveth and maketh a lie. . . . some will turn away from the faith, and give heed to seducing spirits and doctrines of devils, and by them the truth will be evil spoken of."[23]

---

21. *Patriarchs and Prophets*, 124.

22. See 1 Samuel 28:4–20.

23. Ellen White letter to Brethren Daniells and Prescott, October 30, 1905.

"A marvelous work shall take place. Ministers, lawyers, doctors, who have permitted these falsehoods to overmaster their spirit of discernment, will be themselves deceivers, united with the deceived. A spiritual drunkenness will take possession of them."[24]

In their understanding of Revelation 16 Adventists believe that three world forces—spiritualism, Protestantism, and papacy—will unite around two common doctrines that permeate their thinking: "Through the two great errors, the immortality of the soul and Sunday sacredness, Satan will bring the people under his deceptions. While the former lays the foundation of spiritualism, the latter creates a bond of sympathy with Rome."[25]

Many people have made a living on the public stage, proving that many spiritualistic manifestations are a fraud. But there is more to the picture. When Satan works through intermediaries, manifestations of a supernatural order will defy any kind of human explanation—spirits of demons will perform signs that will convince the leaders of the world as well as millions under them. For them who look for signs, these marvelous happenings will be as the great power of God.

Why is spiritualism today so alluring, especially to Bible-believing men and women? Years ago it was recognized for its creepy séances, candles, and levitating tables, but not today. This following quotation is so up-to-date that we get goose pimples:

"Even in its present form, so far from being more worthy of toleration than formerly, it is really a more dangerous, because a more subtle, deception. While it formerly denounced Christ and the Bible, it now *professes* to accept both. But the Bible is interpreted in a manner that is pleasing to the unrenewed heart, while its solemn and vital truths are made of no effect. Love is dwelt upon as the chief attribute of God, but it is degraded to a weak sentimentalism, making little distinction between good and evil. God's justice, His denunciations of sin, the requirements of His holy law, are all kept out of sight. The people are taught to regard the Decalogue as a dead letter. Pleasing, bewitching fables captivate the senses and lead men to reject the Bible as the foundation of their faith. Christ is as verily denied as before; but Satan has so blinded the eyes of the people that the deception is not discerned."[26]

This heady deception began in Eden when Satan told Eve, "Ye shall not surely die" (Genesis 3:4). And "little by little he has prepared the way for his

24. *Last Day Events*, 171.

25. *The Great Controversy*, 588. "The theory of the immortality of the soul was one of those false doctrines that Rome, borrowing from paganism, incorporated into the religion of Christendom."—Ibid., 549.

26. Ibid., 558; emphasis in original.

masterpiece of deception in the development of spiritualism. He has not yet reached the full accomplishment of his designs; but it will be reached in the last remnant of time."[27]

In summary, the subtle virus of the immortal soul disease will permeate all false revivals, all counterfeit Christian movements. These movements will capture the imagination and satisfy the desire for spirituality without careful adherence to Bible truths. It surely leads to a time of great confusion—a time of unparalleled trouble (see Daniel 12:1).

A troubled world will be willing to unite on a counterfeit Sunday-Sabbath in order to foster world brotherhood and thus gain the approval of God.

The underlying issue in the Saturday-Sunday debate is whether to acknowledge the authority of the laws of God or not. Regarding the fourth commandment, the primary argument is often over "who changed the Sabbath from Saturday to Sunday." It becomes a matter of quoting history books. But that usually ends up with tired brains—no real, compelling appeal to the heart and head. It will take more than an argument from history to strengthen those who are about to go through the time of trouble, such as there never was (see Daniel 12:1).

What is so different today in the Christian churches that still emphasize the Reformation motto, "the Bible and the Bible only"? We see an astounding shift that has gone on almost unnoticeably. The Bible is being looked at today, not so much as God's authoritative Word, but as a handbook of how to become a successful person. Let's look again at a previous quotation: "The Bible is interpreted in a manner that is pleasing to the unrenewed heart, while its solemn and vital truths are made of no effect. Love is dwelt upon as the chief attribute of God, but it is degraded to a weak sentimentalism, making little distinction between good and evil. God's justice, His denunciations of sin, the requirements of His holy law, are all kept out of sight."[28]

Those who endure the challenges of the end of time, loyalists "who keep the commandments of God and the faith of Jesus" (Revelation 14:12), will have looked carefully at the Bible's big picture, the overarching picture of the great controversy. They will have settled into the truth that God is their Lord and Refuge when, in the last days, the age-old struggle between the laws of God and the counterfeits of Satan will become a universal test of loyalty.

---

27. Ibid., 561.

28. Ibid., 558.

God's loyalists have learned through experience that the everlasting gospel unfolds a picture of a God who is both holy and merciful—who has chosen to let the law of cause and effect play out. Only then can the universe see the difference between Satan's deceptions and God's plan for universal peace. Note this warning: "If you lower the standard in order to secure popularity and an increase of numbers, and then make this increase a cause of rejoicing, you show great blindness. If numbers were an evidence of success, Satan might claim the pre-eminence; for, in this world, his followers are largely in the majority. . . . It is the virtue, intelligence, and piety of the people composing our churches, not their numbers, that should be a source of joy and thankfulness."[29]

Willingly obedient loyalists have also learned through experience that the Sabbath of the fourth commandment has been their rock—their weekly privilege of "remembering" their Creator God who has been more than sufficient for all their earthly challenges. Of course, they can understand why so many Christians worship on the first day of the week (they have not yet seen the big picture of the great controversy theme), but loyalists base their confidence, in clear skies or stormy weather, on their connection with the One who has promised that He will sanctify and bless those who honor Him on His holy Sabbath. Thus, remembering the Sabbath day to keep it holy (Exodus 20:8) is the open sign to the universe of one's "loyalty to the true God."[30]

So, the final challenge is loyalty—loyalty to the God of the Ten Commandments, not loyalty to the prevailing sentiment that it is more prudent to vote for brotherhood and unity and rally around the one day in the week with which the most people are most comfortable. Thus, the Saturday versus Sunday issue is a matter of not arithmetic or calendars but a face-to-face choice to accept the God of Scripture or the god of counterfeit Christianity (see Revelation 13). And the freedom to make that decision!

In the end time, this issue becomes far more than a theological discussion; it explodes when Sunday supporters enlist the aid of the civil government. Such an event is rapidly gaining ground in most countries of the world today. "The substitution of the laws of men for the law of God, the exaltation, by merely human authority, of Sunday in place of the Bible Sabbath, is the last act in the drama."[31]

How will all this happen? The *first step* will target those who honor the

---

29. White, *Counsels to Teachers*, 94.

30. *The Great Controversy*, 438.

31. White, *Testimonies*, vol. 7, 141.

Bible Sabbath, denouncing them "as enemies of law and order, as break-ing down the moral restraints of society, causing anarchy and corruption, and calling down the judgments of God upon the earth. Their conscien-tious scruples will be pronounced obstinacy, stubbornness, and contempt of authority. They will be accused of disaffection toward the government. . . . A false coloring will be given to their words; the worst construction will be put upon their motives."[32]

The *second step* will eventually follow: "The dignitaries of church and state will unite to bribe, persuade, or compel all classes to honor the Sunday?"

The *third step* is predictable: "Even in free America, rulers and legisla-tors, in order to secure public favor, will yield to the popular demand for a law *enforcing* Sunday observance. Liberty of conscience, which has cost so great a sacrifice, will no longer be respected."[33]

Here we have a classic example of Satan's *modus operandi*—his remark-able ability to blame others for the distress evil itself is causing.

> "Satan puts his interpretation upon events, and they think, as he would have them, that the calamities which fill the land are a result of Sunday-breaking. Thinking to appease the wrath of God, these influential men make laws enforcing Sunday observance. They think that by exalting this false rest day higher and still higher, compelling obedience to the Sunday law, the spurious sabbath, they are doing God service. Those who honor God by observing the true Sabbath are looked upon as disloyal to God, when it is really those who thus regard them who are themselves disloyal because they are trampling under foot the Sabbath originated in Eden."[34]

What will be happening in the United States while all this is being processed? Obviously this country will be going through an enormous period of great distress, causing the majority of Americans to look for scapegoats—somebody to blame—especially those who are appealing for fair-play and responding to undeserved allegations with the logic of reason and history, never mind the logic of the Bible.

Above all else is the issue of freedom—individual and religious free-dom, once guaranteed by the nation's Bill of Rights. Note this unambig-uous forecast: "When our nation, in its legislative councils, shall enact laws to bind the consciences of men in regard to their religious privileges, enforcing Sunday observance, and bringing oppressive power to bear against those who keep the seventh-day Sabbath, the law of God will, to

---

32. *The Great Controversy*, 592.

33. Ibid., emphasis added.

34. White, *Manuscript Releases*, vol. 10, 239.

all intents and purposes, be made void in our land, and national aposta-sy will be followed by national ruin."[35] What that "national ruin" will be, we do not know. It may be an economic collapse or a so-called "natu-ral disaster"—one can think of other possibilities. But one thing is clear: When America enforces Sunday worship (whatever the "good" reasons that may be given), it will be "the last act in the drama. When this substi-tution becomes universal God will reveal Himself. When the laws of men are exalted above the laws of God, when the powers of this earth try to force men to keep the first day of the week, know that the time has come for God to work."[36]

Will there not be some honest men troubled by the unfolding of this drama? Of course! Many lawyers, judges, and legislators will be convinced of the irrefutable logic and integrity of those who are God's loyalists. This peek into the future just around the corner is not all bleak:

> "God also has His agents among the leading men of the nation. The enemy moves upon his servants to propose measures that would greatly impede the work of God; but statesmen who fear the Lord are influenced by holy angels to oppose such propositions with unanswerable argu-ments. Thus a few men will hold in check a powerful current of evil. . . . When the final warning shall be given, it will arrest the attention of these leading men through whom the Lord is now working, and some of them will accept it, and will stand with the people of God through the time of trouble."[37]

Warren would do himself and his loyal followers a great service if he would look more diligently into what he means by *obedience.* What a mighty voice he could be to prepare honest hearts for this immense show-down not too far into the future!

Warren's oft-repeated desire for his followers to please God, so nicely un-folded in chapter 10 of *PDL,* would be amply fulfilled when he joins those who truly honor God by keeping His commandments in the end time.

A world in great distress will join in a dramatic counterfeit peace plan that will unite all nations under one mind in solving this world's international problems

In chapter 1, we reviewed Warren's P.E.A.C.E. Plan that he introduced on April 17, 2005, at Angel Stadium, home of the Angels' baseball team, when the Saddleback Church celebrated its twenty-fifth anniversary. Thirty

---

35. *Last Day Events,* 133.

36. Ibid., 135.

37. *The Great Controversy,* 610, 611.

thousand listened to Warren spell out more clearly his P.E.A.C.E. Plan that, he believes, will mobilize one billion foot soldiers for the Christian church in missions by 2020.

Earlier, on October 27, 2003, Warren had presented his P.E.A.C.E. Plan, titled "God's Dream for You—and the World," telling his Saddleback empire that the "moment of destiny" had arrived, that the plan would "change history," and that it "is going to happen."

On the following Sunday, November 2, 2003, Warren unveiled his five-step P.E.A.C.E. Plan to Saddleback Church and to everyone watching on the Internet. He reviewed his "forty-year commitment" to the church and to the community—the first ten years to "local blessings," the next ten to "national" interests, helping churches around the United States through seminars and resources, and training more than 250,000 churches across this country. But now, he said, it is time to go "global."

Warren said that he had been thinking about this plan for a year and that he had talked to world leaders, getting their opinions. Further, he said that his P.E.A.C.E. Plan would provide the foundation for world peace that everyone craves and that it would hasten the return of Jesus by fulfilling the Great Commission (see Matthew 28:19, 20).

On Larry King's TV program, March 22, 2005, Warren outlined more of how his plan would be implemented. He first would organize pilot programs in sixty-seven countries over a two-year test program (that would extend into 2006). He wants to assist the poor, care for the sick, and educate the next generation on a massive scale involving many millions of dollars and thousands of trained supervisors.

As we have seen previously, Warren clearly sees the advantage of the Christian church over government agencies in accomplishing such goals. Why? Churches have the widest distribution system and the moral authority to face up to these widespread problems—something no government is able to do.

In our second chapter we outlined what each letter in his PEACE acronym means. Warren admits that there is nothing new in any of his plan, but putting it all together, Warren says, is revolutionary! He has seen his plan work on a smaller scale already—Saddleback has already sent out forty-five hundred people on some mission projects, such as Clinic in a Box. Next to ramp up will be Church-in-a-Box and School-in-a-Box. The bottom line is that Saddleback members "all go, all pray, all pay."

Warren's clear-headed analysis of typical church mission programs is "you pay, you pray, and you get out of the way—let the professionals do it!

The revolution I believe in and want to bring about reverses the role—the local church on the front edge."[38]

Worldwide ecumenical umbrella

We have been describing a worldwide ecumenical umbrella that will sweep the nations of the world under the gospel as Warren understands it. He "hopes to enlist 1 billion individuals through their congregations and small groups for mission projects. This mobilization of church and small-group members will walk them through three steps: personal PEACE, local PEACE, and global PEACE."[39] Nobody really believes that Warren's dream will die on the vine.

The cover story of the October 31, 2005, issue of *U.S. News and World Report* is headlined "America's Best Leaders, 2005," leaders who share "a clearly articulated vision, measurable results and . . . 'big hairy audacious goals.'"

Among them is Rick Warren, "Preacher With A Purpose." Highlighted is Warren's "latest, most ambitious project: a worldwide campaign to battle the 'global giants' of poverty, disease, ignorance, egocentric leadership, and spiritual emptiness."

The writer of the magazine article notes that this P.E.A.C.E. Plan "is an unabashedly grandiose undertaking—and it is vintage Warren. In his 25 years in the ministry, no one has ever accused Rick Warren of thinking small."

Even by 2004 Warren's dream was becoming reality. Paul Kagame, president of Rwanda, was given an autographed copy of *The Purpose Driven Life.* Soon, the president wrote to Warren saying, "I am a purpose-driven man." In March 2005, Kagame invited Warren and others to Kigali, Rwanda's capital, where they jointly declared that Rwanda would become the "world's first purpose-driven nation."[40] And that is when Warren turned on the jets, and now all Rwanda knows something new is happening.[41]

---

38. Morgan, op. cit., 36.

39. Ibid.

40. Ibid.

41. In the *Wall Street Journal,* August 26, 2005, Boston College sociologist Alan Wolfe wrote, "Historians are likely to pinpoint Mr. Warren's trip to Rwanda as the moment when conservative evangelical Protestantism made questions of social justice central to its concerns." David Neff noted that the key participants in Warren's 2005 delegation to Rwanda "included Bryan Crute, pastor of Destiny Metropolitan Worship Church, Marietta, Georgia, and Herb Lusk, pastor of Greater Exodus Baptist Church, Philadelphia. By giving black and white pastors from America a new focal point for collaboration, Warren may have created the climate in which racial reconciliation can move beyond festering wounds to creative partnership."—*Christianity Today,* October 2005.

No one can find fault with Warren's motivation and those "global giants" he wants to slay. Who doesn't want world peace? Who wouldn't want to join him in slaying the "giants" of "poverty, disease, ignorance, egocentric leadership, and spiritual emptiness?" We commend him for taking on this Herculean challenge!

In his November 2, 2003, sermon, Warren declared, "God is preparing a platform to do peace . . . . God blesses those who work for peace, for they will be called the children of God." So what is the problem?

Two unsupportable pillars

The issue is not Warren's plan to slay these "global giants" but his underlying message that he leaves with the millions worldwide where he is fighting those "giants." As we have already discussed, Warren's message rests on two unsupportable pillars that will contribute to this earth's crisis in the near future: (1) the muting of the laws of God, specifically the fourth commandment, and (2) the pervasive belief in the immortality of the soul.

The apostle Paul summed up well how the whole world in the end time will be essentially divided between those who look optimistically into solving earth's nagging problems and those who track carefully the closing scenes in the great controversy.

Talking to Christians, he said, "You yourselves know perfectly that the day of the Lord so comes as a thief in the night. For when they say, 'Peace and safety!' then sudden destruction comes upon them, as labor pains upon a pregnant woman. And they shall not escape. But you, brethren, are not in darkness, so that this Day should overtake you as a thief. You are all sons of light and sons of the day. We are not of the night nor of darkness. Therefore let us not sleep, as others do, but let us watch and be sober" (1 Thessalonians 5:2–6).

As we did in chapter 11, note again the remarkable similarities with Neale Donald Walsch's five-step peace plan—one of the foremost New Age leaders whose plan is grossly antagonistic to the Bible.

But even more than Warren's similarities to Walsch and Schuller are the astonishing media events shortly after September 11, 2001, that focused on the new Global Renaissance Alliance of New Age leaders, urging people to be united in small groups to envision and pray for world peace. How would this work out? This world alliance would together dream of world peace through "prayers, meditation, and visualization on the single subject of world peace."[42]

---

42. Warren Smith, op. cit., 139.

An intriguing book

One of the most intriguing books published only days after September 11, 2001, is *From the Ashes—A Spiritual Response to the Attack on America*.[43] In the introduction, Steven Waldman wrote, "At times like this, we can all benefit from hearing a wide variety of voices. That is why we at Beliefnet, the leading multifaith Web site on religion and spirituality, teamed up with Rodale, Inc. to collect the most eloquent and wise voices across the faith spectrum."[44]

One of those "eloquent and wise voices" is Neale Donald Walsch, who wrote,

"The Bible, which is only one of humanity's many sources of spiritual teaching, carries this message throughout, in both the Old Testament and the New. (Have we not all one father? Has not one God created us? Why then are we faithless to one another, profaning the covenant of our fathers?—Malachi 2:10 . . . so we, though many, are one body in Christ, and individually members one of another,—Romans 12:5. . . . Because there is one bread, we who are many are one body—1 Corinthians 10:17).

"This is a message the human race has largely ignored. . . .

"We must change ourselves. We must change the beliefs upon which our behaviors are based. We must create a different reality, build a new society. And we must do so not with political truths or with economic trusts, and not with cultural truths or even the remembered truths of our ancestors—for the sins of the fathers are being visited upon the sons. We must do with new spiritual truths. We must preach a new gospel, its healing message summarized in two sentences:

"*We are all one.*

"*Ours is not a better way, ours is merely another way.*

"This 15-word message, delivered from every lectern and pulpit, from every rostrum and platform, could change everything overnight."[45]

One of the Alliance's co-founders and member of its board of directors, Marianne Williamson, presented these New Age ideas on the *Oprah Winfrey Show* shortly after September 11. She outlined a peace plan based on New Age principles that would be an "alternative to Armageddon." And she announced Walsch would soon be presenting his five-step peace plan.

---

43. Emmaus, Pa.: Rodale, 2001.

44. Ibid., ix.

45 . Ibid., 19–21.

Explosion of peace plans

What shall we make of all this and much more? Since September 11, 2001, this planet has seen an enormous explosion of peace plans based on a new gospel that is the only way to a true and lasting peace. And these plans are not mere wishes.

If Warren, or any other well-known Christian leader, chooses not to be confused with these spiritualistic platforms of the New Age peace platforms, we haven't heard about it.

Let's be unequivocally clear: All of us seek peace. All of us want poverty, ignorance, and disease to be banished from this planet. All of us should seek personal ways to help destroy these "giants," as Warren describes them. Our challenge comes down to one question: What is the gospel message that permeates these various humanitarian uplift plans?

Peace plans are magnificently organized and enchantingly deceptive. What better way could be devised to set the world up with a unified voice that would heap ridicule on any group that would try to expose their errors? Never before has the whole world been wired and connected as today—Web-based computer systems, global cell phone networks, greater international air travel, GPS systems, etc. A united voice, "one mind," would speak, and immediately the whole world would see and hear!

Think again of Revelation 17:13—that dire prediction that the whole world would unite with "one mind" at the end of time. To do what? To "give their power and authority to the beast."

On one hand will be those who rally around the seventh-day Sabbath, knowing that only the return of Jesus will bring genuine peace to planet Earth. On the other, those who rally with "one mind," with one goal in mind—the silencing of those who reject the premises on which five-step peace plans of all kinds are built. Counterfeit peace initiatives will produce visual results so that the whole world will "marvel" (Revelation 13:3) at the almost incredible political changes taking place between nations, in the medical world full of vaccines for cancer of all kinds, and in relief that the energy problem had been solved.

If Rick Warren would pause and read the New Testament carefully, he would continue his marvelous plan to fight the "global giants," fulfilling our Lord's mandate to feed the hungry, relieve the thirsty, look after strangers, clothe the naked, visit the sick and those in prison (see Matthew 25:34-46).

But in reading the New Testament he would also see the higher mandate—to preach the everlasting gospel, including the judgment hour message and

God's power to make His people commandment keepers and loyalists who will represent His truths in a time when truth has been submerged in the sea of relativity. Warren would truly have the thrill of making an eternal difference.

SEVENTEEN

Counterfeits in the End Time—Part 2: New Spirituality

In reviewing the shifts in evangelical Protestantism during the past twenty years, one of the most remarkable legacies has been the emergence of new types of worship services and the burst of megachurches throughout the United States. A tsunami wave of books such as *PDL* are heralded around the world for their practical, spiritual counsel, heavily buttressed with biblical texts. So what's the problem?[1]

But something deeper is going on. The shift is from a traditional biblical base to a more psychological, sociological base, heated by the philosophies of pragmatism and new spirituality. Of course, the Bible is used, but not only is it often misquoted and mistranslated, it becomes a grab bag to support whatever concept the user chooses to promote.[2]

That is the new twist. For more than a century, liberal Protestant thought jettisoned the Bible as a reliable spiritual authority. Today's Evangelicals, once the guardians of the authority of Scripture, do not deny the Bible itself; rather, by its use they give the appearance that the Bible is not really that important on certain points. It is only a short step, then, to other sources of truth that seem more relevant, more personal, more satisfying.

I want to be very clear at this point: I am not saying that Rick Warren and Saddleback Church, in books or church services, are currently promoting new spirituality or the "emergent church" movement or any

---

1. While I was writing these pages, *Newsweek* (Aug. 29–Sept. 5, 2005) featured as its cover story, "In Search of the Spiritual." The subtitle was "Move over, politics. Americans are looking for personal, ecstatic experiences of God, and, according to our poll, they don't much care what the neighbors are doing."

2. See chapter 7, "Faulty Use of Biblical Passages."

form of rampant New Age mysticism. But what I have read concerning the leaders of Saddleback and their affiliations with the promoters of modern mysticism and the new spirituality suggests that they have opened the door.

History seems to show that when those looking for authentic spirituality do not find it in places where the authority of the Bible is upheld, they will seek for some kind of authority for their personal assurance elsewhere. And few return to the Bible; they feel burned over! Such seekers still look for something that seems more personally satisfying without changing the language and feel of Christianity—and that is exactly what is happening.

The new spirituality emphasis has especially captured the attention and commitment of a great number of younger people. New spirituality promises contact with God in ways not experienced in other, more conventional Christian paths.

Distinguish between spiritualism and spirituality

At this point I want to distinguish between age-old spiritualism and rampant new spirituality. As we noted in the last chapter, spiritualism is the open appeal to find reality, God, cosmic consciousness, or whatever through direct contact with the "other" world. It can be through channeling, Ouija boards, séances, certain kinds of extra-sensory perception, etc.

Spirituality, at this point in time, doesn't go in that direction, although it has much in common with spiritualism. Both concepts or movements, however, believe either in the idea of an immortal soul or in the subjective ability to find God or reality within themselves through any number of modalities. Neither believes in the final authority of Scripture.

Modern mood in the twenty-first century

George Gallup stated in his book *The New American Spirituality* that spirituality is very much alive but it is without biblical foundation: "Contemporary spirituality can resemble a grab bag of random experiences that does little more than promise to make our eyes mist up or our heart warm. We need perspective to separate the junk food from the wholesome, the faddish from the truly transforming."[3]

The problem, as he sees it, is the massive level of biblical illiteracy among Christians generally throughout the world. Half, he says, "of those describing themselves as Christians are unable to name who delivered the Sermon

---

3. (Colorado Springs: Victor, 2000), 15.

on the Mount. Many Americans cannot name the reason for celebrating Easter or what the Ten Commandments are. People think the name of Noah's wife was Joan, as in Joan of Ark."[4]

Then Gallup describes the "great disconnect." That is, there is a wide gulf between what Americans in general, and Christians in particular, claim to believe and how they actually live.[5] So he concludes that this "cluster of moral and theological shortcomings seemingly throws into question the transforming power of religious beliefs," leading him to state, "Just because Americans claim they are more spiritual does not make them so."[6] And then he asks the burning question, "Is the church really rediscovering its spiritual moorings, or just engaging in retreat from seemingly insoluble problems?"[7]

Filling the vacuum

Whether the typical church is doing its job or not is a no-brainer. Yet people are still spiritually hungry, and they will find some spiritual guru who promises to satisfy their innate spiritual search.

That is why the tsunami wave of new spirituality is sweeping over the American church. It comes in many forms. Saddleback's philosophy, as expressed in its Web networks and the books it endorses, is riding the waves but not yet visible from shore. But the men and women it *endorses* are riding the cusp of the wave as it rolls over unsuspecting beach walkers. Admittedly, all these men and women Saddleback endorses are on different points of that wave—but new spirituality rolls on.

Promoters of new spirituality generally are gracious, charming, and, in a way, very believable. They believe what they say; they believe that what they have experienced should be shared with the world. And much of what they say is indeed appealing. The issue here is that new spirituality's focus and emphasis is light years from the biblical record.

Richard Foster

For instance, one of the most well-known figures of the new spirituality movement is Richard Foster, founder of Renovaré, which is committed to working for the renewal of the church of Jesus Christ in all her

---

4. Ibid., 30.

5. In chapter 10 we noted the startling research done by George Barna that showed the "great disconnect" between what Christians claimed to believe and their life styles.

6. Ibid., 32, 29.

7. Ibid.

multifaceted expressions. Renovaré holds regional and local conferences bringing Christians together across denominational lines for renewal.

Foster's best known books include *Celebration of Discipline* (hailed by *Christianity Today* as one of the ten best books of the twentieth century[8]), *Streams of Living Water, Freedom of Simplicity,* and *The Challenge of the Disciplined Life.*

Of course, Foster has much that is devotionally helpful. But it doesn't take much to realize that he advocates a prayer movement that has clear, strong links to Eastern mysticism.[9] Contemplative prayer, saturated with New Age, Eastern mysticism, universalism, and pantheism, is now infiltrating Christianity to a large degree.

In addition to his own writings, Foster has a great proclivity to quote or endorse others who are closely linked to Buddhism—such as the Catholic mystic Thomas Merton, whom he quotes thirteen times in *Celebration of Discipline.* Merton wrote, "I think I couldn't understand Christian teaching the way I do if it were not in the light of Buddhism."[10]

In the back of *Celebration of Discipline,* Foster listed Tilden Edward's book *Spiritual Friend* as an "excellent book on spirituality." Edward's position is well known: "This mystical stream [contemplative prayer] is the Western bridge to Far Eastern spirituality."[11]

I mention Thomas Merton and Tilden Edward only as examples of many other indisputable Christian mystics that Foster interacts with—those who are heavily indebted to Eastern mysticism, especially Buddhism. The fascinating, as well as alarming, factor here is that Foster and others wrap their particular goals and methodologies with biblical words so that average readers feel they are truly being blessed.

Most people read only the froth of Foster and don't think twice about what he says regarding visualization, one of the modalities of finding "reality" within: "You can actually encounter the living Christ in the event. It

---

8. *Christianity Today,* April 24, 2000.

9. In *Christianity Today,* October 2005, Richard J. Foster and Dallas Willard are interviewed in "The Making of the Christian." If one read only this article, he or she would have no idea what kind of philosophies and methodologies for which these two gracious men are known. It shows again that most anybody can be received with open arms if they continue to use conventional Christian terms in promoting their core messages that do not begin with the authority of the Bible.

10. Frank X. Tuon, *The Dawn of the Mystical Age* (New York: Crossroad Publishing, 1997), 127.

11. *Spiritual Friend* (New York: Paulist Press, 1980), 18.

can be more than an exercise of the imagination; it can be a genuine confrontation. . . . Jesus Christ will actually come to you."[12]

Further: "In your imagination allow your spiritual body, shining with light, to rise out of your physical body . . . up through the clouds into the stratosphere . . . deeper and deeper into outer space until there is nothing except the warm presence of the eternal Creator." Then he goes on to say that this is more than imagination; it is reality created with the mind.[13]

When Rick Warren highly endorses writers such as Richard Foster[14] and Leonard Sweet[15] one wonders what really is on his mind that doesn't come out too clearly in *PDL* or *PDC*. For instance, in Sweet's *Soul Tsunami* the pages are filled with positive quotes and material from New Agers and globalists such as James Redfield, author of *The Celestine Prophecy,* Sarah Ban Breathnach, Annie Dillard, Tome Sine, and countless others who are well known mystics and New Agers.

Brennan Manning, an inactive Catholic priest, is endorsed often in Saddleback's Web site pastors.com. Here again is a delightful ex-Catholic priest who wrote *The Ragamuffin Gospel,* an emotionally gripping focus on God's forgiving nature and His love for the unworthy—but he works with a limited gospel.

In his *Signature of Jesus,* Brennan wrote that a contemplative spiritualist "looks upon human nature as fallen but *redeemed,* flawed but in essence good."[16] He wrote, "The first step in faith is to stop thinking about God at the time of prayer."[17] The second step is "without moving your lips, repeat the sacred word [or phrase] inwardly, slowly, and often." If distractions come, "simply return to listening to your sacred word."[18] He also

---

12. *Celebration of Discipline* (San Francisco: Harper, 1988), 26.

13. Ibid., 27.

14. *PDC,* 126

15. Endorsement on the cover of Sweet's book, *Soul Tsunami* (Grand Rapids: Zondervan, 1999). "*Soul Tsunami* shows us why these are the greatest days for evangelism since the first century." Sweet is well-known for his focus on unity—a worldwide oneness reflected in the growing union between the East and the West. In Sweet's *Quantum Spirituality,* we read, "Energy-fire experiences take us into ourselves only that we might reach outside of ourselves. Metanoia is a de-centering experience of connectedness and community."—Page 93. "The power of small groups is in their ability to develop the discipline to get people 'in-phase' with the Christ consciousness and connected with one another."—Page 147.

16. *Signature of Jesus* (Colorado Springs, Colo.: NavPress, 2002), 125.

17. Ibid., 212.

18. Ibid., 218.

encourages his readers to "celebrate the darkness" because "the ego has to break; and this breaking is like entering into a great darkness."[19]

This next sentence is common to new spirituality: "If I find Christ, I will find my true self and if I find my true self, I will find Christ."[20]

I could go on and on reading similar statements from individuals that Rick Warren endorses by either quoting or mentioning them in *PDL*—Brother Lawrence,[21] St. John of the Cross,[22] and Catholic priest Henri Nouwen.[23]

Labyrinth

Another remarkable signal of new spirituality is the "labyrinth"[24] that is being featured at many evangelical conferences, especially where younger members are being attracted. Often called A-maze-ing Prayer, the labyrinth feature seems to fill the hunger of those who turn from well choreographed worship services with every minute filled with music, videos, and preaching. Walking the "labyrinth" offers a private, unhurried, mystery-filled, meditative experience.

It seems that hungry experience-seekers are like moths drawn to the flame, ever seeking to know "god" through some kind of spiritual experience. Something seems to click in this pursuit. If you were handed a Ouija board and told that it has been totally redeemed by your spiritual leader and that it would bring you into a greater experience of God, would you

---

19. Ibid., 145.

20. Ibid., 125.

21. *PDL*, 88.

22. Ibid., 108.

23. Ibid., 108, 269.

24. The labyrinth is a path usually designed with intricate passageways and blind alleys. The most famous labyrinth of ancient times was the Cretan lair of the mythological Minotaur. Turf labyrinths still exist in England, Germany, and Scandinavia and were linked to fertility rituals. The Roman Catholic church adopted the practice and Christians made their pilgrimages to cathedrals in Chartres, Rheims, or Amines, where they completed their spiritual journeys in the cathedral labyrinths. The patterns of the labyrinth are similar to Buddhist mandalas and Japanese Zen practice of kinhim "walking meditation." Jean Houston, in the early 1990s, introduced the Christian world again to the practice of seeking enlightenment though walking the labyrinth when she linked up with Lauren Artress, spiritual leader of Grace Cathedral in San Francisco, to bring people back to their center and allow them to experience "Spirit" for themselves. See <www.gracecathedral.org/labyrinth/>. Jean Houston is listed on the Internet as one of the ten top New Age speakers in North America. Many participants at Gorbachev's State of the World forum in 1997 also walked the labyrinth at Grace Cathedral.

take the occult device, looking for the promised higher spiritual experience? The labyrinth is the same as the Ouija board.

In Deuteronomy 12:1–4 and in Exodus 34:10–17, we are admonished not to use anything connected to pagan ritual. No question about it—such pagan gateways do lead to "spiritual" experiences of one's self and "god"—rather, it is the portal to the demonic.

At the National Pastors Conference in San Diego, March 9–13, 2004, the labyrinth path was formed by black lines on a thirty-five-foot square piece of canvas laid on the floor. Participants were given a CD player with headphones to guide the journey through the eleven stations on the passageway. They were told not to rush, but to slow down, breathe deeply, and fully focus on God.

Later in 2004, Graceland at Santa Cruz, California, featured the labyrinth as part of its annual art event and sold "The Prayer Path" kit that transforms a room into a medieval prayer sanctuary. Leaders who promote these labyrinths rejoice that meditative prayer "resonates with hearts of emerging generations."

When I noticed that the National Pastor's Convention on February 22–25, 2006, was sponsored by Zondervan Publishing Company, which is a leading new spirituality publisher, I wondered who else is publishing new spirituality materials. I discovered that so does InterVarsity Press, NavPress (Navigators), Multnomah Books, Integrity, Thomas Nelson, Bethany House, Harold Shaw, and Harper SF. If I listed all the books now available, most readers would be equally shocked—they are the prominent bestsellers in the Christian market.

What is most interesting is the common thread of breath prayers by the labyrinth participants. Many find this link with Rick Warren's emphasis on breath prayers in *PDL*.[25] I wish that Warren had made a clear statement that he does not endorse the extravagance of New Age emphasis on "breath prayers."

Let's summarize: What are the chief distinguishing characteristics of new spirituality? Obviously, not every promoter of new spirituality emphasizes each of these characteristics, but it is very easy to identify its promoters. For the purpose of this chapter, we have probably said enough about the following marks of new spirituality—each characteristic is worth an entire book.

▸ Functional denial of the authority of Scripture

▸ Feelings eclipse reason in seeking truth

---

25. *PDL*, 89.

▸ Contemplative, repetitive prayers

▸ Visualizations to discover inner power and guidance

▸ Abundant references to Roman Catholic mystics

▸ Ancient "disciplines" are to be recovered and celebrated

▸ Unmediated link to the absolute—"god" is within every one

▸ All paths lead to God

▸ Finding one's core, one finds the great mystery called god

Emergent church movement

Another feature of the new spiritualism—but using a different tack—is the emergent church movement of the last ten years. It is a reaction against various forms of evangelicalism with its church structured programs. The emergent church movement finds common ground among those who are doing their spiritual searching in local bars, cafés, and other leisure centers. In other words, they are repotting Christianity into new cultural and intellectual ground.

Some groups seem to emphasize being simple followers of Jesus, avoiding the congregational milieu. They tend to be suspicious of church hierarchy and doctrinal formulations; they talk of "emerging authority." They are less concerned about safeguarding boundaries; they use words such as "liquid" churches. And they are much more open to a wider sphere of activity than just evangelism.

In other words, the emergent church movement is another pleasing counterfeit to the wholesomeness of the everlasting gospel movement. In general, its impulses and desires are those things that the everlasting gospel is meant to fulfill. The issue continues to be how best to unite authority with relevancy—a challenge God's followers have had to meet since Genesis was written.

Emergent church leaders and Jewish leaders

Emergent church Christian and Jewish leaders met in a first-ever meeting on January 16–17, 2006, at the Brandeis-Bardin Institute in Simi Valley, California, to think together in developing congregations that pushed beyond the traditional categories of "left" and "right." Prominent emergent Christian theologian Brian McLaren (author of *A New Kind of Christian*) has met with Synagogue 3000's (S3K) leadership three times in recent months to discuss shared concerns, particularly surrounding attempts by younger Christians and Jews to express their spiritual commitments through social justice. "We have so much common ground on so many levels," he notes. "We face similar problems in the present, we have common hopes for the future, and we draw from shared resources in our heritage. I'm thrilled with the possibility of developing friendship and collaboration in ways that help God's dreams come true for our synagogues, churches, and world."

S3K stress the importance of building a committed religious identity across faith lines. "We inhabit an epic moment," McLaren said, "nothing short of a genuine spiritual awakening. It offers us an opportunity unique to all of human history: a chance for Jews and Christians to do God's work together, not just locally, but nationally, community by community, in shared witness to our two respective faiths."

According to emergent U.S. national coordinator Tony Jones, this meeting has historic possibilities. "As emerging Christian leaders have been pushing through the polarities of left and right in an effort to find a new, third way, we've been desperate to find partners for that quest," he said. "It's with great joy and promise that we partner with the leaders of S3K to talk about the future and God's Kingdom."[26]

The emergent church movement is not a fad; it will find common ground across all denominational lines, especially among the young who search for new ways to express themselves in spiritual pursuits.

---

26. <www.typepad.com/t/trackback/3822640>.

EIGHTEEN

The Purpose and Mission of Seventh-day Adventists

Adventists teach their children that "we are here for a purpose." We believe intently that God has given us a plan for our lives and "desires us to reach the highest standard of development," that we should "constantly be growing in holiness, in happiness, in usefulness," that we should be ambitious "to excel in all things that are unselfish, high, and noble."

Our highest ambition is to cherish Christ's example—an ambition to make the world better for having lived in it. This is the work to which we are called.[1]

This highest ambition embraces the purpose of our church.

To prepare people for translation

Tom Mostert said it well: "Adventists find their strength in remembering why we exist. We were raised up for one purpose: to prepare a people for translation. We are in the end of the end of time. Some generation will surely be the last! We have the awesome challenge of preparing the honest seekers of truth for God's seal of approval described in Revelation 7 and 14. Peter's appeal (2 Peter 3:10–14) will describe that last-day group for which God waits. Our privilege is to join this group and to invite all others from every Christian denomination, from every religious body in the world, to hear our gracious Lord's call, 'Come.' "[2]

That sounds like sermons preached by early Seventh-day Adventists in the nineteenth century! And the purpose and goals have not changed even though the bridegroom has been delayed and the earth's harvest is not yet fully ripe (see Matthew 25:5; Revelation 14:15, RSV).

---

1. *The Ministry of Healing,* 397, 398.

2. *Hidden Heresy?* (Nampa, Idaho: Pacific Press Publishing Association, 2005), 109.

If we believe that we are living in the last days, it follows that we believe that Jesus should come in our day. If we do not die before the Lord returns, we should expect to be translated—if, indeed, we choose to belong to those who "keep the commandments of God and the faith of Jesus" (Revelation 14:12). That is the inescapable opportunity for all the honest followers of God the world over, no matter what religious body they now belong to!

Adventists accept seriously the biblical mandate within the messages of the three angels of Revelation 14 and believe that those messages become increasingly relevant as time goes by:

▶ The focus of the first angel is that the everlasting gospel will finally be delivered to all the world—a promise that has become increasingly possible with the ubiquitous TV and radio and the marvels of the Internet. God's angelic messenger announces that we are living in "judgment" time and that all the universe is involved.

▶ The second angel announces the demise of Babylon—that universal power that has been at war with the everlasting gospel since the beginning of human history. In the end time, Babylon will exert its mightiest force to destroy those who "keep the commandments of God and the faith of Jesus." It will be a death struggle that will end with the return of Jesus (Revelation 14:14–16).

▶ The third angel declares in the clearest words possible that the last generation will be composed of two groups worldwide—false worshipers and those who have the "patience [endurance] of the saints." The final whistle is blown, with no overtime to play further.

As we have noted in chapter 15, the world is awash with reasons to believe that we are living in the end time. The daily news from all over the world screams at us that it is later than we think. We are living during a time when everything imaginable—and unimaginable—is happening with increasing rapidity. We called it the exponential speedup of all things, and it applies not only to technology but also to the moral free fall in the social fabric. These are not times when anyone doubts that we have long gone past what we once called normal.

But on top of all that are the amazing developments in the modern Christian church. Amazingly, those who have made their mark defending the authority of the Bible are often now the chief pied pipers, leading their flocks into the miasma of subjectivism where not only is everyone's opinion as good as anyone else's but Christians are led to seek God within their own inner selves—and then to feel that they are truly relevant and in tune with reality!

A clear, unambiguous, gracious appeal must be voiced by those who have not wasted their lives and their churches listening to siren calls—running onto the rocky shores of the latest fads or philosophy. Those who have not let the pragmatic tail wag the dog of truth! In order to understand the reality of the end time, we must begin with the authority of the Word and not with the changing winds of psychological principles and contemporary charms. Only then will we catch the ear of honest seekers.

Most of God's faithful are yet in Babylon

Adventists are, above all else, inclusivists. We were born of Methodists, Roman Catholics, Presbyterians, and Baptists. That early stream soon flowed with new followers from all denominations and religions, including Muslims, Hindus, and others. We probably are the greatest assortment of various religious groupings in the world! And before the end time, that flow will increase to flood stage as honest and willing seekers find their spiritual home among those who indeed "keep the commandments of God and the faith of Jesus" (Revelation 14:12).

We believe that

▸ the great body of Christ's true followers are still in Babylon.[3]

▸ according to Revelation 18:4, many of God's people must still be in Babylon. That means they must still be in the various Catholic groups, Protestant churches, and other religious groups such as Muslims, Buddhists, Hindus, etc.

▸ "the Lord has His representatives in all the churches. These persons have not had the special testing truths for these last days presented to them under circumstances that brought conviction to heart and mind; therefore they have not, by rejecting light, severed their connection with God."[4]

▸ "God has jewels in all the churches, and it is not for us to make sweeping denunciation of the professed religious world."[5]

We must make clear to all that the fall of Babylon is progressive. When will the last call be made? "Revelation 18 points to the time when, as the result of rejecting the threefold warning of Revelation 14:6–12, the church will have fully reached the condition foretold by the sec-

---

3. *The Great Controversy,* 390.

4. *Testimonies,* vol. 6, 70, 71.

5. White Comments, *Seventh-day Adventist Commentary,* vol. 4, 1184.

ond angel, and the people of God still in Babylon will be called upon to separate from her communion. This message is the last that will ever be given to the world."[6]

What will best frame the final appeal in these last days? (1) The fearful implications of civil coercion against those who observe the seventh-day Sabbath, coercion that boldly defies the guarantees of the United States Constitution and its Bill of Rights; (2) the pervasive inroads of New Age philosophy, especially among those in various levels of government, news-makers, and entertainers as well as among many church members; (3) the siren song of the new spiritualists that appeals to those who plead Christian goals via pagan methodologies; and (4) the amazing hurricane defense of tolerance wherein everyone's opinion is as good as anyone else's and appeals to absolute truth are divisive and troublesome.

Religious interests will unite—not necessarily in doctrinal agreement, but in shared interests

It seems almost unbelievable at the moment to think of a national Sunday law in the United States of America, the "land of the free and the home of the brave." But the will of the people as expressed in "push polls" (asking questions that deliberately direct the answer wanted) will easily cry out to legislators and to judges to do something to protect us against terrorists, against economic collapse when long-awaited pensions are dissolved, against overwhelming moral decline, against any group that declares other groups to be wrong.

Suddenly, Catholics, Protestants, and Jews who have been working together on social issues such as abortion, pornography, and poverty will raise their united voices against those who raise the divisive issue of which day is the Sabbath of the Bible. Such old-fashioned doctrinal arguments show that these seventh-day Sabbath keepers are full of intolerance at a time when America must come together as a united nation.

In other words, we look forward to a time when mental and moral clarity will be the only defense of truth.

This union of all those united by common concerns is one of the unparalleled features of the end time

At the Pew Forum on Religion, May 2005, Rick Warren may have said it best. A reporter questioned him, "So are you saying doctrine won't be important or is not important if you bring together all these [referring to the four thousand pastors of more than one hundred denominations at his

---

6. *The Great Controversy*, 390.

church recently]? Warren interrupted, saying, "No, no, I think, though, it's what Augustine said: 'In the essentials, unity; in the non-essentials, liberty; and in all things, charity.' "

Warren had been discussing what he sees in the future in terms of a third Great Awakening in American Christianity—following the first Great Awakening in early American history and a second Great Awakening focused on individual salvation. According to Warren, "this Third Great Awakening is going to be the coalescing of progressive interest in the social gospel with a sort of revivalist interest in individual salvation." He then went on to note that the

". . . first Reformation with Luther and then Calvin, was about beliefs. I think a new reformation is going to be about behavior. The first Reformation was about creeds; I think this one will be about deeds. I think the first one was about what the church believes; I think this one will be about what the church does.

"The first Reformation actually split Christianity into dozens and then hundreds of different segments. I think this one is actually going to bring them together. Now, you're never going to get Christians, of all their stripes and varieties, to agree on all of the different doctrinal disputes and things like that, but what I am seeing them agree on are the purposes of the church. And I find great uniformity in the fact that I see this happening all the time. . . .

"And I am working toward a second Reformation of the church which could create a Third Great Awakening in our nation or the world."

Earlier in the Pew Forum Warren had said, "Who's the man of peace in any village—or it might be a woman of peace—who has the most respect, they're open and they're influential? They don't have to be a Christian. In fact, they could be Muslims, but they're open and they're influential and you work with them to attack the five giants. And that's going to bring the second Reformation."

The mission of the Adventist Church is to tell the truth about God that has been so grossly distorted and misunderstood

When Adventist preachers enter their pulpits, whether in evangelistic halls or in their houses of worship, they should have no trouble finding *what* to preach. Their sermons should flow out of some direct aspect of the everlasting gospel in the setting of the three messages of those Revelation angels.

One aspect of that gospel is imbedded in the first angel's message: " 'Fear ["revere"] God and give glory to Him . . . worship Him who made heaven and earth, the sea and springs of water' " (Revelation 14:7).

That is exactly the central issue in the great controversy that we have been referring to throughout this book. God has been Satan's target, but God is not the person that Satan has made Him out to be! Look at human history and note the bum rap God has been getting from earliest times down to the latest newspaper. How much truth and glory has been given to God? Real fear, yes. Awful terror, often. But rarely reverence.

Underneath a heavy pile of human neurosis is a misunderstanding of what God is like. Think of the confusion when most people think about how God relates to pain and sorrow, why He doesn't stop evil, and His awful threat of eternal hell fire. Jesus tells us that the Christian's privilege is to tell the truth about the Creator of this world, that our Father God "was in Christ reconciling the world to Himself" (2 Corinthians 5:19).

The Father and Jesus call us "His friends," not even forgiven servants (John 15:15). In some of His last words to His disciples, Jesus told them (and us) how to approach the Father in prayer: " 'In that day you will ask in My name, and I do not say to you that I shall pray the Father for you; for the Father Himself loves you, because you have loved Me, and have believed that I came forth from God' " (John 16:26, 27).

Adventist preachers have hundreds of sermons to preach that honest seekers, baptized believers, and those still seeking truth need desperately. The Gospels are full of sermon outlines—sermons that need to be heard more and more. Sermons that will join the ellipse of salvation and not separate what God has done for us in Christ's death on the Cross from what He wants to do for us in Christ's High Priestly ministry today. Sermons that shout joy to struggling men and women who need to know how the divine-human plan of cooperation works in the rescue of boys and girls, fathers and mothers, caught in the vise of sinful habits.

No wonder a very thoughtful author wrote under inspiration:

> "It is the darkness of misapprehension of God that is enshrouding the world. Men are losing their knowledge of His character. It has been misunderstood and misinterpreted. At this time a message from God is to be proclaimed, a message illuminating in its influence and saving in its power. *His character is to be made known.* Into the darkness of the world is to be shed the light of His glory, the light of His goodness, mercy, and truth. . . .

> "Those who wait for the Bridegroom's coming are to say to the people, "Behold your God." The last rays of merciful light, the last message of mercy to be given to the world, is a revelation of His character of love. The children of God are to manifest His glory. In their own life and character they are to reveal what the grace of God has done for them."[7]

---

7. *Christ's Object Lessons*, 415, 416, emphasis supplied.

Our heavenly Father, our holy, heavenly Friend, hallowed be His name! He is the eternal Rock of the universe, who has shown infinite patience in permitting Lucifer, His "first-created," to have his long day of trying to prove that self-centered living is the happiest way for created intelligences to live their lives. And the laboratory results are almost in. The universe is waiting for the last inning to be played. Unfallen inhabitants of other worlds and heavenly angels are waiting for God's willing loyalists to put the final score on the universal scoreboard. Then judgment day will come, when the willing rejecters of God's mercies are "judged according to their works, by the things which were written in the books" (Revelation 20:12).

Adventists the world over have the privilege of making all this known to men and women on all continents—before the winds blow (see Revelation 7), before everyone crosses that invisible line that marks those who can be trusted with eternal life—and those who can't.

Everyone who thirsts for reality and personal assurance is invited to "come" (Matthew 8:11). All nations of the world will have honest seekers who will find confidence in our Lord who says, "Come" (Revelation 22:17). *Come* is one of the loveliest words in any language.

APPENDIX

Appendix A: Warren's Various Translations and Paraphrases

AMP	*The Amplified Bible,* 1965 (Zondervan)
CEV	*Contemporary English Version,* 1995 (American Bible Society)
GWT	*God's Word Translation,* 1995 (World Publishing)
KJV	*King James Version,* 1611
LB	*Living Bible,* 1979 (Tyndale House Publishers)
Msg	*The Message,* 1993 (Navpress)
NAB	*New American Bible,* 1970 (Catholic Press)
NASB	*New American Standard Bible,* 1973 (Foundation Press)
NCV	*New Century Version,* 1991 (Word Bibles)
NIV	*New International Version,* 1984 (International Bible Society)
NJB	*New Jerusalem Bible,* 1985 (Doubleday)
NLT	*New Living Translation,* 1996 (Tyndale House Publishers)
NRSV	*New Revised Standard Version,* 1990 (Zondervan)
Ph	*New Testament in Modern English,* 1958 (Macmillan)
TEV	*Today's English Version, 1992* (American Bible Society; also called *Good News Translation)*

Appendix B: Relationship Between the Warren Ministry and the Church Growth Movement (CGM)

Elmer Towns provides a crisp definition of the church growth movement (CGM): "Church Growth is that science that investigates the planting, multiplication, growth, function, health, and death of churches. It strives to apply the Biblical and social principles in its gathering, analysis, displaying, and defending of the facts involved in implementing the great commission. The heart of the Church Growth movement involves research into growth to establish principles to guide others in the harvest."[1]

Os Guinness wrote in 1994, before the emergence of Rick Warren as a national phenomenon, "The church growth movement is extraordinarily influential and significant within American churches today. At its best, it should be applauded. Where it is not at its best, it requires criticism so that it might be."[2]

Guinness linked the underlying commitments of the CGM as "Christian renewal through renewal of the church, as opposed to politics or the culture; to renewal of the church through renewal of the local church, as opposed to the denomination or parachurch ministry; to the renewal of the local church through the renewal of mission, as opposed to other priorities; and, most importantly, to the renewal of mission, along one of two avenues—through charismatic renewal or through the employment of the behavioral sciences' insights and tools to aid effective evangelism. In this final area . . . proponents use tools from the fields of management, marketing, psychology, and communications as they seek to 'grow churches.' "[3]

---

1. "The Relationship of Church Growth and Systematic Theology," JETS 29/1 (March 1986), 64.

2. *Dining with the Devil: The Megachurch Movement Flirts with Modernity* (Grand Rapids, Mich.: Baker Book House, 1993), 24.

3. Ibid., 13.

Then Guinness suggests four weaknesses that are imbedded in the CGM. He observes that bigness or size is not the issue by noting that Charles Haddon Spurgeon's Metropolitan Tabernacle in the mid-nineteenth century regularly drew more than ten thousand worshipers.

The first weakness is its name—"church growth movement." Guinness calls the name confusing because of double meanings. Is "church" referring to the "people of God" in general or to a particular local church? If the second, it leads to "consumerist competition" between particular local churches. Likewise, "growth" can be understood quantitatively or qualitatively. Although both are essential to a healthy church, often the two qualities are difficult to see. One megachurch pastor boasted in the *Wall Street Journal* (December 11, 1990) that his church was "the fastest growing church" in the nation. He added, "I want the biggest church I can think of."[4]

Second, CGM has "two common deficiencies." Its " theological understanding is often superficial" and it displays "a minimal sense of historical awareness."[5]

Third, CGM has "two common flaws through which the confusions and deficiencies mentioned above become more serious." On one hand, "it employs a lopsided application of a biblical principle" known as contextualization, or relevance. Paul epitomizes this principle in "I have become all things to all men so that I might by all means save some" (1 Corinthians 9:19–22). But this principle, if not used properly, is also "a recipe for compromise and capitulation."

On the other hand, it opens the door to "an uncritical understanding of modernity and its insights and tool." Thus, "it is amazing to witness the lemming-like rush of church leaders who forget theology in the charge after the latest insights of sociology—regardless of where the ideas come from or where they lead to."[6]

A fourth weakness to watch is CGM's two potential dangers—"no God" and "no grandchildren." On one hand, modern tools and insights can "be so brilliant and effective that there no longer appears to be any need for God. On the other, the tools of one generation may not be as successful and sustainable in the next."[7]

---

4. Ibid., 26.

5. Ibid., 26, 27.

6. Ibid., 27–29.

7. Ibid., 29, 30. "Without truth, relevance is meaningless and dangerous," 63.

Guinness insists that after all is said and done, the CGM will stand or fall by one question: "Is the church of Christ a social reality truly shaped by a theological cause, namely the Word and Spirit of God? In sum, What—in practice—is the church's decisive authority?"[8]

In summary, the CGM is an inherently pragmatic approach to church-centered evangelism, following the innovative techniques of its founding father, Donald McGavran (of Fuller Seminary), who in turn borrowed the techniques of Charles Finney.[9] It is interesting, as a historical note, that Finney and his followers realized after years of pragmatic evangelistic techniques, that not much lasting results remained.[10] Finney went on to become a teacher and later president of Oberlin College (1835–1875).

Appendix C: Saddleback's Doctrinal Statements

WE BELIEVE

ABOUT GOD

God is the Creator and Ruler of the universe. He has eternally existed in three persons: the Father, the Son and the Holy Spirit. These three are co-equal and are one God. Genesis 1:1, 26, 27; 3:22; Psalm 90:2; Matthew 28:19; 1 Peter 1:2; 2 Corinthians 13:14.

---

8. Ibid., 35.

9. See John Muether, "Contemporary Evangelicalism and the Triumph of the New School," *WTJ* 50/2 (Fall 1998) 343.

10. "The pragmatic approach, rampant in American life, where anything that got results was commended, was applied to evangelistic endeavour. It is universally admitted that the pioneer in the new methods was Charles Finney. . . . Finney himself said, 'I was able to bring many to temporary repentance and faith.' He said again in 1835, 'They soon relapse into their former state.' In his Systematic Theology he confesses that the greater number of his 'converts' were a disgrace to religion. As for the lasting aspect the results in the churches were disastrous." This article was one of a series of papers delivered in 1973 for the Annual Evangelical and Reformed Conference of South Africa, at Koegheim in Natal. Clive Tyler was a tutor at the Kalk Bay Bible Institute in the Cape at that time.

ABOUT MAN

Man is made in the spiritual image of God, to be like Him in character. He is the supreme object of God's creation. Although man has tremendous potential for good, he is marred by an attitude of disobedience toward God called "sin." This attitude separates man from God. Genesis 1:27; Psalm 8:3–6; Isaiah 53:6a; Romans 3:23; Isaiah 59:1, 2.

ABOUT ETERNITY

Man was created to exist forever. He will either exist eternally separated from God by sin, or in union with God through forgiveness and salvation. To be eternally separated from God is Hell. To be eternally in union with Him is eternal life. Heaven and Hell are places of eternal existence. John 3:16; John 2:25; John 5:11–13; Romans 6:23; Revelation 20:15; 1 John 5:11, 12; Matthew 25:31–46.

ABOUT JESUS CHRIST

Jesus Christ is the Son of God. He is co-equal with the Father. Jesus lived a sinless human life and offered Himself as the perfect sacrifice for the sins of all men by dying on a cross. He arose from the dead after three days to demonstrate His power over sin and death. He ascended to Heaven's glory and will return again to earth to reign as King of kings, and Lord of lords. Matthew 1:22, 23; Isaiah 9:6; John 1:1–5, 14:10–30; Hebrews 4:14, 15; 1 Corinthians 15:3, 4; Romans 1:3, 4; Acts 1:9–11; 1 Timothy 6:14, 15; Titus 2:13.

ABOUT SALVATION

Salvation is a gift from God to man. Man can never make up for his sin by self-improvement or good works. Only by trusting in Jesus Christ as God's offer of forgiveness can man be saved from sin's penalty. Eternal life begins the moment one receives Jesus Christ into his life by faith. Romans 6:23; Ephesians 2:8, 9; John 14:6, 1:12; Titus 3:5; Galatians 3:26; Romans 5:1.

ABOUT ETERNAL SECURITY

Because God gives man eternal life through Jesus Christ, the believer is secure in salvation for eternity. Salvation is maintained by the grace and power of God, not by the self-effort of the Christian. It is the grace and keeping power of God that gives this security. John 10:29; 2 Timothy 1:12; Hebrews 7:25; 10:10, 14; 1 Peter 1:3–5.

ABOUT THE HOLY SPIRIT

The Holy Spirit is equal with the Father and the Son as God. He is present in the world to make men aware of their need for Jesus Christ. He also lives in every Christian from the moment of salvation. He provides the Christian with power for living, understanding of spiritual truth, and guidance in doing what is right. The Christian seeks to live under His control daily. 2 Corinthians 3:17; John 16:7–13, 14:16, 17; Acts 1:8; 1 Corinthians 2:12, 3:16; Ephesians 1:13; Galatians 5:25; Ephesians 5:1.

ABOUT THE BIBLE

The Bible is God's word to all men. It was written by human authors, under the supernatural guidance of the Holy Spirit. It is the supreme source of truth for Christian beliefs and living. Because it is inspired by God, it is truth without any mixture of error. 2 Timothy 3:16; 2 Peter 1:20, 21; 2 Timothy 1:13; Psalm 119:105, 160, 12:6; Proverbs 30:5.

Appendix D: Examples of Faulty Use of Biblical Texts

PDL: Introduction (9–12)

▸ *Romans 12:2, NLT (10)—" 'Let God transform you into a new person by changing the way you think. Then you will know what God wants you to do.' "*

In reading Romans 12:1, 2 together in a more faithful translation, you get an entirely different context of "presenting your bodies a living sacrifice, holy, acceptable to God. . . . And do not be conformed to this world." The NLT gives us a true statement, but it is not what the biblical text says.

▸ *2 Timothy 2:7, NIV (10)—" 'Reflect on what I am saying, for the Lord will give you insight into all this.' "*

There is nothing wrong with the translation, but Warren wants to lift the text completely out of context and apply it to his own book!

Paul is specifically urging Timothy to become more proactive in his ministry, to be "strong in the grace that is in Christ Jesus." Think of the "good soldier," the committed "athlete," "the hard-working farmer," Timothy. "Consider what I say, and may the Lord give you understanding in all things."

Chapter 1 (17–21)

▶ *Job 12:10, TEV (18)—" 'It is God who directs the lives of his creatures; everyone's life is in his power.' "*

Of course, we all are within and under God's power—He is our Creator. I agree, as long as we do not think that His Sovereignty overrules our personal power of choice. This, of course, highlights the differences between John Calvin and John Wesley and suggests how *PDL* tends to muddy this difference.

▶ *Romans 8:6, Msg (18)—" 'Obsession with self in these matters is a dead end; attention to God leads us out into the open, into a spacious, free life.' "*

Marvelous poetry, but is that what Paul is saying? "For to be carnally minded is death, but to be spiritually minded is life and peace." Paul gives us the choice between life and death, in this world and the next, not depending on how we dwell with the "righteous requirement of the law" that "might be fulfilled in us who do not walk according the flesh but according to the Spirit" (8:4). We should stay in context.

▶ *Matthew 16:25, Msg (19)—" 'Self-help is no help at all. Self-sacrifice is the way, my way, to finding yourself, your true self.' "*

Strange paraphrase! Jesus is not rebuking "self-help." The phrase *self-sacrifice* is a fair translation, but Peterson omits "for my sake," which puts the whole verse in perspective. "Finding yourself" is another pop-psychology phrase we have heard since the middle 1960s. Peterson's paraphrase misses Christ's point and turns the text upside down: Jesus is addressing not self-understanding but eternal life and eternal reward.

The use of this paraphrase is what may be called bait and switch. Just before Warren uses this text he writes, "You need more than self-help advice." Then afterwards, "This is not a self-help book." Here the author is tapping into the modern mind's "felt" need regarding one's true self. "Self-sacrifice" for Christ's sake (omitted in the quote) is much different than "self-sacrifice" to find one's "true self." It may seem a subtle shift, but that is the way *PDL*, at times, turns the reader. Reality is that we find our "true self" when we focus our thoughts and actions on obeying Christ's teachings and example, but that is a different route from where *PDL* takes the reader.

▸ *1 Corinthians 2:7, Msg (20)—" 'God's wisdom . . . goes deep into the interior of his purposes. . . . It's not the latest message, but more like the oldest—what God determined as the way to bring out his best in us.' "*

Again, very creative reading. It depends on what anyone means by "his best in us."

▸ *Ephesians 1:11, Msg (20)—" 'It's in Christ that we find out who we are and what we are living for. Long before we first heard of Christ and got our hopes up, he had his eye on us, had designs on us for glorious living, part of the overall purpose he is working out in everything and everyone.' "*

This paraphrase seems to be tailor-made for *PDL*. When the whole context is read—verses 3 through 12—an entirely different direction is discovered. Paul said nothing about discovering our purposes through a relationship with Christ; he speaks about God's purpose for us—that we have been made heirs of God through no merit of our own. That is God's purpose, not ours.

Chapter 2 (22–26)

▸ *James 1:18, NCV (24)—" 'God decided to give us life through the word of truth so we might be the most important of all the things he made.' "*

This translation completely overlooks the intent of the New Testament word *firstfruits* (Romans 8:23; 16:5; 1 Corinthians 15:20, 23; and Revelation 14:4). In no case does this text refer to the "importance" of a certain group today, but to James's contemporaries—the first of those now called Christians.

▸ *Isaiah 46:3, 4, NCV (25)—"God says, 'I have carried you since you were born; I have taken care of you from your birth. Even when you are old, I will be the same. Even when your hair has turned gray, I will take care of you. I made you and will take care of you.' "*

This may be a comfortable verse to some, but God is talking to Israel, not to mankind in general nor to believers in the church today. This text does not say that God made any one of us today in order to show how much He loves us.

▶ *Romans 12:3, Msg (25)*—" 'The only accurate way to understand ourselves is by what God is and by what he does for us.' "

This may be a very proper sentence, but that is not what Paul is saying. The thrust of the text is the problem of pride—that we should not be proud and that we should think soberly because each one has been given some capacity for faith to be used in recognizing the Lordship of God. Paul is not giving us a formula of how to find ourselves.

▶ *Isaiah 44:2 CEV (26)*—" 'I am your Creator. You were in my care even before you were born.' "

Isaiah is referring to Israel as a nation, not to individuals in Israel. The sentiment in this paraphrase is true but does not reflect Isaiah's meaning.

Chapter 3 (27–35)

▶ *Ecclesiastes 4:4, LB (27)*—"I observed that the basic motive for success is the driving force of envy and jealousy!"

Is this what Solomon meant? "I saw that for all toil and every skillful work a man is envied by his neighbor." It seems that Solomon is noting that for every successful man there would be envious neighbors—a far different idea than given in the paraphrase.

▶ *Jeremiah 29:11, NCV (31)*—" 'I know what I am planning for you. . . . "I have good plans for you, not plans to hurt you. I will give you hope and a good future." ' "

This text has been a great motto for many and is one of Warren's favorites. But God is promising Israel a future after its captivity in Babylon. This verse is not a promise that wonderful changes will happen once we believe our purposes. Warren quotes this text several times in *PDL*.

▶ *Isaiah 49:4, NIV (30)*—" 'I have labored to no purpose; I have spent my strength in vain and for nothing.' "

Here again is another example of not reading all the text. Isaiah is responding to God with some regret that it seems he does not have much to show for his preaching. But he finishes his sentence with the ringing affirmation that he is confident that his "just reward is with the LORD, and my work with my God." Just the opposite of the way Warren is using this text.

> *Isaiah 26:3, TEV (32)—" 'You, Lord, give perfect peace to those who keep their purpose firm and put their trust in you.' "*

I think Warren must search concordances to find texts that use the word *purpose* regardless of the text's meaning. This text promises peace to those "whose mind is stayed on" God, not especially to those who "kept their purpose firm."

Chapter 4 (36–40)

> *1 Corinthians 2:9, LB (38)—" 'No mere man has ever seen, heard or even imagined what wonderful things God has ready for those who love the Lord.' "*

Warren uses this text, that Paul imported from Isaiah 64:4, to suggest that heaven and eternity are indescribable. That is no doubt true, but that is not what the context says. The next verse says, "But God has revealed them to us through His Spirit."

Chapter 5 (41–46)

> *James 4:14b, NIV (41)—"What is your life?"*

Warren uses this text to build his own question: "How do you see your life?" And he uses this text as a springboard for his own teaching message—that we should have our own "life metaphor." But he does not read on to note that James answers this question differently than Warren would choose: "It is even a vapor that appears for a little time and then vanishes away."

> *1 Corinthians 4:7b, NLT (44, 45)—" 'What do you have that God hasn't given you? And if all you have is from God, why boast as though you have accomplished something on your own?' "*

There is nothing wrong with this statement. But Paul is really talking about how the Corinthian Christians are responding to the teachings of himself and Apollos—and how they are puffed up with pride.

Chapter 7 (53–59)

> *Proverbs 16:4, NLT (53) "The Lord has made everything for his own purposes."*

This is another example in which Warren searches in his arsenal of fifteen translations and paraphrases for particular words to suit his primary message in *PDL.* For his overriding purpose, he chose not to complete the text: "Yes, even the wicked for the day of doom."

▶ *John 3:36, Msg (58) " 'Whoever accepts and trusts the Son gets in on everything, life complete and forever!' "*

I find it interesting that here, again, Warren chooses that part of a text that affirms his primary message but neglects to use the whole verse—"and he who does not believe [Greek: "obey"] the Son shall not see life, but the wrath of God abides on him."

Chapter 8 (63–68)

▶ *Revelation 4:11, NLT (63) "You created everything, and it is for your pleasure that they exist and were created."*

The Greek word translated *pleasure* means "choice." The King James Version also uses the word *pleasure*. In 1611, *pleasure* may have been a valid way to translate this text, but not so today. A more literal translation would say, "You created all things; they came into existence and continue to exist because of your decision." This verse has nothing to do with making God feel good, although He was surely pleased with His creation on planet Earth (see Genesis 1:31).

▶ *Psalm 147:11, CEV (64) " 'The LORD is pleased only with those who worship him and trust his love.' "*

This is a true statement, but it is not what the psalmist is saying. The word here translated "worship" should be translated "fear." Of course God is pleased when we worship Him, but this text is saying something quite different.

Chapter 9 (69–76)

▶ *1 Timothy 6:17, TEV (75) " 'God . . . generously gives us everything for our enjoyment.' "*

We must place this text within its context. Paul is rebuking the rich who are misusing their riches and urges them to "do good . . . rich in good works." In other words, "scale back the misuse of riches, always remembering that God is pleased with 'everything' you have, but would be more pleased with the right use of it." Some of Warren's readers could easily suppose that as long as we thank God for "everything" we can enjoy our immediate pleasures—after all God gives generously for our "enjoyment." Perhaps everyone can define his own "enjoyment."

Chapter 10 (77–84)

▶ *Romans 6:13, TEV (77) "Give yourselves to God. . . . Surrender your whole being to him to be used for righteous purposes."*

The idea of "surrender" is the keynote of chapter 10 of *PDL,* but is this what the text is saying? Of course, Warren is right: *surrender* is understood by New Testament Christians as "stop fighting against God." But God is asking for more, and the New Testament calls it obedience. The whole text can be translated, "Don't make a daily habit of offering yourselves (physically and mentally) as weapons with which the rule of unrighteousness may be maintained, but offer them once and for all to God in the service of righteousness."

In other words, when Warren says that the "heart of worship is surrender," he should quickly emphasize that worship is wholehearted obedience to God wherever the light of truth leads. Passivity is part of worship, but active commitment to follow the Lord in cheerful obedience completes the worship experience.

▶ *1 Timothy 6:17b (78). Warren paraphrases in saying God "gave you the capacity to enjoy all kinds of pleasure."*

The same comments we made about *PDL* chapter 9 apply. This is not what Paul is telling Timothy, although Warren's intent is acceptable if we know what he means by "all kinds of pleasure."

▶ *Job 22:21, NLT (82) " 'Stop quarreling with God! If you agree with him, you will have peace at last, and things will go well for you.' "*

This is Eliphaz speaking, of whom God said later, "My wrath is aroused against you and your two friends, for you have not spoken of Me what is right, as My servant Job has" (Job 42:7). Eliphaz was dead wrong in using these words against Job. He was sure that Job must have sinned greatly in order to be so afflicted, but Job remonstrated that he did not sin to bring all this on himself. Context is everything!

▶ *Romans 6:17, Msg (82) " 'Offer yourselves to the ways of God and the freedom never quits. . . . [his] commands set you free to live openly in his freedom!' "*

God does set us free, but from what? And to what? Paul provides the context to these questions in Romans 6: "But God be thanked that though you were slaves of sin, yet you obeyed from the heart that form of doctrine to which you were delivered. And having been set free from sin, you become slaves of righteousness. . . . so now present your members as slaves of righteousness for holiness" (verses 17–19, NKJV). Warren is correct as far as he goes, but he must read further to get Paul's full meaning.

Joshua 5:13–15 (82) Warren says that Joshua "surrendered his plans" to God before the battle of Jericho. The text says that Joshua "fell on his face . . . and worshiped, and said to Him, 'What does my Lord say to His servant?' Then the Commander of the LORD's army said to Joshua, 'Take your sandal off your foot, for the place where you stand is holy.' And Joshua did so."

There is no reference to Joshua "surrendering" *his* plans, just a willingness to listen to counsel.

Chapter 11 (85–91)

▸ *Exodus 34:14, NLT (86) " 'He is a God who is passionate about his relationship with you.' "*

This is taken way out of context! This text does not prove that God wants me "for a close friend." The whole context concerns engaging in idolatry of all kinds and the fact that God punishes idolatry with death (see Exodus 32, Leviticus 20, and Numbers 25). A better translation would be, " 'For you shall worship no other god, for the LORD, whose name is Jealous, is a jealous God.' "

▸ *Jeremiah 9:24, TEV (87) " 'If any want to boast, they should boast that they know and understand me. . . . These are the things that please me.' "*

This is a misuse of a grand text! Warren omits

> "That I am the LORD, exercising
>   lovingkindness, judgment, and
>   righteousness in the earth.
> For in these I delight," says the LORD.

Of course, the Lord is pleased with people knowing and understanding Him, but the verse points us in a different direction.

▸ *Psalm 25:14, LB (91) " 'Friendship with God is reserved for those who reverence him. With them alone he shares the secrets of his promises.' "*

This may be true, but it is not what Psalm 25 is saying. The immediate context begins with verse 10:

> All the paths of the LORD are mercy and truth,
> To such as keep His covenant and His testimonies. . . .
> The secret of the LORD is with those who fear Him,
> And he will show them His covenant.

The Hebrew word for *covenant* is the same in both verses. The covenant was hardly a secret to the Israelites. Established during the time of Moses, it was the basis of God's relationship with Israel. In many ways the Israelites had broken the covenant with their idolatries and self-interests; in many ways God had called them back to a faithful obedience to the covenant. When Warren settled for this paraphrase, he missed the whole intent of Psalm 25. To talk about "secrets of his promises" when the psalmist is talking about a known covenant at the center of Israel's relationship with God is a strange stretch.

Chapter 12 (92–99)

▶ *1 Timothy 6:21a, LB (99) " 'Some of these people have missed the most important thing in life—they don't know God.' "*

This is certainly a true statement, but it is not what Paul had in mind. Here is a more accurate translation: "O Timothy! Guard what was committed to your trust, avoiding the profane and vain babblings and contradictions of what is falsely called knowledge—by professing it, some have strayed concerning the faith." From the wording of *The Living Bible*, the reader would have no idea what Paul is writing to Timothy.

Chapter 14 (107–113)

▶ *Job 34:13 (111)*

Warren refers to this text to show that Job felt that God "is in control." But this is Elihu speaking, one whom God reproved by saying that Elihu and his two friends "have not spoken of Me what is right, as My servant Job has" (42:7). Surely Job rejected this reasoning as Elihu developed his thought in this whole chapter.

Chapter 17 (130–137)

▶ *Genesis 2:18 (130) " 'It is not good for man to be alone.' "*

In the first half of this verse that is not quoted, God states the reason why Adam and all men should not be alone—he needed a "helper"— a female helper! Warren redirects this text to suggest that the church community is the solution. God's reason seems better.

Chapter 19 (145–151)

▶ *Ephesians 4:15 (146) " 'speak the truth in love.' "*

Warren uses this text in saying, "We can't have community without candor." But that is not what this text is saying; it is not about candor or frankness, but about opposing deceptive teachings with love.

Chapter 20 (152–159)

▸ *2 Corinthians 5:18, GWT (152) "[God] has restored our relationship with him through Christ, and has given us this ministry of restoring relationships."*

Clearly, this text is not about restoring relationships between people, although that may be a secondary consequence. The context, including verse 20, focuses on us being "ambassadors for Christ" by "pleading through us," for others to "be reconciled to God."

▸ *Psalm 73:21, 22, TEV (155) "When my thoughts were bitter and my feelings were hurt, I was as stupid as an animal."*

Warren lifts this text out of context to underline his point that "resentment makes us act and think in foolish ways." The psalmist, rather, is surveying life as it often is—the triumph of evil reflected in the prosperity of the wicked. All of this, he said,

> *was too painful for me—*
> *Until I went into the sanctuary of God;*
> *Then I understood their end (73:16, 17).*

Until the psalmist saw the bigger picture that the sanctuary service was teaching, he indeed was "vexed in my mind . . . like a beast before You." But he continues,

> *Nevertheless I am continually with You;*
> *You hold me by my right hand.*
> *You will guide me with your counsel,*
> *And afterward receive me to glory (73:21–24).*

In other words, when the psalmist looked at life in the short term, everything looked awful and unfair. In the long look, from the standpoint of the great controversy as taught in the sanctuary service, everything would be sorted out. This text has nothing to say about resentments in human relations that make us "bitter" and act as "stupid as an animal."

Chapter 21 (160–167)

▸ *Jude 1:19, Msg (165) " 'These are the ones who split churches, thinking only of themselves.' "*

Jude speaks of "mockers" in the last days that cause divisions. Mocking is different from gossip—which is the application Warren makes.

Chapter 30 (234–239)

▶ *Isaiah 43:21, NJB (234) "The people I have shaped for myself will broadcast my praises."*

Warren's use of this verse is opposite to what Isaiah is saying. The whole context focuses on the wild animals that honor God, but *not* the Israelites, O Jacob, O Israel (see verses 22–24). I think Warren used this text because, in this paraphrase, the word *shape* is used.

▶ *Ephesians 2:10, NIV (235) " 'We are God's workmanship, created in Christ Jesus to do good works.' "*

Here Paul refers to one's conversion, not to his birth—contrary to Warren's point.

Chapter 31 (241–248)

▶ *Exodus 31:3–5, NIV (242) " 'skill, ability, and knowledge in all kinds of crafts to make artistic designs . . . and to engage in all kinds of craftsmanship.' "*

Warren is using this verse to highlight "the natural talents you were born with" (241). Such a use would have been appropriate if he did not deliberately omit the beginning of the verse: " 'I have filled him with the Spirit of God . . .' " These skills are *supernatural* abilities that God gave to particular people.

Chapter 32 (249–255)

▶ *Hebrews 12:l, LB (253) " 'run with patience the particular race that God has set before us.' "*

Warren is looking for support for his idea that God has assigned boundaries to us, that each of us has "a field or sphere of service. . . . When we try to overextend our ministry reach beyond what God shaped us for, we experience stress." So to validate this thought he reads into Scripture the elaboration of *The Living Bible*! Paul is speaking of the Christian race of faith in general; he is not saying that each Christian has his own "particular race" to run.

▶ *2 Timothy 2:15, Msg (255) " 'Concentrate on doing your best for God, work you won't be ashamed of.' "*

This is good advice, except that is not exactly what Paul is telling Timothy. Paul is urging Timothy to stay on track, always cutting straight the word of truth.

Chapter 34 (265–271)

▶ *Nehemiah 6:3, CEV (268) " 'My work is too important to stop now and . . . visit with you.' "*

This text is not about Nehemiah refusing to waste time defending himself against criticism. It refers to his excuse to keep from spending time with enemies who were planning to kill him (see verse 2).

Chapter 35 (271–278)

▶ *2 Corinthians 12:7, Msg (274) " 'So I wouldn't get a big head, I was given the gift of a handicap to keep me in constant touch with my limitations.' "*

In a way, this wording is very comforting for many, but it is still a very misleading paraphrase! True, the thorn, "a messenger of Satan," kept Paul from being "exalted above measure." But he is not talking here about a human limitation that he may or may not have had from birth. His thorn was a supernaturally induced burden that Satan sent to "buffet" (to "beat," as the word is used in Matthew 26:67, describing soldiers who beat Jesus) Paul to offset the supernatural knowledge that God was giving him and which he was sharing. To extrapolate this verse into comfort for the physically handicapped is to reduce—and even misapply—Paul's point.

Chapter 36 (281–288)

▶ *Acts 1:7, 8, NIV (285) " 'It is not for you to know the times or dates the Father has set by his own authority. But you will receive power when the Holy Spirit comes on you; and you will be my witnesses in Jerusalem, and in all Judea and Samaria, and to the ends of the earth.' "*

Warren says this text is in response to the disciples' question regarding the end of the world. But this question was asked before the crucifixion (see Matthew 24). Warren, however, does skip back to Matthew 24 in the next verse he quotes: " *'No one knows about that day or hour, not even the angels in heaven, nor the Son, but only the Father' "* (Mathew 24:36). Acts 1:7, 8 describes the question the disciples asked Jesus just before He ascended—whether He was now setting up His kingdom on earth, not when He was returning at the end of the world.

▶ *Luke 9:62, NLT (286) " 'Anyone who lets himself be distracted from the world I plan for him is not fit for the Kingdom of God.' "*

This is a poor paraphrase because Jesus is talking to prospective, full-time disciples about continuing to be connected in some way to their previous way of life, before they put their "hand to the plow"— perhaps trying to hold on to some part of their earlier livelihood, not quite sure that the Lord could take care of them. Jesus is saying we should make a clean break, look forward, and wholeheartedly follow Him, especially if the person wants to do full-time service.

Chapter 37 (289–295)

▶ *1 John 5:10a, GWT (289) "Those who believe in the Son of God have the testimony of God in them."*

This version represents a real switch of meaning. John is referring to the "testimony from God" *about* Jesus—the source of eternal life (see 1 John 5:9, 10). Certainly John, in this text, is *not referring to our testimony about God* that we develop through our own personal experiences.

▶ *Psalm 119:33, Msg (291) " 'God, teach me lessons for living so I can stay the course.' "*

The psalmist is referring not to lessons we all should learn from life's experiences but to what we can learn from the law that God etched in stone and gave through Moses—as reinforced in almost every other verse in Psalm 119.

Chapter 38 (297–304)

▶ *1 Corinthians 14:20, CEV (299) " 'My friends, stop thinking like children. Think like mature people.' "*

Once again, this is great advice but not what Paul is saying. This text does not tell us, as Warren says, to "shift from self-centered thinking to other-centered thinking." Paul is speaking about the problem of tongues in a group of believers. Incidentally, are children always "self-centered?"

▶ *Psalm 2:8, NCV (300) " 'If you ask me, I will give you the nations; all the people on earth will be yours.' "*

Without question, this text is not about praying for countries to be saved. That is a good prayer but not what the psalmist meant. In this text, God the Father is promising His Son, the Messiah, will be given kingship rule over all the world, regardless what the rulers of earth have in mind (see verses 1–3).

Chapter 39 (305–311)

▸ *Numbers 33:2, NLT (308) " 'At the LORD's direction, Moses kept a written record of their progress.' "*

This verse does not refer to any spiritual journal that Moses was writing. Verse 2 is simply referring to the record that Moses kept regarding where the Israelites stopped to camp throughout the wilderness after leaving Egypt. Of course, at some later time, Moses wrote the Hebrew record that we know today as Genesis through Deuteronomy, but that is not what this verse is referring to.

Chapter 40 (312–319)

▸ *Philippians 4:7, Msg (314) " 'A sense of God's wholeness . . . will come and settle you down. It's wonderful what happens when Christ displaces worry at the center of your life.' "*

Of course, this general statement is true. But it is far from what Paul wrote: "The peace of God, which surpasses all understanding, will guard your hearts and minds through Christ Jesus." What does "a sense of God's wholeness" mean? It does not mean "the peace of God." *The Message* Bible simply manipulates but does not exegete.

▸ *2 Corinthians 10:13, LB (318) " 'Our goal is to measure up to God's plan for us.' "*

This concept is right, but how this paraphrase ever saw the light of day tests our imagination! The New King James Version is very close to the literal translation: "We, however, will not boast beyond measure, but within the limits of the sphere which God appointed us— a sphere which especially includes you." Paul is referring to his experience at Corinth—that it is appropriate for him to boast of the preaching of the gospel in Corinth, but that he will not boast beyond what is appropriate. He says nothing about "plans" and "goals."

Appendix E: A Sampling of New Testaments Texts That Spell Out the Purpose of the Everlasting Gospel

Matthew

▶ *"You shall call His name Jesus, for He will save His people from their sins" (1:21).*

John

▶ *"Neither do I condemn you; go and sin no more" (8:11).*

Acts

▶ *"To you first, God, having raised up His Servant Jesus, sent Him to bless you, in turning away every one of you from your iniquities" (3:26).*

▶ *"Now as he [Paul] reasoned about righteousness, self-control, and the judgment to come, Felix was afraid" (24:25).*

▶ *" ' "to open their eyes and turn them from darkness to light, and from the power of Satan to God, that they may receive forgiveness of sins and an inheritance among those who are sanctified by faith in Me" ' " (26:18).*

Romans

▶ *"For I am not ashamed of the gospel of Christ, for it is the power of God to salvation for everyone who believes [has faith], for the Jew first and also for the Greek" (1:16).*

▶ *"Who 'will render to each one according to his deeds': eternal life to those who by patient continuance in doing good seek for glory, honor, and immortality" (2:6, 7, emphasis in original).*

▸ *"But God be thanked that though you were slaves of sin, yet you obeyed from the heart that form of doctrine to which you were delivered. And having been set free from sin, you became slaves of righteousness. . . . But now having been set free from sin, and having become slaves to God, you have your fruit to holiness, and the end, everlasting life"* (6:17, 18, 22).

▸ *"That the righteous requirement of the law might be fulfilled in us who do not walk according to the flesh but according to the Spirit"* (8:4).

1 Corinthians

▸ *"No temptation has overtaken you except such as is common to man; but God is faithful, who will not allow you to be tempted beyond what you are able, but with the temptation will also make the way of escape, that you may be able to bear it"* (10:13).

▸ *"Awake to righteousness, and do not sin; for some do not have the knowledge of God. I speak this to your shame"* (15:34).

2 Corinthians

▸ *"Therefore, having these promises, beloved, let us cleanse ourselves from all filthiness of the flesh and spirit, perfecting holiness in the fear of God"* (7:1).

▸ *"Examine yourselves as to whether you are in the faith. Prove your-selves. Do you not know yourselves, that Jesus Christ is in you?—unless indeed you are disqualified"* (13:5).

Galatians

▸ *"I say then: Walk in the Spirit, and you shall not fulfill the lust of the flesh"* (5:16).

Ephesians

▸ *"For by grace you have been saved through faith, and that not of yourselves; it is the gift of God, and not works, lest anyone should boast. For we are His workmanship, created in Christ Jesus for good works, which God prepared beforehand that we should walk in them"* (2:8–10).

▸ *"For you were once darkness, but now you are light in the Lord. Walk as children of light (for the fruit of the Spirit is in all goodness, righteous-ness, and truth), proving what is acceptable to the Lord"* (5:8, 9).

▶ *"That He might sanctify and cleanse it with the washing of water by the word, that He might present it to Himself a glorious church, not having spot or wrinkle or any such thing, but that it should be holy and without blemish" (5:26, 27).*

▶ *"Above all, taking the shield of faith with which you will be able to quench all the fiery darts of the wicked one" (6:16).*

Philippians

▶ *"Being confident of this very thing, that He who has begun a good work in you will complete it until the day of Jesus Christ" (1:6).*

▶ *"Only let your conduct be worthy of the gospel of Christ" (1:27).*

▶ *"Work out your own salvation with fear and trembling; for it is God who works in you both to will and to do for His good pleasure" (2:12, 13).*

▶ *"I can do all things through Christ who strengthens me" (4:13).*

Colossians

▶ *"That you may have a walk worthy of the Lord, fully pleasing Him, being fruitful in every good work and increasing in the knowledge of God; strengthened with all might, according to His glorious power, for all patience and longsuffering with joy; giving thanks to the Father who has qualified us to be partakers of the inheritance of the saints in the light" (1:10–12).*

▶ *"To present you holy, and blameless, and irreproachable in His sight—if indeed you continue in the faith, grounded, and steadfast and are not moved away from the hope of the gospel" (1:22, 23).*

1 Thessalonians

▶ *"Walk worthy of God who calls you into His own kingdom and glory" (2:12).*

2 Thessalonians

▶ *"God from the beginning chose you for salvation through sanctification by the Spirit and belief in the truth" (2:13).*

Titus

▶ *"For the grace of God that brings salvation has appeared to all men, teaching us that, denying ungodliness and worldly lusts, we should live soberly, righteously, and godly in the present age, looking for the blessed hope and glorious appearing of our great God and Savior Jesus Christ, who gave Himself for us, that He might redeem us from every lawless deed and purify for Himself His own special people, zealous for good works" (2:11–14).*

Hebrews

▶ *"For we do not have a High Priest who cannot sympathize with our weaknesses, but was in all points tempted as we are, yet without sin. Let us therefore come boldly to the throne of grace, that we may obtain mercy and find grace to help in time of need" (4:15, 16).*

▶ *"Pursue peace with all men, and holiness, without which no one will see the Lord" (12:14).*

James

▶ *"Blessed is the man who endures temptations; for when he has been proved, he will receive the crown of life which the Lord has promised to those who love Him" (1:12).*

1 Peter

▶ *"As He has called you is holy, you also be holy in all your conduct" (1:15).*

▶ *"Since Christ suffered for us in the flesh, arm yourselves also with the same mind, for he who has suffered in the flesh has ceased from sin, that he no longer should live the rest of his time in the flesh for the lusts of men, but for the will of God" (4:1, 2).*

▶ *"For the time has come for judgment to begin at the house of God; and if it begins with us first, what will be the end of those who do not obey the gospel of God?" (4:17).*

2 Peter

▶ *"His divine power has given to us all things that pertain to life and godliness, through the knowledge of Him who called us by glory and virtue, by which have been given to us exceedingly great and precious promises, that through these you may be partakers of the divine nature, having escaped the corruption that is in the world through lust" (1:3, 4).*

▶ *"Therefore, since all these things will be dissolved, what manner of persons ought you to be in holy conduct and godliness, looking for and hastening the coming of the day of God, because of which the heavens will be dissolved being on fire, and the elements will melt with fervent heat? Nevertheless we, according to His promise, look for new heavens and a new earth in which righteousness dwells. There-fore, beloved, looking forward to these things, be diligent to be found by Him in peace, without spot and blameless" (3:11–14).*

1 John

▸ *"If we confess our sins, He is faithful and just to forgive us our sins and to cleanse us from all unrighteousness" (1:9).*

▸ *"He who says, 'I know Him,' and does not keep His commandments, is a liar, and the truth is not in him" (2:4).*

▸ *"If you know that He is righteous, you know that everyone who prac-tices righteousness is born of Him" (2:29).*

▸ *"And everyone who has this hope in Him purifies himself, just as He is pure" (3:3).*

▸ *"For this is the love of God, that we keep His commandments. And His commandments are not burdensome. For whatever is born of God overcomes the world. And this is the victory that has overcome the world—our faith" (5:3, 4).*

▸ *"We know that whoever is born of God does not sin [does not prac-tice sinning] but he who has been born of God keeps himself, and the wicked one does not touch him" (5:18).*

Jude

▸ *"Now to Him who is able to keep you from stumbling, and to present you faultless before the presence of His glory with exceeding joy" (24).*

Revelation

▸ *" 'To him who overcomes . . .' " (2:7; 2:11; 2:17; 2:26; 3:5; 3:12; 3:21).*

▸ *"The dragon was enraged with the woman, and he went to make war with the rest of her offspring, who keep the commandments of God and have the testimony of Jesus Christ" (12:17).*

▸ *"Here is the patience of the saints; here are those who keep the com-mandments of God and the faith of Jesus" (14:12).*

▸ *" 'Let us be glad and rejoice and give Him glory, for the marriage of the Lamb has come, and His wife has made herself ready.' And to her it was granted to be arrayed in fine linen, clean and bright, for the fine linen is the righteous acts of the saints" (19:7, 8).*

▸ *"Blessed are those who do His commandments, that they may have the right to the tree of life, and may enter through the gates into the city" (22:14).*

INDEX

If you found this book useful, you'll want to read these books:

They Were There
Herbert E. Douglass

They were there. They saw Ellen White. They heard her speak. Why do their stories matter to us today?

Each of the individuals involved in these stories was directly affected by Ellen White and her visions. They were there and saw for themselves the power of God that accompanied her work as she dealt with perplexing situations. Some continued to resist, but for many, the result was a mighty confirmation of their faith in her life and ministry. In each case, Ellen White, ever the soul winner, urged individuals to a closer walk with the Lord.

Paper, 128 pages.   08163-2117-5   US$11.99

Should We Ever Say, "I Am Saved"?
Herbert E. Douglass

What it means to be assured of salvation—now!

The compelling insights found in *Should We Ever Say, "I Am Saved"?* summarize Dr. Herbert E. Douglass's study and personal discovery through the years of what it means to be assured of salvation. In these pages you will learn the difference between genuine and false assurance; how to have genuine assurance now; what Ellen White really said about assurance; how grace relates to faith; what works, legalism, and perfection have to do with assurance; and much more.

Paper, 158 pages.   0-8163-1967-7   US$6.97

Hidden Heresy?
Thomas Mostert

Is spiritualism influencing the Adventist Church?

How could something so foreign to the very heart of Adventism possibly gain entry into this church? That just isn't possible! Or is it?

Author Tom Mostert, president of the Pacific Union Conference of Seventh-day Adventists, looks at some of the current trends in popular churches—trends and methodologies that are being eagerly embraced in Adventism—and asks, "Can you identify veiled spiritualism?" Using statements from the Spirit of Prophecy, Mostert probes the mega-/giga-church movement—its leaders, philosophies, and articles of faith—and draws conclusions that may startle you.

Paper, 112 pages.   0-8163-2115-9   US$10.99

Order from your ABC by calling **1-800-765-6955,** or get online and shop our virtual store at **<www.AdventistBookCenter.com>.**
- Read a chapter from a book
- Order online
- Sign up for email notices on new products